SO MUCH MORE THAN THE ABCs

THE EARLY PHASES OF READING & WRITING

REVISED EDITION

MOLLY F. COLLINS &
JUDITH A. SCHICKEDANZ

National Association for the Education of Young Children
Washington, DC

National Association for the Education of Young Children

1401 H Street NW, Suite 600
Washington, DC 20005
202-232-8777 • 800-424-2460
NAEYC.org

NAEYC Books
Senior Director, Publishing & Content Development
Susan Friedman

Director, Books
Dana Battaglia

Senior Editor
Holly Bohart

Editor II
Rossella Procopio

Senior Creative Design Manager
Charity Coleman

Senior Creative Design Specialist
Gillian Frank

Creative Design Specialist
Makayla Johnson

Creative Design Specialist
Ashley McGowan

Publishing Business Operations Manager
Francine Markowitz

Through its publications program, the National Association for the Education of Young Children (NAEYC) provides a forum for discussion of major issues and ideas in the early childhood field, with the hope of provoking thought and promoting professional growth. The views expressed or implied in this book are not necessarily those of the Association.

Permissions
NAEYC accepts requests for limited use of our copyrighted material. For permission to reprint, adapt, translate, or otherwise reuse and repurpose content from this publication, review our guidelines at NAEYC.org/resources/permissions.

Figure 3.1 on page 48 is from *Negative Cat,* by Sophie Blackall, copyright © 2021 by Sophie Blackall. Used by permission of Nancy Paulsen Books, an imprint of Penguin Young Readers Group, a division of Penguin Random House LLC. All rights reserved.

The vignette in Box 4.1 on page 90 is adapted from V.B. Fantozzi, "Exploring Elephant Seals in New Jersey: Preschoolers Use Collaborative Multimedia Albums," *Young Children* 67, no. 3 (2012): 42.

Figure 5.9 on page 120 is from *Elkonin Boxes: A Literacy Tool for Beginning Readers,* copyright © 2015 by Ross McNamara. Used by permission of Ross McNamara.

The vignette in Box 8.6 on page 186 is adapted from J.A. Schickedanz, "Setting the Stage for Literacy Events in the Classroom," *Child Care Information Exchange* 123, Sept./Oct. (1999): 54.

Figure, Illustration, and Photo Credits
Created by NAEYC with graphics copyright © Getty Images: cover and Figures 3.2, 4.6, 5.4–5.8, and 5.10

Copyright © Getty Images: Photos on pages 1, 5, 7, 19, 20, 34, 45, 47, 51, 68, 81, 90, 99, 125, 127, 134, 135, 154, 157, 182, and 186

Courtesy of the authors: Figures 4.1–4.5

Courtesy of Annmarie Blaney: Figure 7.2

Courtesy of Christina M. Cassano: Photo on page 30

Courtesy of Marco Melgar: Photo on page viii (bottom)

Courtesy of Kathleen A. Paciga: Figure 7.22

Courtesy of Kimberly Pierpont: Photo on page 10

Reprinted with permission of the creator or their guardian: Figures 5.1–5.3, 6.1–6.5, 7.1, 7.3–7.21, 7.23, and 8.1–8.61

So Much More than the ABCs: The Early Phases of Reading and Writing, Revised Edition. Copyright © 2024 by the National Association for the Education of Young Children. All rights reserved. Printed in the United States of America.

Library of Congress Control Number: 2023945426

ISBN: 978-1-952331-32-9

Item: 1172

CONTENTS

ABOUT THE AUTHORS

Molly F. Collins, EdD (Boston University), associate professor of the practice of literacy in the Department of Teaching and Learning at Vanderbilt University's Peabody College, has taught graduate and undergraduate courses in cognitive development, language acquisition, linguistics, and storybook reading. She has also provided multiyear professional learning experiences on language and literacy for preschool teachers in national and international settings. Previously, she taught toddlers and preschoolers.

Collins directed early literacy and professional educator projects funded by the US Department of Education, foundations, and universities, and she served as principal investigator for foundation- and university-sponsored grants to explore monolingual and multilingual children's vocabulary learning and comprehension from story reading. She is a member of the American Educational Research Association, the Literacy Research Association, the National Association for the Education of Young Children, and the Society for Research in Child Development, and she serves as part of the National Early Education Council at Jumpstart.

Judith A. Schickedanz, PhD (University of Illinois at Urbana-Champaign), professor emerita at Boston University, taught courses in child development, early literacy, and curriculum and instruction; served as director of the laboratory preschool; coordinated the early childhood program; and helped launch the Jumpstart volunteer program. She taught preschool and has worked extensively with early childhood teachers on funded projects, including Early Reading First.

Schickedanz has authored numerous articles, book chapters, and books, including *Understanding Children and Adolescents* (Allyn & Bacon, 2000); *Increasing the Power of Instruction* (NAEYC, 2008); *Writing in Preschool* (International Reading Association, 2009); *Inside Preschool Classrooms* (Harvard Education Press, 2018); and *What Are Preschoolers Thinking?* (Harvard Education Press, 2022). She lives with her husband, David, in Southern California near their son's family and enjoys their two grandchildren, a 10-year-old and a 3-year-old.

ABOUT THE CONTRIBUTORS

Christina M. Cassano, EdD (Boston University), is professor at Salem State University. Her scholarship and teaching focus on supporting literacy and language acquisition for all children, particularly young multilingual learners and children living in poverty. She was a kindergarten teacher and a reading specialist in public schools for over a decade and has also worked with multilingual preschoolers in Head Start. Cassano coauthored *Guided Drawing with Multilingual Preschoolers* (Teachers College Press, 2023).

Jessica L. Hoffman, PhD (University of Illinois at Chicago), is an urban literacy specialist consultant for the Ohio State Support Team, supporting school-based early childhood program administrators. Previously, she worked with preschool children and teachers through research in two Early Reading First grants, taught in early childhood classrooms, and mentored preservice and practicing early childhood teachers. Her current interests include supporting system-level literacy improvement in large urban school districts.

Kathleen A. Paciga, PhD (University of Illinois at Chicago), is associate professor of education at Columbia College Chicago. She started in the field as a kindergarten teacher and has worked with preschool children and teachers through research in two Early Reading First projects. Her research and service focus on several aspects of early literacy instruction, including the ways in which media, in all its diverse forms, are integrated into children's literate lives. Paciga coauthored *Guided Drawing with Multilingual Preschoolers* (Teachers College Press, 2023).

ACKNOWLEDGMENTS

We thank the multitude of teachers and children from whom we have learned so much over the years and continue to draw inspiration. We also thank the many early literacy researchers whose work informed this book. We are grateful to our invited contributors—Christina Cassano, Kathleen A. Paciga, and Jessica L. Hoffman—especially to Christina for taking responsibility for Chapter 2. We are grateful, as well, for the editorial support that NAEYC provided, including Rossella Procopio's incomparable detail and keen organization in transforming this edition into an insightful revision. Her final editing, feedback, and photograph selection imbued the revision with coherence and beauty. It's a gift to both authors and readers when a book's details are given such thoughtful attention.

Last, but certainly not least, we thank our families, immediate and extended, for their support and patience throughout.

It is a joy to learn from and learn with one's mentor over a professional lifetime. I (Molly) am grateful to Judy for decades of generosity, collaboration, and friendship.

INTRODUCTION

A TIME TO BEGIN

If asked when children learn to read and write, the average person would probably say, "in first grade." Although true for most children, success in first grade relies on more than the instruction at this time. Its foundation also depends on the knowledge and skills acquired during experiences starting all the way back in infancy.

Children who struggle with learning to read in first grade often lack this essential foundational knowledge. Moreover, this struggle is pervasive and persistent. Over three decades ago, 75 percent of children who struggled with learning to read in first grade continued to experience major reading difficulties throughout their years of schooling, never reading within the typical range for their grade level (Spira, Bracken, & Fischel 2005; Torgesen 2004). Those trajectories are substantially different when children receive early reading intervention for foundational skills (Gersten et al. 2020).

Some children succeed in *learning* to read in first grade but then experience difficulties starting in the middle grades. This difficulty, known as "the fourth grade slump," is related to insufficient content knowledge, vocabulary, and overall language, as well as difficulty in drawing inferences (Chall & Jacobs 2003; Lesaux & Kieffer 2010; Sweet & Snow 2002). These children struggle to comprehend the content in their subject-area texts, such as a biology or history book. This challenge is experienced more often by children from families with low incomes and who attend urban schools, and it is especially prevalent in children from families with low incomes and who primarily speak a language that is not English at home (Crosson & Lesaux 2010).

It is essential to help children build strong foundations for both *learning to read* and *reading to learn* in the years *before* formal schooling (Paratore, Cassano, & Schickedanz 2011). By engaging infants, toddlers, and preschoolers in experiences that foster oral language skills, content knowledge, reasoning/thinking skills, and literacy skills, early childhood educators help ensure children's later academic success (NICHD 2008; Sénéchal, Ouellette, & Rodney 2006; Storch & Whitehurst 2002). Maintaining children's interest and motivation is also crucial, given that these factors account for a significant portion of later reading achievement (Wigfield, Gladstone, & Turci 2016).

This book was written and has been updated throughout the years to support early childhood educators and families in helping young children acquire the understandings, knowledge, and skills needed for later success in learning to read and write. It addresses four main points:

1. What children need to learn in these early years
2. The strategies that teachers can use to help children acquire these foundations
3. The features of emergent literacy and language understandings and skills
4. The design features of the materials and physical environment in early childhood programs that support language and literacy learning

Seasoned early childhood educators will find information that both updates their current knowledge and validates much of what they already do to support young children's early language, literacy, and content knowledge acquisition. The book also addresses a wide range of basics useful to preservice teachers and other students of early childhood education, as well as to educators who are just beginning their careers. Families will also find this an informative resource for learning about the many early literacy experiences that early childhood programs provide and about ideas for literacy experiences that can be implemented at home.

This book is based on a great deal of research, although we authors also drew on our own experiences with young children and early childhood educators, given that research has not yet addressed all important questions or provided sufficient information on all topics (Duke & Carlisle 2011). It is critical to also acknowledge that a wide variety of interconnected factors are at play in each child's emergent literacy development. Because one size does not fit all, teachers must adapt instruction for each child's individual characteristics, experiences, and contexts (NAEYC 2020, 2022).

Many examples of children's work and thinking are offered throughout the book. The names of children featured in the writing samples and other examples are a mixture of pseudonyms and actual names, which are used with permission.

Topics and Their Organization

This book is organized into two parts, addressing the following key topics.

In **Part One: Building a Foundation for Reading**

> Chapter 1 provides an overview of two reading processes and two phases of reading development following the emergent literacy period. This overview offers a framework for understanding how experiences in the early years contribute to later success in conventional reading.

> Chapter 2 links motor, cognitive, language, and social development milestones from birth to 30 months to children's book interests and interactions.

> Chapter 3 discusses selecting picture storybooks and goals and strategies for reading stories to preschoolers.

> Chapter 4 focuses on selecting informational books and on goals and strategies for using these with preschoolers.

> Chapter 5 details the literacy skills comprising early foundations for learning to read and write and the support necessary for their acquisition.

In **Part Two: Building a Foundation for Writing**

> Chapter 6 outlines phases of emergent writing and discusses the conventional writing that follows.

> Chapter 7 considers mark making between 12 and 30 months, toddlers' attributions of meaning to these marks, and infant and toddler knowledge acquisition.

> Chapter 8 focuses on word and picture creation, the different organization used for pictures and writing marks, literacy skills, and language and content knowledge involved in drawing and writing in children between 30 months and 5 years old.

Using This Book

A reader interested in the entire span of the emergent literacy years (birth through 5 years old) will want to start at the beginning of this book and read the chapters consecutively. However, the book's layered organization by topic and age also makes it easy to find information of most interest without reading chapters in order. For example, a reader interested primarily in infants and toddlers might start with Chapters 1, 2, 6, and 7, and then turn to the other chapters to build an understanding of literacy development during the preschool years. A reader primarily interested in preschoolers, meanwhile, might take a different path, reading Chapters 1, 3, 4, 5, 6, and 8 before examining the infant and toddler chapters. In this situation, examining the infant and toddler chapters can provide an understanding of the experiences that support language and literacy development in the preschool years.

Lists of both children's literature and research references cited throughout the text are provided at the end of the book. Readers interested in learning more about the many topics introduced in this resource are encouraged to read some of these studies, books, reports, and position statements.

This Book's Goals

This book focuses on more than just the understandings and skills that ensure success in learning to read. As previously mentioned, it instead takes a long view: the early years are a launching pad for both *learning to read* and *reading to learn*. Discussing both of these phases of reading is important because each one involves unique factors. (See Chapter 1.) If teachers and families emphasize one set of understandings and skills over the other, children's early literacy experiences will not effectively support them in reaching their full potential.

The book's goals also include keeping motivation to learn at the forefront. Learning from books right from the beginning, when adults read to children, is key. As a consequence of concern over insufficient early learning, early childhood educators and families sometimes rely on narrow and tedious lessons with little appeal and too few here-and-now applications. Playful, interesting, and useful instructional approaches support robust and meaningful early language, literacy, and content knowledge learning.

With such a long road of school and learning stretching out before children, a primary goal of early literacy experiences is to build children's interest in reading- and writing-related activities and learning. Without interest, children will not be motivated to read or write; without motivation, children will read and write relatively little and only what and when they must. Children who read little are unlikely to become good readers. Children who write little are unlikely to become good writers. Therefore, promoting children's *desire* to read and write is as important as helping children develop the necessary understandings and skills essential for learning *how* to read and write.

It is not this book's goal to encourage early childhood educators or families to teach children to read and write conventionally before kindergarten or first grade. Of course, some children will develop enough skill early on to do so. Most children, however, will follow the more typical course, progressing to conventional reading and writing after the emergent literacy period on which this book focuses.

Teachers at all levels recognize the importance of meaningful literacy experiences during early childhood. It is still the case, however, that many children entering the early primary grades have not had the benefit of a full range of enriching literacy experiences at home, in preschool, or in other early childhood settings that foster not only *knowledge about* reading and writing but *love for* them.

Early childhood educators have both the opportunity and the privilege to shape the progress young children make in acquiring the literacy skills, oral language, and background knowledge that are vital to their later success in learning to read and write. They also have the chance to shape children's basic social and emotional attachments to reading and writing. This book focuses on the range of considerations that help educators achieve these complementary goals.

PART ONE
BUILDING A FOUNDATION FOR READING

WHAT'S INVOLVED IN LEARNING TO READ?

Meaningful, enriching early language and literacy experiences provide children with a crucial foundation for later conventional reading, which involves two processes and two phases of development. Basic information about these processes and phases is provided in this chapter to support the reader's understanding of how early emergent literacy experiences contribute to children's success in both learning to read and in long-term reading proficiency.

Reading Processes and Phases

Readers engage in two different processes: ***decoding*** and ***comprehending***. Decoding involves translating printed words into their spoken counterparts. Comprehending involves striving to understand what the connected words and sentences mean. Although both processes occur simultaneously and constantly influence one another, they involve different sets of behaviors. Reading development occurs in two fairly distinct phases: ***learning to read*** (decoding words) and ***reading to learn*** (obtaining new information). When children are first learning to read, they must devote virtually all of their time and attention to decoding—to figuring out what the words mean. But because reading is a meaning-making activity, it is also important for children to understand what they read from the beginning. To make this possible for children who are just beginning to read (i.e., to decode), the first books they use are written and designed for easy comprehension. The writers and designers of materials for beginner readers meet this goal by making sure that the books contain words and content that children already know. These beginner books also include short sentences, have words with simple spelling patterns, and use relatively few words, some of which are repeated numerous times. Phrases and similar sentences (e.g., out went the duck, out went the sheep) might also be repeated. All of these characteristics, which are featured in books intended for children through the second grade, help children who are just learning to read also understand what they are reading.

After second grade, most children can read many words at a glance because they have encountered them repeatedly while reading. After a while, they can also decode new words more quickly by drawing on patterns they have observed, such as individual spoken sounds (phonemes) and correspondences between sounds and the letters that represent them (graphemes) (Adams 1990).

Of course, while children are learning to read, they still benefit from hearing adults read aloud to them. Just as they did during their infant, toddler, and preschool years, children in kindergarten and first grade can comprehend material that is much richer than what they can read by themselves. Moreover, adults' comments and explanations continue to enhance children's comprehension. Children's motivation to engage with books is also likely to remain high when adults continue to read to them.

Once children can decode well, they enter a second phase of reading development. For most children, this phase begins in third grade. In this second phase, the child reads to obtain new information; in other words, they read to learn. Previously, reading to learn was a minor goal, and the content featured in books children read was quite familiar to them. By third grade, the books children read have a considerable amount of unfamiliar content, as well as new vocabulary and longer, more complex sentences. Consequently, the task of comprehension becomes more difficult, and it increases in difficulty with each successive school year.

It is important to continue to read aloud to children during all of the primary grade years—even longer if a child still enjoys it. When children hear books above their own reading level and adults discuss these books with them, children develop language, content knowledge, and the reasoning skills that are needed to comprehend texts they read on their own.

By fourth grade, children begin reading textbooks for content areas such as science and history, but many find these textbooks very challenging. There are several reasons that transitioning to these books can cause difficulties. For one thing, the textbook content introduces mostly, if not entirely, new information for children to process. The language is also denser and more abstract than the language found in storybooks, and the vocabulary is more sophisticated and technical (Kelley et al. 2010; Nagy & Townsend 2012). Young children typically hear more narratives (i.e., stories) than informational texts because teachers' and families' own reading preferences favor stories over informational texts (Price, van Kleeck, & Huberty 2009).

It is also the case that many books for readers in kindergarten through second grade are stories, not informational texts (Duke 2000; Fang 2008). Moreover, informational books for young children are often written as narratives or in verse (e.g., *Mama Built a Little Nest*, by Jennifer Ward, illustrated by Steve Jenkins; *Water Is Water,* by Miranda Paul, illustrated by Jason Chin;

Chickens Aren't the Only Ones, by Ruth Heller) rather than in expository text form. Verse and story text structures differ from the more technical writing found in informational textbooks for older children. While books in narrative or verse form are delightful and should be used to engage children's interest, it is important to balance them with informational texts. Using bona fide informational texts in addition to storybooks at the preschool level helps to build children's content knowledge and the vocabulary associated with it, which in turn helps children succeed later when reading textbooks. This is explored more in Chapter 4.

We authors have observed more informational book reading by teachers now than we did 10 years ago, and most curricula, even for preschool, include more informational books written in expository, not narrative or verse, form. More research is needed to understand the extent to which preschool teachers read more informational texts, feel prepared to do so, and enjoy the genre (Robinson 2020).

Understandings and Skills Needed When Learning to Read

Decoding and comprehending require different understandings and skills. The two processes also differ in relationship to one another during the two phases of reading development. This section discusses each of the major code-related skills necessary for learning to read and how they contribute. It also explores how oral language and content knowledge assist in the final steps of the decoding process.

Print Conventions

Print conventions specify how print is organized on a page and how words in print are designated. For example, in English and many other languages, print is organized on a page from left to right and top to bottom. Clusters of letters are separated with spaces to indicate where one word stops and another begins. Other conventions specify when and where to use uppercase versus lowercase letters and how to use each punctuation mark.

Children begin to learn about the directionality of print during preschool, and they solidify this understanding during kindergarten and first grade. During preschool, children also notice that their names feature capital letters at the beginning, followed by lowercase letters. This awareness is a first step for young children in learning that alphabet letters have a "big" (capital) form and a "small" (lowercase) form. They continue to learn about case use in the primary grades. Knowledge of other conventions is also acquired over an extended period of time. For example, although children might be interested in punctuation as early as preschool, learning about its use continues well into the intermediate grades and beyond.

The Alphabet and Phonological Awareness

To decode words, a reader must translate individual letters (graphemes) or letter pairs into speech sounds (phonemes) and then blend these into the spoken form of the word. Decoding skill requires letter-name knowledge and ***phonological awareness*** (i.e., knowing that each spoken word consists of a series of individual sounds). Phonological awareness helps children understand that decoding is a matter of translating letters in a printed word into sounds that comprise its spoken form. (See Chapter 5 for further discussion of phonemic and phonological awareness.)

Children must also learn many specific connections between individual letters or letter pairs and the phonemes they represent. For example, the letter *B* represents the /b/ sound, the letter *T* represents the /t/ sound, and *C* and *H* together represent the first sound heard in *cherry*.

Of course, in English, some words begin with the same sound but are spelled with a different beginning letter or letter pair (e.g., city/silly; fun/phone), while others begin with different sounds but are spelled with the same first letter (e.g., eat/enter; Connie/Cindy). No wonder it takes children several years to learn the basics of the English spelling system. The fact is, adults continue to learn about spelling throughout their lives—and, of course, look up word spellings in (primarily online) dictionaries.

Oral Language

Although oral vocabulary and grammatical understanding are not central to decoding, they do provide some support, both indirectly and directly. For example, oral vocabulary is thought to affect decoding skill indirectly (Dickinson, Golinkoff, & Hirsh-Pasek 2010). According to one explanation, words are first stored in the brain as holistic units. As vocabulary increases and the phonological structures of some words overlap (e.g., cut/cat; mouse/house), words in these clusters are reorganized and stored as smaller units of sound. This finer-grained storage is thought to provide a foundation for phonological awareness (Metsala 1999; Metsala & Walley 1998).

A child's oral vocabulary also helps them reformulate an approximate pronunciation that they obtain after the initial steps of decoding a printed word (i.e., the pronunciation does not at first match the printed word). This happens somewhat frequently in the early stages of learning to read, when children's letter-sound knowledge is not yet secure and the many spelling irregularities found in English still puzzle them.

Consider, for example, a beginner reader's difficulty in decoding the words *peanut* and *butter* as they try to read a new book to their mother at home:

1. *P* (correctly pronounced /p/)
2. *E* (correctly pronounced /e/, as in *pediatric*)
3. *A* (incorrectly responded to single letter, pronounced /a/, as in *ate*)
4. *N* (correctly pronounced /n/)
5. *U* (incorrectly pronounced /u/, as in *chute*)
6. *T* (correctly pronounced /t/)
7. The child repeated the word *peanut* with an extra syllable—pronouncing /a/, as in *ate*—and looked puzzled.
8. The child then sounded out/read *butter* but produced "beauter."
9. The child stopped to think.
10. Suddenly, the child said, "Peanut butter!"

How might such a sudden correction in pronunciation happen? First, the child knew the story was about a picnic and that animals were making sandwiches because they and their mother had discussed an illustration in the book that depicts a sandwich-making scene. Using knowledge of both this context and the kind of sandwich, the child suddenly transformed the sound approximations they had obtained into the actual words in the book. Had these words not already been in the child's vocabulary, they might not have found their way past the approximations.

Oral vocabulary and background knowledge help only *after* a reader has engaged in basic decoding to arrive at a sound approximation (Adams 1990; Share 1999). However, this assist is useful to a young child just learning to read, especially when they have interesting books at home that might not be simplified to the same degree as the beginner books they read at school. Additionally, linking the visual pattern of letters in a word to its pronunciation and meaning helps to anchor this pattern in the child's mind. As a consequence, they can read it much faster the next time they encounter the word in a book or some other context (Pikulski & Chard 2005).

Understandings and Skills Needed When Reading to Learn

In addition to good decoding skill, reading to learn requires good oral language skills, solid background knowledge, and reasoning skills. After first explaining how decoding affects comprehension, each of these items is discussed.

Decoding Skill

If children make serious errors in recognizing words, the meanings of sentences and passages are distorted. Additionally, if children struggle to sound out each word instead of recognizing some words automatically and decoding others relatively easily, they have fewer cognitive resources available for thinking about meaning. In short, unless word recognition is fairly accurate and somewhat automatic, comprehension suffers (LaBerge & Samuels 1974; Pikulski 2006).

Oral Vocabulary and Other Oral Language Skills

Oral vocabulary knowledge is very important to reading comprehension because readers need to know the meanings of individual words to understand the text as a whole. Oral vocabulary learning begins in infancy and happens when children hear the adults who care for them, such as teachers and family members, say words (Rowe, Romero, & Leech 2023). The repetition of words and exposure to diverse words impact vocabulary size and growth in children's early years (Newman, Rowe, & Ratner 2016; Rowe 2012).

Syntactic and grammatical skills also matter because word forms and meanings differ depending on the position and order of words in a sentence. Consider the difference between *wave* used as a verb and a noun:

1. *Wave* bye-bye to Grandma.
2. When we went to the beach, I saw a very large *wave*.

The position of *wave* used as a verb in the first sentence differs from the position of *wave* used as a noun in the second sentence, and the nearby words in each sentence also differ.

Skill with grammar and syntax helps children know whether a word is the name of something, stipulates an action, or modifies the meaning of another word. Similar to vocabulary, language exposure affects children's syntax comprehension and use (Language and Reading Research Consortium 2015). Good language skills become absolutely essential for good comprehension of books, especially those that children read to learn about content areas, such as science, history, or geography (Nagy & Townsend 2012). A strong foundation of oral language skills in early childhood supports this later success.

Background Knowledge

Background knowledge is everything a person knows about the physical, biological, and social worlds. Young children use background knowledge to comprehend books they hear read aloud, just as older children use it to comprehend books they read independently (Smith et al. 2021).

For instance, consider the effects of background knowledge (or lack thereof) on story interpretation in a preschool example during a reading of *Whistle for Willie,* by Ezra Jack Keats (Schickedanz & Collins 2012). Immediately after the teacher read, "He jumped off his shadow, but when he landed, they were together again," a child shouted, "He found another one!" Adults and older children understand that "He jumped off his shadow" means that Peter's (the main character's) body made the shadows. But unless a child understands that shadows are nonmaterial objects—which many preschoolers do not (Carey 1985)—they could easily think a shadow stays where cast and that someone coming along later might find it.

Background knowledge is also critically important for comprehending informational books. Although these books are written and designed to help children acquire information, when used in isolation from related concrete experiences, children can find it difficult to understand the concepts these books are trying to teach (Leung 2008). If a child's science or geography book is not coupled with meaningful real-life experiences that use key words, children will rarely learn terms at the depth required to understand the book. Prior subject knowledge (including associated vocabulary) aids children's comprehension, even when using books that are intended to teach about specific topics. Good knowledge of grammar and syntax helps too.

Children also apply knowledge about different text structures. For example, informational texts usually do not have characters, a problem, or a plot, while narratives do. Additionally, informational texts are denser with ideas than narratives and contain considerably more technical terminology (Kelley et al. 2010; Nagy & Townsend 2012). Knowledge about these differences in text structures, gained from experience in hearing adults read them aloud and discuss them, helps children comprehend different kinds of books (Best, Floyd, & McNamara 2008).

Reasoning

Children must learn to use background knowledge in conjunction with information provided in a book's text and illustrations. This learning occurs as adults read books to children, model reasoning by sharing their thoughts, and ask questions that prompt the children to reason. Authors often leave gaps in stories and expect readers or listeners to use reasoning to fill them in. For example, at the beginning of *One Dark Night*, by Hazel Hutchins, illustrated by Susan Kathleen Hartung, Jonathan (the main character) is awake in bed, looking out his window. The text tells readers that a storm is approaching; lightning flashes and thunder booms. Although the text does not state that Jonathan was kept awake by the storm, background knowledge helps readers to infer this.

Table 1.1 lists other events from *One Dark Night*, as well as gaps in the story that must be inferred. This filling in requires reasoning based on the integration of information from the book's text and illustrations and the reader's or listener's background knowledge.

Consider a classroom example that occurred as the teacher finished reading *The Snowy Day*, by Ezra Jack Keats. At the end of this story, Peter (the main character) is going out to play in the snow with a friend who is not named in the text. One child suggested that Peter's friend was Gilberto, a character the children knew well from hearing their teacher read *Gilberto and the Wind*, by Marie Hall Ets. Like Peter, Gilberto had also played outside by himself. Apparently, the child thought that Peter and Gilberto would make good friends. Although it is unlikely that Peter's friend at the end of this story is Gilberto, this is an example of a child's engagement in reasoning. What the child did not understand is that Peter lived in the city and Gilberto lived in the country. A lack of knowledge leads the preschooler to draw erroneous conclusions, even when the child engages in drawing inferences—in high-level reasoning.

Table 1.1. Examples of Thinking Needed to Fill in Gaps in *One Dark Night*

Event	Inference
An illustration shows Jonathan is in pajamas in bed, looking through the window. The text tells readers it is nighttime and that Jonathan sees lightning and hears thunder. Readers can infer that Jonathan should be asleep or trying to sleep.	Readers use background knowledge about lightning and thunder to help understand why instead he's awake and looking out his window. He looks concerned. Readers' experiences with thunderstorms help them understand why Jonathan is a bit frightened.
The text says that Jonathan sees something small outside and that it is looking back at him. Readers see the outline of a cat's head and its two green eyes in the darkness.	Readers can infer that Jonathan might not know what the animal is; the text only says he sees "something small." Perhaps it's an owl, dog, or cat. Readers can use background knowledge to infer that it is an animal because of the eyes. They can also guess that it is a cat, given the shape of the head.
The text says Jonathan runs downstairs, opens the door, and lets a stray cat in. He's depicted near the door, as a cat runs in. Jonathan tells his grandparents the cat is afraid of thunder. Grandfather says stray cats are not afraid of thunder. Grandmother says she thinks the cat has a mouse in its mouth.	Jonathan's grandparents are introduced here; readers might infer that he lives with them or was sleeping over. Readers might also infer that the grandparents were awakened by the storm and heard Jonathan get out of bed and run downstairs. Perhaps they wondered what was going on and got out of bed to find out. Grandfather may have said something, such as, "Hey! Why are you opening the door?" which prompted Jonathan to say the cat was afraid of thunder. Finally, Grandmother might have thought the cat had a mouse because cats catch mice and like to show what they have caught.
An illustration shows a kitten on a rug. Jonathan is not shown, but the text says he announces, "It's a kitten!"	Readers can infer that the large cat is the kitten's mother. Readers don't see Jonathan with the kitten, but they can infer that he's there because he identifies it. They can also infer that his grandparents had not joined him because he calls to them as if they are in another part of the house. Finally, readers might infer from Jonathan's announcement that he is excited and wants Grandmother to know there is no mouse.

What Are Preschoolers Thinking? (Schickedanz, Collins, & Marchant 2022) explores many examples like this one, where higher-level reasoning about some aspect of a plotted narrative yields a wrong conclusion because the child lacked essential knowledge.

Over time, preschoolers' reasoning becomes more accurate because they learn from teacher feedback and comments to take account of more information (Duke & Carlisle 2011). They also learn to reason when teachers ask higher-level questions in a discussion that follows a first reading (Collins 2016). It is important to note that questions asked *during* a first reading can interrupt thinking. Think about watching a film in a theater and having it stopped every 10 minutes for a question. Adults would be outraged if this happened! After children have had opportunities to hear the story uninterrupted in its entirety, questions can be used strategically during later readings on subsequent days.

Different Learning from Different Experiences

Different experiences in the early years yield different kinds of learning. Some things children learn influence decoding, while other things they learn influence comprehension (Language and Reading Research Consortium 2015; NICHD Early Child Care Research Network 2005). Moreover, because beginner books are simplified, educators do not see the full effect of the understandings and skills that primarily affect comprehension until a reader moves past the first phase of reading development and encounters more challenging texts.

Refer to Table 1.2. The first column lists a selection of early literacy practices similar to typical preschool standards for language and literacy. Additional standards, such as science and social studies, also impact reading development because background knowledge in these domains provides critical support for comprehension. The most important contributions that each experience makes are featured in the table's second column. The third and fourth columns indicate whether a contribution is very important (i.e., strong) for either decoding or comprehension or less important (i.e., weak). Early childhood experiences that support oral vocabulary development and background knowledge significantly aid comprehension and make some contribution to decoding skill. Good decoding skill is necessary, though not sufficient, to support good comprehension, as noted for the decoding items listed in the third column.

Adopting a Long View

Children benefit more when teachers and families emphasize language development, background knowledge, and comprehension strategies rather than focus primarily on code-related skills, such as alphabet learning. Likewise, encouraging deep levels of word understanding by using a rich language and content knowledge curriculum benefits children's comprehension more than settling for only simple labels to increase vocabulary (Kelley et al. 2010; Ouellette 2006). These instructional issues matter because the reading comprehension levels of school-age children in the United States—already low in most national assessments (NCES 2022)—were further exacerbated by the COVID-19 pandemic. Early childhood programs are encouraged to reach beyond the use of minimal approaches to vocabulary development and provide a balanced, more thorough approach to language and literacy that will benefit children in the long term.

Table 1.2. Selected Early Practices and Their Contributions to a Foundation for Reading

Teaching practice	Contributions	Importance in decoding (learning to read)	Importance in comprehension (reading to learn)
Reading storybooks	Print conventions	Strong	Weak
	Oral language/vocabulary	Weak	Strong
	Reasoning	Weak	Strong
Reading informational texts	Print conventions	Strong	Weak
	Oral language/vocabulary	Weak	Strong
	Background knowledge	Weak	Strong
	Reasoning	Weak	Weak
Reciting songs and nursery rhymes	Phonological awareness	Strong	Weak
	Oral language/vocabulary	Weak	Strong
Explaining word meanings	Oral language/vocabulary	Weak	Strong
Playing with the sounds in words	Phonological awareness	Strong	Weak
Teaching alphabet letters	Alphabet letter identification	Strong	Weak
	Print conventions (uppercase and lowercase letter forms)	Strong	Weak
Underlining book and poem titles	Print conventions	Strong	Weak
Going on field trips	Background knowledge	Weak	Strong
	Oral language/vocabulary	Weak	Strong
Having conversations	Oral language/vocabulary	Weak	Strong
	Reasoning	Weak	Strong

Alphabet letter identification is the ability to label alphabet letters by their names. *Background knowledge* is information about the physical, biological, and social worlds. *Oral language/vocabulary* includes grammatical and syntactic skills, plus oral vocabulary support. *Phonological awareness* is the ability to recognize and manipulate sounds in spoken words. *Print conventions* include left-to-right scanning of print, top-to-bottom scanning of a page, and putting spaces in between words. *Reasoning* includes thinking about text and illustrations to infer information, as well as abstract thinking in decontextualized conversations.

Looking Beyond Code-Related Skills

Sometimes early childhood educators adopt a code-related focus without realizing that different sets of understandings and skills affect decoding and comprehending, or that young children must start building both sets before formal learning begins. This misunderstanding results in an overemphasis on decoding skill because teachers know that these are needed when children learn to read. Although children learn to read first, they must simultaneously begin to develop knowledge and skills that influence reading to learn (Neuman & Kaefer 2018).

Some kindergarten and first grade teachers want children to recognize and name the alphabet letters and to write their names by the time they finish preschool. While this expectation is acceptable, preschool teachers must in turn emphasize to kindergarten and primary grade teachers that code-related understandings and skills and comprehension-related skills must be addressed and instructed with more balance (Shanahan 2016; Stahl 2012). In fact, research has indicated for years a need for this balance in the early primary grades.

One of the first longitudinal studies spanning preschool through fourth grade (Storch & Whitehurst 2002) advocates supporting code-related skills and oral language comprehension skills simultaneously. Children do not need proficiency in decoding before receiving instruction in oral language skills. Children need both, beginning in preschool and continuing throughout the *learning to read* and *reading to learn* years.

Strong support for oral language must begin during the infant and toddler years (Rowe, Romero, & Leech 2023) and must continue not only during preschool, but *forever* after that.

Looking Beyond a Narrow Focus on Recognition-Level Oral Vocabulary

The oral language focus in curricula used in some early childhood programs is often too narrow. Learning words only as labels of objects within the confines of books alone develops oral vocabulary at a simple recognition level. A deeper focus that provides children with information about words is of considerably more benefit to their comprehension in the short and long term (Ouellette 2006). Encountering words in authentic contexts, such as hands-on science experiences, is a critical part of meaning making (Gelman & Brenneman 2004). Children must also have multiple encounters with a word in a variety of contexts, rather than in just one or two (Nagy & Townsend 2012). In short, meaningful firsthand experiences (historically a mainstay in preschool programs) are part and parcel of good emergent literacy programs that have long-term effects.

Concluding Thoughts

The truth is, early childhood educators must keep many balls in the air, right from the beginning. The alphabet is not *the* place to start, nor is oral language or content knowledge. Teachers must start on many fronts simultaneously, which is why early educational standards include literacy, language, math, science, social studies, and more, and why curriculum frameworks suggest a wide range of experiences.

CHAPTER 2

THE BEGINNING—READING WITH INFANTS AND TODDLERS

Christina M. Cassano and Jessica L. Hoffman

Grandma Judy reads to 8-month-old Ana, as she always does when visiting. Their story time routine begins with a book that has a distinct beat capable of eliciting a smile or a giggle and, in time, Ana's participation. *Dr. Seuss's ABC: An Amazing Alphabet Book* and *Mr. Brown Can Moo! Can You?,* both by Dr. Seuss, are favorites. From there, Grandma Judy usually reads *Goodnight Moon,* by Margaret Wise Brown, illustrated by Clement Hurd. This book also invites participation, though in a quieter way. Because Ana continues to be interested and engaged, Grandma Judy finishes story time by reading two more books that have a soft musical quality, such as *Everywhere Babies*, by Susan Meyers, illustrated by Marla Frazee; *Ten Little Fingers and Ten Little Toes,* by Mem Fox, illustrated by Helen Oxenbury; and *Te amo, bebé/Love You, Baby,* created by Amy Pixton, illustrated by Stephan Lomp. When they are finished, Grandma Judy places the books in the nearby basket so they are easily accessible for the next time she and Ana read together.

Long before they can read—even before they can talk—infants learn a multitude of skills, concepts, and values from reading with an adult (Franks et al. 2022; Price & Kalil 2019). They learn, for example, to attend to new words and structures in the language they hear (Rowe & Snow 2020; Weisleder & Fernald 2013). Infants also begin to learn about the concepts these words and language structures represent (Karrass & Braungart-Rieker 2005; Muhinyi & Rowe 2019). With exposure, infants learn that the language of books differs from spoken language and that stories communicate human experiences (Birckmayer, Kennedy, & Stonehouse 2008; Montag, Jones, & Smith 2015). Infants also learn some physical things about books, such as how to orient them and turn their pages. Most importantly, perhaps, infants and toddlers become acquainted with learning from others and begin to observe and acquire cultural practices and values, such as learning to wonder, seeking answers, and reading as a pleasurable activity (Tamis-LeMonda, Kuchirko, & Song 2014; Tamis-LeMonda & Song 2012). Through reading, even the youngest children begin to see themselves and their families reflected in the images of the texts and are exposed to new information, experiences, and languages (Bishop 1990; NAEYC 2019). Reading to young children has many benefits for adults too. These experiences make for powerful bonding moments, such as a time of shared quiet after lunch or at the end of the day as part of a bedtime routine.

Understanding infant and toddler development, including how to select interesting and appropriate books and engage infants and toddlers in reading experiences, is essential to ensure story reading is enjoyable for both young children and adults. Reading with infants and toddlers requires a more individualized approach than reading to older children; adult responsiveness to the unique needs of the infant or toddler is necessary (Tamis-LeMonda, Kuchirko, & Song 2014). This chapter focuses primarily on reading to individual children. Later in the chapter, there is a short discussion about reading to small groups (three or four) of older toddlers.

The information in this chapter is grounded in decades of research. The age ranges, developmental milestones, reading practices, and recommended books are general guidelines based on current understanding of child development and learning. Early childhood educators and families will want to consider this information in combination with their own deep knowledge of an individual child's behaviors, contexts, and interests when choosing books for them. The goal is for early childhood educators and families to act as both interested followers and knowledgeable guides when sharing books with very young children. In this balanced approach, the child is given ample opportunity to guide what is shared and how, while the adult scaffolds engaging learning experiences with books.

Engaging Infants and Toddlers with Reading

This part of the chapter is organized into six specific infant and toddler age groups. Each discusses what most children can do, book recommendations, and ways to engage the children with books. Table 2.1 provides additional recommendations organized by formats, types, and features important for these age groups.

From Birth to 3 Months

What the infant can do. Because a newborn cannot raise their head, adults must support it when holding them. Over the first few months, infants become able to raise their heads for increasingly longer periods of time while lying on their stomachs. Infants also grasp objects placed into their hands reflexively, and they become more skilled in directing their hands to their mouths to suck on them.

At this age, infants do not yet have fully developed visual acuity, so objects are not clear when they look at them. This is why they prefer images with high contrast and large shapes and patterns (Johnson 2011). Newborns attend more closely to images resembling human faces than to other objects because faces have high-contrast features (i.e., skin, eyes, eyebrows, lips), making them visually distinct and easier to perceive and focus on (Frank, Vul, & Johnson 2009; Simion et al. 2001).

With respect to oral language development, infants attend well to speech with high pitch, longer pauses, and exaggerated intonation (Golinkoff et al. 2015; ManyBabies Consortium 2020). Infants can perceive the sounds of all languages spoken to them, enabling them to learn any language. This ability declines over time as they become more attuned to the specific sounds they hear in the languages adults use with them most (Kuhl et al. 2014). Though their speech perception is keen, young infants do not yet understand the words they hear. Newborns communicate through sounds. They begin with crying, but within a few months, their verbalizations include gurgles and coos.

Choosing books for the infant. High-contrast books target the visual abilities and interests of infants. Examples include *Babies Love Animals,* by Susanne König, and *Tummy Time!* created by Mama Makes Books. Because babies prefer looking at human faces, books with close-up photographs of people are also good choices (e.g., *Baby Faces,* by Jim Harbison; *Hugs and Kisses,* by Roberta Grobel Intrater). Educators and families can also create personalized books with faces familiar to the infant using albums with transparent plastic sleeves for printed photos or websites such as Snapfish or Chatbooks for creating and printing digital photo books.

Of course, not all books need to focus on infants' visual development. Any read aloud or other language-rich vocal experience is appealing to most babies. Early literacy researchers Zambo and Hansen (2007) noted that "being held, feeling good, and hearing a familiar, comforting voice are more important than the kind of book or the content of a story" (33). Adults can recite nursery rhymes or poems (e.g., *¡Pío Peep!* selected by Alma Flor Ada and F. Isabel Campoy, illustrated by Viví Escrivá), sing songs, or read storybooks and literature geared toward older children.

Table 2.1. Book Recommendations for Infants and Toddlers

Format/type	Features	Select recommended titles
Accordion books	• Include panels folded in a zigzag pattern • Can be propped open or unfolded to view multiple pages at once	*Animal Parade*, by duopress labs, illustrated by Jannie Ho *In the Air*, by Natasha Durley *Tummy Time!* created by Mama Makes Books
Basic concept books	• Focus on a single concept (e.g., colors, shapes, numbers, body parts) • Each page includes a single image and an accompanying word or phrase	*Baby Eye Like* series, by PlayBac *Bilingual Bright Baby* series, by Roger Priddy *Hey, Water!* by Antoinette Portis *Little Nature Explorers* series, by Amber Hendricks, illustrated by Gavin Scott
Bath (plastic) books	• Designed to be chewed, mouthed, and wiped clean easily • Waterproof for bath play	*Color Me: Who's in the Water?* by Surya Sajnani *My Neighborhood*, by Maddie Frost *Tub Time Books* series, by Land of B.
Cloth (fabric, rag) books	• Soft and durable • Include different textures	*Nursery Times* series, by Jo and Nic's Crinkly Cloth Books *Tails* series, by beiens
Die-cut books	• Have firm, thick pages with cut-outs to help convey information and story content	*8 Little Planets*, by Chris Ferrie, illustrated by Lizzy Doyle *In My Barn*, by Sara Gillingham, illustrated by Lorena Siminovich *Nighty Night, Little Green Monster*, by Ed Emberly
High-contrast books	• Include pictures and patterns with black-and-white contrasts that appeal to young infants	*Babies Love Animals*, by Susanne König *Black on White*, by Tana Hoban *California, Baby!* by Csongor Szalay
Interactive books (simple)	• Include a basic interactive feature, such as flaps for lifting or tabs for pulling, that is used to reveal key components of the story • Feature a simple story on a single topic (e.g., daily routines, animals, hide-and-seek)	*Getting Dressed*, by Pauline Oud *Let's Find the Tiger*, by Tiger Tales, illustrated by Alex Willmore *Things That Go*, by Scarlett Wing, illustrated by Martina Hogan

Format/type	Features	Select recommended titles
Interactive books (complex)	• Require participation and interaction through one or more features—such as elements that can be lifted, turned, slid, pulled, popped up, or otherwise moved—to reveal or engage with key components of the story. • Have simple storylines with opportunities to learn new information through the interactive features • May include other features, such as textures, technology, or sounds	*Don't Tickle the Monkey!* by Sam Taplin, illustrated by Ana Martin Larranaga *I Thought I Saw a Crocodile!* by Templar Books, illustrated by Lydia Nichols *Tails*, by Matthew Van Fleet
Language play books	• Include opportunities to play with language through alliteration, repetition, rhyme, and rhythm	*Happy in Our Skin*, by Fran Manushkin, illustrated by Lauren Tobia *Sumo Counting*, by Sanae Ishida *Whose Knees Are These?* by Jabari Asim, illustrated by LeUyen Pham
Predictable books	• Repeat phrases and refrains that encourage chiming in during reading and memorization of text • Include stories, poems, and songs on new and familiar topics	*Ducks Away!* by Mem Fox, illustrated by Judy Horacek *Go Sleep in Your Own Bed!* by Candace Fleming, illustrated by Lori Nichols *Goodnight, Goodnight, Construction Site*, by Sherri Duskey Rinker, illustrated by Tom Lichtenheld
Texture (touch-and-feel, sensory) books	• Include a variety of textures for a young infant's hands to explore	*10 Things I Love About You!* by Danielle McLean, illustrated by Grace Habib *In the Wild*, by Little Hippo Books, illustrated by Sarah Muthomi *The Touch Book*, by Nicola Edwards, illustrated by Thomas Elliott
Theme books	• Feature a series of sequentially related events and illustrations • Have a simple plot with limited characters and familiar settings • Include familiar routines, experiences, or traditions	*Dinosaur Dance!* by Sandra Boynton *Stir Crack Whisk Bake: A Little Book About Little Cakes*, by America's Test Kitchen Kids and Maddie Frost *Sunny Days*, by Deborah Kerbel, illustrated by Miki Sato
Topic books	• Focus on broader, more complex subjects, such as vehicles, nature, or emotions • Text provides more information than basic concept books • Feature clear photographs or illustrations	*Animals Move*, by Jane Whittingham *Kindness*, by Paloma Rossa, illustrated by Katia Klein *My Big Truck Book*, by Roger Priddy

Box 2.1. Making Books Available to Infants Younger than 4 Months

At this age, an infant can have books set in their crib or placed nearby on the floor when they are awake and on their stomach or when sitting upright in an infant seat. A book placed to stand upright on the floor near an infant lying prone should be positioned at a viewing distance that allows the infant to choose, using a simple head turn, when and for how long to look.

Traditional board books stand up well and stay open to a selected page. Accordion books that have panels folded in a zigzag pattern can be spread out to display multiple pages at once. Infants will grasp a book reflexively if one is handed to them. Because they will mouth items they hold, soft plastic or cloth books are ideal.

Engaging the infant. Much of a very young infant's daily life is spent eating, sleeping, and experiencing diaper changes. While reading does not hold a prominent place, families and educators can weave experiences with books into the infant's day.

Though books for infants typically have limited text, adults can invent language to accompany the images when sharing these books. By talking about images (whether in the text's original language, the family's home language, or both), adults help infants connect language sounds with the objects, actions, or attributes they refer to (Bergelson & Aslin 2017; Gogate & Hollich 2016).

Because young infants cannot yet support their heads when held upright, adults usually cradle them in their arms while reading. As infants develop more head control, they can explore books more independently during tummy time. (See Box 2.1.)

The infant's attention and reactions should guide how the adult explores books with them. Some infants are calmed and quieted when an adult reads to them; others might coo differently, imitating the rise and fall of a reader's voice. When a bit older, an infant may even gurgle and coo with delight (Holland 2008; Torr 2023). However, infants might sometimes indicate overstimulation or disinterest in the experience. When their behavior indicates discontent of any kind, the adult should discontinue reading and try again another time.

From 4 to 6 Months

What the infant can do. Infants at this age grab, grasp, and mouth just about everything, including books. They are learning how things work and how to move their bodies to accomplish their goals. The infant can now support their own head and sit upright comfortably with support when held in someone's lap. By 6 months, some babies might begin to sit up independently.

Although infants this age are still prelinguistic—that is, not yet uttering understandable words— by 6 months, they understand the meanings of many common nouns (Bergelson & Swingley 2012). At this age, infants communicate through ***paralinguistic communications***, including vocalizations such as cooing, laughing, and crying; body language and gestures; and gazing and facial expressions. Some adults and older children interpret these communicative efforts and vary their own speech to engage infants' attention using ***child-directed speech (CDS)***. Characteristics of CDS, as compared to normal speech, include (Jones et al. 2023; Saxton 2009)

> - A slower rate
> - Longer pauses
> - A higher and greater range of pitch
> - Exaggerated intonation
> - Clearer enunciation

> - More gestures and facial expressions
> - Simpler, shorter phrases that emphasize important words
> - Some use of the child's own vocabulary (e.g., "go bye-bye" instead of "leave")

CDS is used by speakers of many different languages and fosters the mutual engagement needed for social and linguistic development (Jahdhami 2023; Rowe & Snow 2020). During this time, infants learning more than one language are also becoming increasingly adept at distinguishing between them (Byers-Heinlein & Lew-Williams 2013).

Choosing books for the infant. Because infants now grasp and mouth objects to explore them, adults can introduce cloth, board, or soft plastic books that can withstand crumpling, chewing, and drooling. Waterproof bath books are also a good choice. Books with simple, high-contrast illustrations or photos are still appropriate, but with infants' color vision more fully developed, adults can also include books with more colorful illustrations. Basic concept books, which focus on a simple concept and feature an image and maybe a word or two on each page, are good options.

Texture books that invite infants to touch and feel various items on the pages capitalize on an infant's budding interest in manual exploration. For example, *Little Feet Love,* by Anthony Nex; the *Touch and Feel/Tacto y textura* series, by DK; and the *See, Touch, Feel* series, by Roger Priddy, include a variety of materials (e.g., terrycloth, sandpaper, stringy grass) and textures (bumpy, rough, shiny, smooth, furry) for a young infant's hands to explore alongside the theme or topic of the book.

Engaging the infant. Infants are now sitting upright with support when held, which frees an adult's hands to hold a book for shared viewing. Because the infant will likely grasp and physically explore the book, durable books are the best option. Providing the infant with a toy or teether to manipulate while looking at books with an adult can satisfy and distract the infant from physical exploration of the book the adult is sharing and may increase the infant's engagement.

Of course, there is nothing wrong with allowing an infant to touch and manipulate books. The educator or family member can comment about the infant's actions, such as opening the book or pointing to items on the pages. Infants this age are usually out of their cribs more often but not yet walking. Thus, adults must still bring books to them.

When reading, adults might draw the infant's attention to the images in the book and then label, describe, or explain them using CDS, facial expressions, and gestures like pointing. By reading expressively and including other attention-getting behaviors, the adult enhances the meaning of the words and images in the book while making the experience interactive and engaging.

From 7 to 9 Months

What the infant can do. During this period, the infant's gross motor skills are developing rapidly. They sit up independently and become mobile by crawling, scooting, and creeping. Soon after, they begin to pull themselves up to stand. With these new motor skills, infants enjoy spending a lot of time on the move.

When manipulating objects, infants will often hold an object in one hand while patting, poking, or pulling on it with the other. While they will still explore objects with their mouths, this kind of exploration decreases with their improved visual inspection and manual manipulation capabilities. By the end of this period, most infants have developed their ability to use a thumb and index finger in opposition (i.e., a pincer grasp) to pick up small objects. A pincer grasp dramatically increases an infant's dexterity and ability to manipulate objects, including books. Infants this age also become interested in ***deformation manipulations*** and may intentionally crumple or tear paper to explore what happens (Corbetta & Snapp-Childs 2009; Karniol 1989).

Infants understand an increasing number of words in the languages they hear regularly, even though they may not produce their first words for several more months (Bergelson & Swingley 2012; Hoff et al. 2012). If adults establish ***joint attention*** (i.e., shared focus) with infants by looking at, pointing at, and commenting about the same objects, vocabulary learning can occur (IOM & NRC 2015; Newman, Rowe, & Ratner 2016). The infant also begins to point with their index finger, which aids them in establishing joint attention by directing the adult to an object, person, or phenomenon of interest (Colonnesi et al. 2010).

Choosing books for the infant. With a pincer grasp at their disposal, babies begin to turn the pages of certain books, particularly the thick, stiff pages of board books that can be moved easily with an index finger. Board books and the more paper-like format of Indestructibles books are durable options that withstand attempts to crumple, chew, or tear pages. Adults can support larger and heavier, lap-size board books when reading with an infant this age. Smaller board books are better suited for infants' hands when they explore books independently. Topic books—featuring clear photographs or illustrations of different types of objects, people, and actions and more information than basic concept books—can facilitate language learning.

Engaging the infant. Infants this age are busy beginning to crawl, and this new motor skill limits their interest in sitting still to read with an adult. This is perfectly okay; reading should be an enjoyable experience, not a chore. There are, however, ways to encourage book engagement in even the busiest infant. Reading can occur in very short spurts during quieter moments, such as during a mealtime while the child sits in a high chair, before a nap or bedtime, or during car rides while an adult or older sibling sits in the back with the child. These opportunities can add up to a significant amount of reading time over the course of the day. While reading, the adult can follow the infant's lead by allowing them to turn the book around, turn pages, or open and close it. When the infant looks at or points to particular objects, the adult can label and describe them. Infants who do not spontaneously express interest in books should still be invited to explore them with an adult. They can become engaged in reading if allowed to participate in meaningful ways.

Other babies often enjoy listening to the adult read while they move about and play. Judy's son, Adam, often scooted out of her lap to walk around near her chair. At first, Judy would stop reading because she thought he was no longer interested. However, Adam would ask her to continue ("Read, mommy, read"), so she read while he played. He would come stand by her chair every once in a while to look at the book and its pictures, then resume walking around.

The two key developmental achievements of understanding words and learning to point are closely related. As the infant begins to understand that words refer to particular people, objects, and actions, pointing provides a new and highly effective tool for requesting words. For infants who are not yet pointing, gaze facilitates joint attention and word learning (Brooks & Meltzoff 2015; Hollich et al. 2000). In other words, when infants point to or intently gaze at a book's illustrations, they call the adult's attention to the object, and the adult can reply with a label or explanation using CDS (Fletcher & Reese 2005).

To support infants' developmental interests, educators and families can adapt their book-sharing strategies, shifting away from reading extended selections of text (which simply sounded interesting to a younger infant) and toward more labeling of and talking about illustrations. "Reading" to infants this age can feel like an ongoing series of pointing, labeling, and making personal connections to the images, which makes the language of the text less important to consider when choosing books. For example, although a book written for preschoolers might include lengthy and complex text that is far beyond the comprehension of a 9-month-old, an infant can still enjoy the book if the topic and illustrations are of interest. When the adult uses the book as an opportunity for joint attention, talking about the illustrations (instead of reading the book as one would with a preschooler), and responding to the infant's interests and communication attempts, the experience can be engaging for both participants and provide rich opportunities for language exposure for the infant (Tamis-LeMonda, Kuchirko, & Song 2014).

From 10 to 12 months

What the infant can do. As their fine motor skills continue to develop, infants become more intentional in manipulating objects. For example, they might press buttons on toys and lift the flaps in books. They are also crawling, cruising furniture, and possibly even taking their first wobbly steps. With their increased mobility, infants are sometimes less interested in sitting with an adult for extended periods to read books.

Language development is also accelerating with ongoing exposure to rich language (Cartmill et al. 2013). Although individual differences are common, by 12 months old, most infants understand dozens of words across all the languages they hear regularly (Hoff et al. 2012) and begin to produce their first recognizable words (Bates & Goodman 1997). Their receptive language continues to exceed their expressive language—that is, they can understand more words than they can speak. This pattern is true for all phases of language development and for all speakers of any language.

Choosing books for the infant. Because the infant now expresses their individuality and shows budding interests in and preferences for toys, activities, and books, educators and families can begin to rely more on content than physical characteristics when choosing books. The infant is more likely to be engaged by a book when its topic is familiar and of interest to them (e.g., transportation, animals).

Books with interactive parts, such as lift-the-flap books and move-turn-slide books, also become of interest because they allow infants to engage in manipulating the book on a topic of interest. Examples include *Bedtime for Duckling,* by Amelia Hepworth, illustrated by Anna Doherty, and *Let's Find the Tiger,* by Tiger Tales, illustrated by Alex Willmore.

Infants no longer purposefully damage books as they explore how paper tears; however, because their fine motor skills are still developing, there can still be unintentional page tearing. For this reason, board books are still a good format for this age range. A wide range of stories is available as board books, although some are more engaging than others. Those with relatively simple language and clear connections to illustrations are the best as these features help the infant understand the language of the book when supported with adult talk, gestures, and expressions. Examples include

› Topic books with a specific focus and representative examples on each page, such as Byron Barton's transportation books (e.g., *Boats, Planes, Trains*)

› Books that provide opportunities to play with language through alliteration, repetition, rhyme, and rhythm, such as *The Going to Bed Book,* by Sandra Boynton, and *Give Me a Snickle!* by Alisha Sevigny

Engaging the infant. Infants this age begin to bring toys or books to a family member or educator as a way to ask, "Play this with me" or "Read this with me." Children who experience consistently warm and responsive support in play usually have better social and cognitive outcomes and later literacy achievement (Landry, Smith, & Swank 2006; Tamis-LeMonda, Kuchirko, & Song 2014). Therefore, adults should follow the infant's lead in play. For example, they can share a book when the infant is interested and, when their interest wanes, allow them to return to other play.

Adults can also sustain active infants' engagement in reading by making reading itself active. For example, when reading language play books, adults can emphasize the cadence, vary the pace, sing the words, or create movement or dance to accompany the words. Interactive books also invite infants to participate in the reading as they manipulate books. Pointing, labeling, and asking questions about the book fosters engagement and supports language development (Olson & Masur 2015; Ünlütabak et al. 2022).

> Saira and her 11-month-old son, Liam, read one of his favorite books, *Where's Spot?* by Eric Hill. They are seated on the floor in the living room. Saira holds the book on her lap facing outward so that Liam, who is facing her, can see the pictures. As Saira expressively reads the question ("Is he under the . . . ?") that is the culmination of the text on each page, Liam is prompted to lift the flap to see if Spot is hidden there. Following the lift, he robustly shakes his head *no,*

and Saira verbally repeats "no" to reinforce that Spot is indeed not the animal discovered. This exchange repeats for every page, Liam joyfully responding to his mother's intonation and the familiar routine.

Now that infants are beginning to understand and use more language, shared reading also provides opportunities to extend infants' utterances. For example, when a child says "choo choo," a responsive adult affirms the child's response and models more complex language with, "Yes, that's a train, a choo-choo train." Similarly, pointing to relevant illustrations, acting out actions, and using facial expressions support infants' understanding because words are linked to meanings in concrete ways. Making connections between concepts in the book and an infant's familiar experiences also supports understanding. For example, the adult might point from an illustration of a bunny to the pet curled up in their lap and say, "This is a bunny, just like your bunny."

Adults support an infant's ability to produce language by encouraging talk during the book reading interaction, which supports the infant's expressive language (i.e., **output**) (Muhinyi & Rowe 2019). Consider this common interactive sequence (Ninio & Bruner 1978):

1. **Get the infant's attention.** The adult might say, for example, "Oh, look!" while pointing to a book's illustration (e.g., a puppy).

2. **Ask the infant a labeling question.** To prompt the infant's attempt at saying *puppy,* the adult asks, "What do you see?"

3. **Wait for the infant to respond, or provide the answer if necessary.** The infant might reply with a word, gesture, or even just a smile of recognition.

4. **Offer feedback by labeling, confirming, and extending.** If the infant responds with the correct label or gesture, the adult replies, "Yes, that's a puppy!" If the label or gesture offered is incorrect (e.g., the infant attempts to say *kitty*), the adult supplies language, saying, "This animal does have four legs and a tail like a kitten, but it is a puppy. Kittens have longer fur than most puppies have and smaller ears too." The adult points at and traces the puppy's ears with an index finger.

This kind of adult language interaction supports or **scaffolds** a child's language development and leads infants toward more independent language use (Mermelshtine 2017). After several months of responding to requests for labels during book reading interactions, toddlers often begin initiating responses. For instance, a toddler might label objects while turning the book's pages. Independent labeling behaviors represent the first steps toward emergent reading of books, which is an early but essential precursor to conventional reading (Teale & Sulzby 1986).

Toward the end of this age range, infants begin to associate objects with routines and events. For example, when an adult reaches for keys, the infant might say "bye-bye;" upon seeing a sippy cup, the infant might ask, "¿Leche (milk)?" The infant's ability to make connections between objects and events can be used to establish routines for reading. For example, since Lily's infancy, book reading often took place before bedtime. By age 2, Lily responded to the word "bedtime" by gathering an armload of books and bringing them to a parent to read. Similarly, 28-month-old Alex disliked riding in the car, but his mother, Christina, realized combining book reading with riding in the car would make the activity more manageable. While Alex flipped through books

like *Truckery Rhymes,* by Jon Scieszka, illustrated by David Shannon, Loren Long, and David Gordon, Christina recited verses from memory as she drove.

From 13 to 18 months

What the toddler can do. Increasingly steady on their feet, toddlers can accomplish more of their goals. For example, when standing, they can bend down to pick up objects from the floor. They also begin to climb onto furniture or into the lap of an adult. Fine motor skills are also developing as toddlers become better at manipulating objects, such as turning the book pages and engaging with interactive book features (e.g., move-turn-slide books).

Early in this period, toddlers use single words to name familiar objects and people. Within a few months, their language begins to include two-word phrases and sentences (e.g., "More milk" or "Go outside") in the languages they hear frequently. Toddlers also use ***expressive jargon***, or nonsensical strings of sound that resemble actual speech and include intonation, emphasis, pauses, and even gestures. Sometimes, when looking at books, toddlers make utterances that mimic the overall sound of reading. This kind of vocalizing, called ***book babble***, is another early form of emergent reading. It indicates the child's understanding that book language differs from conversational language.

Choosing books for the toddler. With supervision, some toddlers can have access to books with paper pages because they are increasingly able to turn pages without tearing or crumpling them. Toddlers continue to develop preferences in foods, toys, books, and more. They might express likes and dislikes by bringing books they like to an adult or pushing a book away during shared reading. If the toddler pushes a book away or says "no," offer alternative choices; their protests might be due to a lack of interest in the specific book, not the activity of reading itself. Adults should pay attention to a child's movements and body language as they typically offer additional information. Wiggling and squirming, for example, often signal the message "I want to get down!" A toddler who stays close to keep viewing is still interested while one who moves away is not.

As the toddler's capacity for language develops, they enjoy slightly more complex books and are fascinated by more detailed illustrations (Mohammed, Afaya, & Abukari 2023; Scherer et al. 2019). Theme books about new and familiar topics are good choices for this age (Towell et al. 2021). Unlike basic concept books that consist of examples of one particular topic (e.g., cars, animals, shapes), theme books feature a series of sequentially related events and illustrations.

A common theme features a child's daily activities and routines (e.g., getting dressed, eating, going to bed). Theme books offer a transition from basic concept books to actual stories because, although they have a limited number of characters, familiar settings, and simple events, they lack a complex plot (i.e., they have no problem to resolve). (See Box 2.2 for a discussion of setting up a book nook.)

Engaging the toddler. Now that toddlers understand words represent real things, they are more interested in labeling and describing objects pictured in books and less interested in listening to extended readings of the text. Toddlers point to things they recognize and often label them while asking for the names of unknown objects. With simple books, toddlers might fly through the pages labeling objects quickly: "Yep, that's a chicken (*turns page*), okay, that's a pig (*turns page*)." More complex illustrations, such as those in *Hidden Hippo,* by Joan Gannij, illustrated by Clare Beaton, take much longer to "read," and toddlers may spend considerable time poring over every detail, sometimes repeatedly. Repetition is important to toddlers' learning from book reading (Horst, Parsons, & Bryan 2011; Simcock & DeLoache 2008). Adults provide repetition by reading the same book again and again, each time the toddler wants to hear it, and by sharing books that have highly repetitive language.

At this age, the adult and toddler can engage in more extended discussion about illustrations. Prompts that elicit conversation (e.g., wh-questions) are positively related to toddlers' language growth (Rowe, Leech, & Cabrera 2017). Discussion can include descriptions of details in the illustrations (rather than just simple labels) and connections between the book and the child's world. For example, if the child points and says "airplane" the adult might say, "Yes, that is an airplane. It is flying high in the sky. We saw an airplane flying up in the sky at the park today, didn't we? What else do you see?"

Adults can also support a book's language by using words that are more familiar to an individual child (Martin 1998). For instance, an adult might say "nanna" alongside "grandma" if that is what the child calls their grandmother or add to the phrase "fell fast asleep," often found in books, the more familiar "is sleeping." Adults who scaffold reading experiences in this way have been described as using a *storytelling* or *interactive* approach. Interactive reading invites the child's participation as the adult asks questions and makes comments to support meaningful connections. Interactive reading that includes talk that goes beyond just reading the written text is highly effective in promoting language development (Luo & Tamis-LeMonda 2017; Rowe, Leech, & Cabrera 2017).

Children differ in their interest and engagement in book reading; however, research suggests that promoting interaction positively affects a child's engagement (Son & Tineo 2016). Some toddlers simply require interaction to be engaged at all in book reading. If an adult only reads extended portions of text to such a child, the child's attention often fades quickly, as if to say, "If you're going to read so that I can't understand and participate, then I'm not interested." That same toddler might become highly engaged when an adult uses interactive reading strategies to support comprehension and participation. Adults should attend to children's cues!

Box 2.2. Placement of Books in the Toddler Early Learning Setting

A book nook for toddlers differs from those designed for preschoolers. Here are some considerations when setting up and maintaining this area.

Location and furniture. A book nook in a corner of the room is preferred to limit traffic through the area. Carpeting or a rug makes sitting more comfortable. Pillows are neither necessary nor safe because toddlers might trip over them. Instead, toddler-size armchairs that help children use books in their laps could be included, provided they are easy to clean and are not placed in ways that create tripping hazards.

Book displays. The typical upright book display racks found in preschool early learning settings are not functional or safe in a toddler room. First, toddlers are not tall enough to reach the higher shelves. Second, unseasoned walkers may lose their balance as they reach to obtain materials. Third, and more serious, the book display rack itself can topple over if toddlers try to climb on it. (Furniture should, of course, be bolted or otherwise secured to walls or the floor.)

Instead, books can be propped up on the floor to catch a toddler's attention from a distance. A few additional books can be laid flat nearby or placed in shallow tubs or baskets. A limited number of books should be on display so the space is not visually overwhelming. Rotate books frequently to support exploration and interest. Damaged books should be discarded.

Other considerations. Although book nooks are a staple of the older toddlers' early learning setting, books need not stay there. A book nook can be thought of not so much as where books permanently belong but as a place to find them.

Toddlers between 14 and 18 months old like to be up and about. They often get a book, look at it briefly, and then carry it as they go to another area of the room. With this knowledge about children's mobility at this stage, educators can also proactively include books in a variety of places throughout the early learning setting alongside other toys. This helps ensure that children will have the option to look at a book no matter where they wander. For example, books on transportation may be placed next to a collection of toy vehicles to foster meaningful connection between the books and the toy cars, trucks, and trains. Furthermore, placing books throughout the space fosters more opportunities for organic reading interactions between toddlers and adults.

Books should be made of sturdy materials (e.g., board books, cloth books) to withstand the wear and tear of mouthing and being moved throughout the room. Although it is expected that young children will mouth, suck, and chew on books, interactions with adults can prompt other book-related behaviors. Even a brief interaction with only eye contact and a smile from a nearby adult or perhaps a question (e.g., "Oh, what do you see in your book?") can encourage children to explore books with their eyes instead of their mouths.

From 19 to 30 Months

What the toddler can do. Adults' book selections for and ways of reading to the toddler at this age are influenced more by the toddler's language and cognitive development and less by their motor development. Toddlers now use more extended and complex language structures and multiword utterances that qualify as sentences (e.g., "I not want it" or "Mommy go there"). They are also learning six to 10 new words a day (Gilkerson et al. 2018), most of which are acquired through language interactions that take place in the context of real-life experiences (Rowe & Snow 2020). Interestingly, a toddler's expressive language development, or use of words, is also affected by their story-reading experiences (Montag, Jones, & Smith 2015; Richman & Colombo 2007). If toddlers are frequently engaged in read alouds, up to one-third of the new words they speak are acquired from these experiences (Hepburn, Egan, & Flynn 2010).

Consider the following scenario, which shows a toddler's increased engagement with concepts in books and familiar ideas, enjoyment in shared reading, and growing language skill:

> Lucy, Molly's 26-month-old niece, wants to "read" *Feast for 10,* by Cathryn Falwell, to herself while Molly is nearby. Legs outstretched, Lucy sits on the floor with the book on her lap, turning pages and labeling several pictures as she reads aloud. Upon seeing a picture of hands that help with grocery shopping, Lucy clasps her own hands, makes a few hand motions while babbling to a tune, and then points to the illustration. When Lucy gets to the last page of the story, she points to the picture of a sleeping baby held in the mother's arms and looks up at Molly, who is watching quietly.
>
> **Lucy:** Look, a baby! Look, a baby! Hey, that. (*Points to the baby on the page.*)
>
> **Molly:** (*Looks at the baby and then smiles at Lucy.*)
>
> **Lucy:** (*Repeats.*) Look, a baby! Baby. Love baby!
>
> **Molly:** Yes, I see the baby! Yes—
>
> **Lucy:** (*Interjects.*) It nap.
>
> **Molly:** Yes, she's going for a nap. She's sleepy.
>
> **Lucy:** He tired.
>
> **Molly:** Yes—
>
> **Lucy:** (*Interjects and points to the dad taking the baby from the mom.*) Yat, dad! It dad!
>
> **Molly:** It *is* dad. What a nice dad!

Toddlers are capable of thinking and acting in increasingly abstract ways. For instance, they might pretend to read to a doll or put a bandage on a teddy bear with a hole. Around 18 to 24 months, toddlers begin to show empathy toward others (Zahn-Waxler et al. 1992). For example, when they hear a sibling crying, they may offer them the toy they have been playing with.

Toddlers' growing understanding of emotions, coupled with their new representational abilities (e.g., pretend play, attributing meaning to their scribbles), helps them to understand the content in books that adults share with them.

During this period, toddlers also start to join more in conversations that involve recalling and talking about recent events they have experienced in their daily lives (Olaussen 2022). For example, when asked, "What happened to your knee?" a toddler between 24 and 29 months old might reply, "I was falling. I hurt!" to indicate that they fell and hurt themself earlier in the day. Recounting life events in this fashion is an emergent form of one type of story, the ***personal narrative***. Personal narratives share characteristics (e.g., characters, a setting, a series of events) with the ***fictional narratives*** found in storybooks. When adults help toddlers include the important people, places, and actions while relating their own immediate past events, eventually the child is better able to understand these key features in the fictional narratives that adults read to them. They will use these key features in the stories they compose orally for an adult to write down and later when they write stories independently (Peterson & McCabe 2004).

Choosing books for the toddler. Educators should continue using books with clear illustrations that have direct connections to the written text on each page. As the adult reader points to illustrations that represent words they read to the toddler, this interaction structure supports the toddler in making connections between language and images.

Through their second year, toddlers' life experiences affect their book interests. The adult uses their knowledge of a toddler's recent and upcoming experiences to choose books of interest to them. Basic concept, topic, and theme books, such as those already described, remain good choices. With the vast array of children's literature available, adults can find appropriate books about almost any topic. Books about seasonal or holiday activities (e.g., *LunarTale: A New Year's Adventure,* by Stella Hong; *Hanukkah Nights,* by Amalia Hoffman) or special family events (e.g., *Time for a Trip,* by Phillis Gershator, illustrated by David Walker) allow toddlers to make connections to their own experiences.

Toddlers also enjoy predictable books because the repetitive nature helps them anticipate words and chime in with the reading. Predictable books also support word learning, providing opportunities to hear new words repeatedly and say them as toddlers join in with the reading. Examples include storybooks like *Hush! A Thai Lullaby,* by Minfong Ho, illustrated by Holly Meade, and song books like *The Wheels on the Bus,* illustrated by Yu-hsuan Huang.

As toddlers develop their ability to recount events from their own lives, they begin to understand and enjoy books with a plot. When choosing stories for toddlers, adults look for simple story problems that contain events familiar to the toddler. Familiarity makes it more likely that a toddler will engage with and understand a story. Examples include a new sibling at home (e.g., *On Mother's Lap,* by Ann Herbert Scott, illustrated by Glo Coalson), going to the doctor (e.g., *Leo Gets a Checkup,* by Anna McQuinn, illustrated by Ruth Hearson), and missing a family member (e.g., *Llama Llama Misses Mama,* by Anna Dewdney).

Older toddlers (i.e., 24 to 30 months) might watch television programs or movies occasionally. Books related to TV programs generally fall into two categories: (1) original books that were made into shows (e.g., the *Curious George* series, by Margaret Rey, illustrated by H.A. Rey) and (2) original shows that were made into books (e.g., *Sesame Street*). Original books usually have higher-quality writing and illustrations than books based on shows. It is wise to offer selections of high-quality books from which the toddler may choose.

Engaging the toddler. Because toddlers are now capable of understanding and producing more complex language, conversations around books become even more integral to the reading experience. The adult assumes multiple roles during shared reading. The first is scaffolding the child's understanding of the book by commenting about the text and illustrations to provide background knowledge. The second is making connections to the child's personal experiences and labeling and explaining unfamiliar objects and concepts. The third is promoting expressive language by asking questions and inviting the child's comments and questions.

As toddlers accumulate more life experiences and acquire more language, they can make increasingly complex connections between their lives and the lives of characters in the books. Toddlers are more likely to make these connections when adults consistently model connections as they read (e.g., "She has a teddy bear she sleeps with, just like you sleep with your bear"). Before long, the toddlers make connections themselves. This often begins by expressing connections physically, such as by showing the adult their teddy bear. Older toddlers will voice their connections (e.g., "I sleep with my teddy too!").

In learning to talk about the immediate past, toddlers make connections between events in books that mirror their own experiences (e.g., "See elephants at zoo"). As they develop empathy, they also begin connecting the emotions portrayed in books with their own emotions or those observed in family members. As educators recognize toddlers' growing ability to think about emotions, they begin to include discussion about ***narrative intangibles***, such as characters' feelings and motivations, in shared reading (McArthur, Adamson, & Deckner 2005). For example, the adult might explain, "Oh, I think the little girl in the story is feeling sad now. See? She's crying. She misses her mommy, just like you miss your mommy sometimes." With age and experience, children also begin to ask more questions about these intangibles (Tompkins et al. 2017).

Questioning toddlers during shared reading supports language development by encouraging expressive language use (Luo & Tamis-LeMonda 2017). Many adults naturally shift toward more questioning as a child becomes more familiar with a particular text through repeated readings (Fletcher & Finch 2015). As educators and families ask more questions, children assume a more active role in the reading experience (McArthur, Adamson, & Deckner 2005).

When reading *Olivia . . . and the Missing Toy,* by Ian Falconer, 30-month-old Livi and her mother, Christina, turn to the page where Olivia is looking for her toy under the cat.

Christina: Oh my! Where is Olivia looking now?

Livi: Under the cat.

Christina: Does the cat look happy about being picked up like that?

Livi: No. Him mad.

Christina: Yes. He does look mad, doesn't he? He might also be a little shocked—surprised to be lifted up like that. (*Turns page.*) Where is she looking now?

Livi: Wooshee gaga

Christina: Who said "wooshee gaga"?

Livi: Baby.

Christina: That's right. Baby William said it. What did Olivia say to William?

Livi: What did you do with my toy? Wooshee gaga!

Christina: That's right! Babies sometimes talk like that, don't they? Does William have Olivia's toy?

Livi: No. The puppy ate it.

Children's interest in book reading is also associated with adults' use of questioning and other language interactions around the text (Luo & Tamis-DeLemonda 2017; Rowe, Leech, & Cabrera 2017). However, frequent questioning during the first reading of a book is not recommended; it can frustrate a child who would like to find out what is going to happen next. After the first reading, children have some knowledge and understanding of a book, and they are more likely to be interested in answering questions.

Toddlers this age also begin ***emergent reading***, or "pretend reading." For example, they chime in with particular words in well-known or predictable books or describe illustrations when browsing through books on their own. Educators can encourage emergent reading by pausing to prompt the child to complete a well-known phrase (i.e., ***cloze reading***). Or, if an older toddler is narrating a book by describing illustrations in succession, the adult can ask the child to "read" the book to them.

All of these research-based suggestions might seem like a lot to manage with a toddler, but they become a natural part of interacting with a toddler around books when the adult's goal is to make a book meaningful to the child. Box 2.3 features an example of how one parent wove specific support strategies into a very natural interactive conversation with an older toddler while reading *The Mitten,* by Jan Brett.

Box 2.3. Engaging Toddlers in Shared Reading: Putting It All Together

This very brief snapshot of a reading experience shows how a parent connects a book (*The Mitten,* by Jan Brett) to her child's experiences with yarn and knitting at his grandmother's.

Adult: (*Reads text.*) "But Nicki wanted snow-white mittens so much that grandma (*Substitutes for* Baba.) made them for him." Oh, look at all that yarn. See the yarn balls? (*Points.*) His grandma is going to knit some mittens. See here? She knits yarn just like your grandma does.

Child: Balls . . . yarn . . . mitten.

Adult: Yes, those are balls of yarn, and his grandma is going to knit and make mittens out of that yarn, just like grandma does. (*Continues reading and discussing next few pages.*)

Child: Rabbit coming!

Adult: Oh, yes, there's the rabbit. See here. Nicki is stepping on top of the rabbit's house? I don't think the rabbit likes that. He's scared, and he's going to run away. (*Discusses for a moment.*) Where is he going? (*Turns page.*)

Child: Coming in mitten.

Adult: Yes, here comes the rabbit to snuggle in the mitten. (*Reads text.*) "A rabbit came hopping by. He wiggled in next to the mole." (*Snuggles in closer to child and points to illustration.*) He's snuggling in. (*Continues reading and discussing next few pages.*) Oh, look. Nicki is stepping on another animal's house and scaring him. Who is that?

Child: Doggie. Where Sadie go? (*Looks for own dog.*)

Adult: I don't know where Sadie is. (*Points back to book.*) This does look like a dog, but it's a fox. Remember fox with the pointy ears?

Child: Fox.

Adult: Mm hmm, there's the fox, and it looks like he's going to run to the mitten too.

This parent warmly accepted the child's contributions, clarified or extended his language attempts, and asked questions that prompted his language use. She also explained the cause-and-effect relationship between Nicki's intrusions on the animals' homes and their fear and flight away to take refuge in the mitten.

Reading Daily to Older Toddlers in Groups

Early childhood programs sometimes schedule a daily read aloud for toddlers 2 years old and older to help ensure that all toddlers benefit from book experiences. However, whole group reading can make it difficult for all children to see the book's pictures, which leads to decreased attention. This approach also makes it difficult for educators to encourage responses from children and for children to respond adequately. For these reasons, research suggests reading to toddlers in small groups of four children or fewer (IOM & NRC 2015).

There are several options to consider to make this manageable. One educator might read to rotating small groups while a second educator supervises children during their play in other areas. Educators might also try reading to a different small group each day for only the first 10 minutes of play or center time to ensure that every child regularly benefits from small group story experiences. Programs might also enlist the help of volunteers (e.g., children's families, members of the wider community) to help with story reading during short visits. No matter the approach, appropriate teacher-child ratios must be kept in mind.

Because of the benefits of reading to toddlers individually or in very small groups, families can also be encouraged to share books at home. Educators can provide workshops that focus on strategies for reading to very young children, as well as direct families to resources for obtaining books beyond their local library. (See Box 2.4.)

Box 2.4. Resources for Obtaining Free Books for Infants and Toddlers

Dolly Parton's Imagination Library (www.imaginationlibrary.com) mails free books to children from birth through age 5 once a month. Currently, there are participating communities in the United States, Canada, Australia, Ireland, and the United Kingdom.

Freecycle (www.freecycle.org) and similar websites offer a place of connection for individuals and groups looking to either donate or request items, promoting the reuse and recycling of goods to reduce waste. This includes opportunities to pick up gently used books donated by families whose children have outgrown them.

Little Free Library (www.littlefreelibrary.org) fosters a network of book-sharing boxes where anyone can take or share a book. Volunteers have installed more than 90,000 book-sharing boxes near sidewalks and other places people tend to walk to provide 24/7 access to free books.

Reach Out and Read (www.reachoutandread.org) is a pediatric program that gives books to children at each well-child visit from 6 months through 5 years. To encourage families to read to children, the program also provides families with other tools and information.

Box 2.5. Sharing Digital Books with Older Toddlers

The American Academy of Pediatrics recommends that adults not use digital media of any form with children younger than 2 years old because their extensive review of the research indicates that real-life experiences—free play, hands-on experiences, and traditional book reading—provide better support for language development (AAP Council on Communications and Media et al. 2016). An exception is the use of video calling software, such as FaceTime, with adults. Even after age 2, which includes the older toddler range (24 months to 30 months) included in this chapter, children's total exposure to all forms of digital media (e.g., electronic games, television, tablets) should be limited to relatively brief periods that total no more than about one hour per day. This hour includes any educational television coviewed with an adult (AAP Council on Communications and Media et al. 2016).

When choosing digital books for toddlers with audio narration included as a feature, educators look for selections that allow for the pacing of the narration to be controlled. They should also look for books that allow the narration to be turned off so that the adult can read the text aloud (Labbo 2009).

Rather than rely on booksellers alone for access to and information about digital books, educators and families can look to independent sources, such as

> **Children's Books Online: The Rosetta Project** (www.childrensbooksonline.org), a digital library of scanned historical children's books, many of which are translated into several languages.

> **International Children's Digital Library** (http://en.childrenslibrary.org), which offers thousands of free digital books in dozens of languages.

> **Open Library** (https://openlibrary.org), a nonprofit library that has millions of free books, movies, music, and more.

> **Storyline Online** (www.storylineonline.net), which streams videos featuring celebrities reading children's books.

> **Tumble Book Library** (www.tumblebooks.com/library), an online collection of animated, narrated picture books available by subscription, which many public library systems offer for their members. It includes Spanish, French, and English titles.

Although many digital books are designed for older toddlers to use independently, children benefit more from digital books when adults interact with them during the experience (AAP Council on Communications and Media et al. 2016; NAEYC & Fred Rogers Center for Early Learning and Children's Media 2012). Adults can use the same practices with digital books that have been discussed throughout this chapter, including labeling illustrations (or animations) and referencing them to the story. Adults can also scaffold the physical actions needed when using digital books (i.e., scrolling, swiping, clicking) and use verbal descriptions as they model and prompt children's use of the interactive features (Labbo 2009; Smith 2001).

Early Reading-Related Behaviors

Young children differ significantly in all aspects of early reading-related behaviors. While some snuggle right up to hear a story, others pause their active play only briefly to listen. These behaviors result from the accumulated experience of infants and toddlers with books and reading, as well as from their motor, cognitive, language, and social development. For example, some children are provided with baskets of books designed for infants and toddlers, while others have fewer opportunities to engage in book reading. These variations in experience greatly influence how infants and toddlers interact with a particular book.

The following reading-related behaviors are precursors to more conventional forms of reading (e.g., NICHD 2008; Paciga, Hoffman, & Teale 2011):

> **Book handling** describes children's manipulations and uses of books, in both traditional print and digital formats. (Digital book or e-book experiences are appropriate only for children 2 years and older. See Box 2.5.) An infant's book handling depends not only on their age, motor skills, and previous book experiences, but also on specific book characteristics. For example, a very young infant typically maintains eye contact best with simple, bright, and high-contrast pictures, while the size of a book and the composition of a book's pages (i.e., cardboard versus paper) influence a toddler's ability to turn pages independently.

> **Language understanding and use** with books includes both verbal and nonverbal communications with adults. This behavior includes the older toddler's use of story language to interact playfully with others (e.g., asking "Mommy, mommy, what do you see?" after reading *Brown Bear, Brown Bear, What Do You See?* by Bill Martin Jr., illustrated by Eric Carle).

> **Comprehension** behaviors indicate the child's developing verbal and nonverbal skills in constructing meaning from both the pictures and the written texts that adults share. Opportunities for language and social interaction help very young children understand both fictional and informational genres and express their comprehension of both.

> **Emergent reading** behaviors indicate children's developing understanding of how reading works and their desire to engage in it. For example, a young toddler who chants some of the phrases in *Brown Bear, Brown Bear, What Do You See?* demonstrates the understanding that the text language remains constant (i.e., readers do not "make up" unique language to go with pictures each time they read a book). Or a toddler might express a developing love of reading by insisting that an adult read their favorite book again and again (and again) (i.e., reading is an enjoyable act). Some items in the emergent reading behavior list overlap items in the language and comprehension lists. However, most emergent reading items focus on the child's active initiation of book reading, both by assuming the role of reader and participating in book reading by chiming in on repetitive text.

For more information about these behaviors, including examples of typical behaviors exhibited by infants and toddlers early versus later, see Table 2.2. Although most children exhibit early reading-related behaviors within the approximate age ranges discussed, each child's interests, interaction style, and cumulative book-reading experiences affect their specific timetable. For example, a 12-month-old with intense interest in books, coupled with extensive experience with book reading, may exhibit the behaviors typical of older toddlers, while a 3-year-old with limited book reading experience may exhibit behaviors that are more typical of a younger toddler. Infants and toddlers exhibit the behaviors listed both while sharing books with adults and when exploring books independently.

Table 2.2. Early Reading-Related Behaviors

Behavior: Book handling	
Early	**Later**
• Makes eye contact with a book's pictures but no attempts to handle a book (2–4 months) • Explores a book by grasping and bringing it to the mouth to suck and chew (5–10 months) • Shakes, crumples, and waves the book (5–10 months) • Holds board books with both hands and explores how the book works by making it open and close and turning pages (6–8 months) • Deliberately tears paper pages (7–15 months) • Helps the adult turn the pages (7–8 months) • Shows a notable increase in visual attention to books and decrease in physical manipulation of books (8–12 months)	• Might accidentally tear pages due to difficulty in handling books, but intentional tearing of pages to explore decreases (12–14 months) • Turns pages awkwardly because of difficulty in separating pages (8–12 months) • Turns pages well (11–15 months) • Flips through a book by gathering clumps of pages and letting them fly past (14–15 months) • Turns an inverted book right side up, or tilts head as if trying to see the picture right side up (11–15 months) • Operates the basic functions of digital books (e.g., opens applications, turns pages, clicks animations) (24–30 months)
Behavior: Language understanding and use	
Early	**Later**
• Looks intensely at pictures for several minutes (2–4 months) • Coos and gurgles while adult reads (4–6 months) • Understands words for familiar objects in pictures (7–9 months) • Laughs or smiles when a picture is recognized (8–12 months) • Points to individual pictures (8–12 months) • Makes animal or other appropriate sounds (e.g., "beep beep" in *Little Blue Truck,* by Alice Schertle, illustrated by Jill McElmurry) (10–13 months) • Points to familiar objects when asked "Where is the . . . ?" (11–14 months) • Names objects pictured, although articulation may not be accurate (11–14 months) • Uses book babble (13–18 months)	• Joins in during reading of predictable story or song (16–30 months) • Points to a picture and asks, "What's that?" or requests a label in another way (e.g., "Dat?" or questioning intonation) (13–20 months) • Begins to use two- to four-word sentences; for instance, describing pictures or events in books (e.g., "baby crying") (18–24 months) • Uses more complex sentences when talking about the book or favorite characters (e.g., "That not Dora backpack, that *my* backpack") (24–30 months) • Asks and answers simple questions during the story reading (e.g., "Where Momma go?" when listening to *Owl Babies,* by Martin Waddell, illustrated by Patrick Benson); might ask the same question each time the story is read (27–30 months) • Plays with the story language outside of the story-reading context (e.g., "Mommy, mommy, what do you see?" after reading *Brown Bear, Brown Bear, What Do You See?* by Bill Martin Jr., illustrated by Eric Carle) (27–30 months)

Table 2.2. Early Reading-Related Behaviors (continued)

Behavior: Comprehension	
Early	**Later**
• Understands words for familiar objects in pictures (6–9 months) • Relates an object or action in a book to the real world (e.g., retrieves a teddy after adult has read *That's Not My Teddy . . .* by Fiona Watt, illustrated by Rachel Wells) (10–14 months) • Selects books based on content, demonstrating some understanding of what certain books are about (e.g., picks up a book with a picture of a duck after playing with a toy duck; selects a book about a doctor's visit after a check-up) (10–15 months)	• Shows preference for a favorite page by searching for it or holding the book open at that page, as if that part is particularly well understood or appreciated (11–14 months) • Performs an action shown or mentioned in the book (e.g., pretends to throw a ball when book mentions playing baseball) (12–23 months) • Shows empathy for characters or situations depicted in books (e.g., repeats distress words ["hurt," "boo-boo," "miss mommy"] while looking at pictures, and displays sad or concerned facial expression; pretends to cry after hearing that a child in the book is sad) (18–24 months) • Makes associations across books (e.g., gets two books and shows the adult similar pictures or events in each one) (20–24 months) • Talks about the characters and events during the reading in ways suggesting understanding of what has been read or said (e.g., saying "Shhh! Bunny sleeping" at end of *Goodnight Moon,* by Margaret Wise Brown, illustrated by Clement Hurd) (20–26 months) • Relates events in texts to own experiences during shared reading (e.g., saying "I play freight train," referring to own toy trains when reading *Freight Train,* by Donald Crews) (20–26 months) • Links situations from a book to situations outside of the book sharing context (e.g., reenacting events and reciting lines from *The Snowy Day,* by Ezra Jack Keats, when playing in the snow) (20–30 months)

Behavior: Emergent reading	
Early	**Later**
• Coos or gurgles when read to (3–6 months) • Gazes at and/or points to illustrations while adult is reading (7–9 months) • Vocalizes (unintelligibly) while pointing at pictures (7–10 months) • Points to the pictures and vocalizes (more intelligibly), such as with rising intonation, to indicate "What's that?" (10–12 months)	• Imitates adult's behaviors by pointing to the words or pictures when sharing the book (15–20 months) • Describes illustrations or familiar parts of books in own words (e.g., says "piggy's dancing" when adult reads *Moo, Baa, La La La!* by Sandra Boynton) (16–20 months) • Fills in the next word in the book when the adult pauses, says the next word when the adult reads it, or reads along with the adult when the text is highly predictable (16–24 months)

Behavior: Emergent reading (continued)

Early	Later
• Makes animal or other appropriate sounds (e.g., "beep beep" in *Little Blue Truck* by Alice Schertle, illustrated by Jill McElmurry) (10–13 months) • Names objects pictured, although articulation may not be accurate (11–14 months) • Brings books to an adult to read, and hands a book back after reading it, suggesting the adult should read it again (12–16 months) • Uses book babble (13–18 months) • Search more thoroughly through books on shelf or in baskets to find preferred books (16–20 months)	• "Reads" to self and pretends to read to dolls or stuffed animals, holding the book so that they can see (17–25 months) • Recites entire phrases from a favorite story if the adult pauses at the opportune time (20–30 months) • Protests when an adult misreads or skips a word in a familiar, and usually predictable, text; typically offers the correction (28–30 months) • Asks to read books to the adult and may be able to recite several books quite accurately, especially if simple and predictable (28–30 months)

Concluding Thoughts

Each infant and toddler is unique, and each reading experience with an infant or toddler occurs at a unique point in the child's development. Adults consider the motor, cognitive, language, and social development of each child, along with their interests and experiences, when choosing books and ways of reading. Moreover, because children are growing and changing, the books that are read and the ways they are shared must continuously adapt to the child. Adults who make careful, intentional, and flexible decisions about reading with infants and toddlers create experiences that engage and enthrall, supporting the beginning of a child's lifelong passion for reading and learning.

CHAPTER 3

READING STORYBOOKS WITH PRESCHOOLERS

Much of this chapter is devoted to a discussion of storybook reading strategies because *how* books are shared determines in large part what young children actually learn from them (Cunningham & Zibulsky 2011). The chapter also discusses criteria for selecting storybooks, goals for storybook reading, and strategies for reading stories in ways that support meaning and language development.

Selecting Storybooks

The goal for an educator is to select high-quality stories suitable for a specific group of children. Three-year-olds need somewhat different stories than 4-year-olds, and a mixed-age group needs especially thoughtful consideration. Book selection also depends on the topics children are learning about, family experiences, and community characteristics, including local customs and celebrations.

It is helpful to keep several criteria in mind when selecting a storybook: (1) its complexity; (2) its potential interest to young children; (3) the richness of its language; (4) the values it conveys; (5) its representation of diversity and inclusivity; and (6) the appropriateness of its illustrations and size. (See Box 3.1 for a discussion of book genres.)

Box 3.1. Considering Book Genres

Familiarity with various book genres aids a teacher's book selection and influences the range of understandings and skills the teacher can support through book reading. Four different kinds of books are described here: narrative, informational, predictable, and concept.

Narratives

Narratives are fictional stories that have at least one character, a problem, and a plot that leads toward the resolution of the problem. Fiction is the most popular book genre for young children in the United States (Curcic 2023). Most storybooks for preschoolers are picture books in which words (i.e., written text) and creative illustrations work together, sometimes in complex ways, to provide information about the story's characters, settings, and events. Stories are usually written in the past tense because they relate events that have already occurred. In narratives, characters try to resolve the story's problem by taking action. Through these actions, characters reveal their knowledge, viewpoints, and motivations to the reader or listener (Temple, Martinez, & Yokota 2019). Unlike informational books that sometimes focus on physical cause and effect (e.g., lightning is the cause of thunder), narratives involve mostly psychological causation (e.g., losing a friend makes a character sad).

Examples include *Last Stop on Market Street,* by Matthew de la Peña, illustrated by Christian Robinson, and *Knuffle Bunny,* by Mo Willems.

Informational Books

Informational books are a type of nonfiction. Topics found in these books include animals and plants; natural habitats (e.g., deserts, swamps); human-made places (e.g., zoos, construction sites); natural events (e.g., water freezing into ice, wind spinning to create tornadoes); customs and celebrations (e.g., the clothing worn and food eaten by people in different parts of the world, holidays and other special occasions); and transportation and commerce (e.g., airplanes and airports, grocery stores, pizza restaurants). The common feature of these books is a focus on factual content, including processes that pertain to the social, physical, or biological worlds.

Because informational books convey factual information that applies all the time, they are commonly written in the present tense (Duke et al. 2003; Duke, Halvorsen, & Knight 2012). Like narrative storybooks, informational books use both illustrations and text to convey meaning. But unlike in a storybook, the illustrations in an informational book are realistic. That said, while traditional graphics (e.g., diagrams, charts, graphs, photographs) are used, more recently published informational books also include more creative (but still accurate) artwork, including paintings and collages. (See Chapter 4.)

Examples include *The Street Beneath My Feet,* by Charlotte Guillain, illustrated by Yuval Zommer, and *Can an Aardvark Bark?* by Melissa Stewart, illustrated by Steve Jenkins.

Predictable Books

Predictable books use one or more literary devices that make a text easy for young children to remember and anticipate after hearing it just a few times. These literacy devices include (1) rhyming and alliteration; (2) repetition of a basic sentence frame with only one or two words varied each time; (3) use of a refrain; (4) use of cumulative text (one new sentence is added on each page, and text introduced previously on each successive page is repeated); (5) a close relationship between illustrations and text (every item or action mentioned in the text is pictured); and (6) depiction of only one idea or thought on each page. Young children enjoy the flow and rhythm of the language in predictable books. They also enjoy these books because they can begin to chime in as the teacher reads them and can soon "read" the books independently (i.e., read the book from memory).

Examples include *Bathe the Cat,* by Alice B. McGinty, illustrated by David Roberts, and *Bee-Bim Bop!* by Linda Sue Park, illustrated by Ho Baek Lee.

Concept Books

Concept books introduce a concept (e.g., colors, numbers, body parts, feelings, opposites) or explore the names of objects along a theme (e.g., a transportation book about trains, planes, and boats) in enjoyable ways. Most concept books lack main characters, a problem, and a plot; instead, the concept itself provides the book's framework. Some concept books, however, do convey information and events in chronological order, with a hint of a problem to solve. This feature makes some concept books resemble a simple story.

Examples include *Alphabet Under Construction,* by Denise Fleming, and *Vámonos a Tegucigalpa/Let's Go to Tegucigalpa,* by Patty Rodriguez and Ariana Stein, illustrated by Ana Godinez.

Interest, Cognitive Engagement, and Story Complexity

Preschoolers enjoy books with humor, imagination, and a surprise or two. They also like genuine, unique, and endearing characters through which they can see or imagine themselves. While a good story must not be over the children's heads, it should also provide new information to think and wonder about across several readings.

Both younger and older preschoolers enjoy stories that vary in complexity, although older preschoolers can engage better than younger ones with stories that are more complex. A story's complexity depends on a number of things, but the main difference between simple and complex stories is that complex stories have a story problem and a plot through which the problem is solved, while simple stories do not.

For example, in the simple stories *Gilberto and the Wind,* by Marie Hall Ets; *Dog's Colorful Day,* by Emma Dodd; and *Windows,* by Julia Denos, illustrated by E.B. Goodale, each main character has multiple experiences of a specific kind—with wind, color stains, and a neighborhood walk, respectively. Yet without a central problem, a story's events are not interrelated. Instead, a simple story has a series of events whose order could be altered considerably without repercussion.

In return, Max leaves hairballs on the rug,

his tail in the butter,

and poop in the vestibule.

He eats the flowers

and deletes my email to Grandma.

Figure 3.1. Max's misbehavior in *Negative Cat.*

Characters in complex stories also learn quite a lot throughout the story, and usually change remarkably in their understanding of self and others as a consequence. For example, in *Peter's Chair,* by Ezra Jack Keats, Peter has a "change of heart" after realizing two things: he can no longer use his little blue chair and his parents still love him. As the plot unfolds, Peter expresses his thoughts and concerns, and experiences complex emotions. In contrast, although Gilberto in *Gilberto and the Wind* learns something about wind, the range of his emotions is more limited, and he has no major insights about himself or others. Gilberto is very much the same little boy at the end as he was at the start of the story.

Compared to simple stories, complex stories typically have richer language and more sophisticated vocabulary, including words that describe mental states (e.g., thought, surprised, knew, decided, wondered). Complex stories also have a main theme, such as friendship, perseverance, or family-child relationships, not just a central topic focus (e.g., wind, color stains, the neighborhood).

Complex stories also prompt reasoning. For example, to understand *Negative Cat,* by Sophie Blackall, children must reason about how a boy's exuberant efforts to care for Max, a cat that rebuffs him and misbehaves, affects the boy's morale and self-confidence and how the boy's ingenuity leads to an unconventional but far-reaching solution. (See Figure 3.1.) Because the author does not state explicitly that the boy feels daunted or worried that Max will have to leave, children must draw inferences about his perseverance and connect story events to understand how they work together for the boy's and Max's mutual benefit. And background knowledge about cats underscores the precious ending!

Vocabulary and Language Structures

High-quality stories also have many words that are not yet in most preschoolers' vocabularies. Complex stories typically have an abundance of new words, while simple stories usually have only a few. For example, the complex story *Some Smug Slug,* by Pamela Duncan Edwards, illustrated by Henry Cole, has roughly 10 sophisticated words (e.g., *antennae, sauntered, sinister*), while the simple story *Dog's Colorful Day* has about five (e.g., *stains, pollen, trots*).

Complex stories expose children to diverse sentence structures that support overall language development. For example, these sentences convey characters' thoughts through dialogue, relate events in past tense, and say things efficiently (e.g., "Afraid to jump into the dark water, he stared back at the mud bank" in *Raccoon on His Own,* by Jim Arnosky).

The language in high-quality stories is also crafted differently—is more literary—than language used in everyday conversation. For example, *Duck in the Truck,* by Jez Alborough, is written in verse and includes lines like "This is the ear that hears the shout . . . " and "These are the feet that jumped the Duck down into the muck all yucky and brown." In ordinary conversation, you would likely say, "The goat heard the duck shout" and "The duck jumped feet first into the mud." Part of the pleasure experienced from reading or listening to stories comes from the beautifully crafted language that differs from the ordinary. But children must hear book language to understand and learn to enjoy it.

Values and Diversity of Characters, Cultures, and Family Structures

The values in good storybooks apply to all people, everywhere (i.e., are universal). Universal values include concern and consideration for others, friendship, patience, courage, embracing differences, personal fortitude, perseverance, belonging, love, and responsibility.

The best stories have genuine characters with diverse cultures, races, linguistic backgrounds, abilities, and family structures. These characters display a full range of complex behaviors as they deal with relatable problems and themes. Although diversity of every kind cannot be present in a single book, all aspects of diversity can be addressed in the collection of books read over a year (Smith, Brady, & Anastasopoulos 2008).

Goals for Story Reading

Hearing stories read aloud in a group helps build a classroom community. High-quality stories help children learn about emotions, support their language development, and help them acquire general knowledge about many aspects of the world.

Build Community

Story reading in the early years provides a context for building positive emotional bonds between adult and child (Bus, van IJzendoorn, & Pellegrini 1995). In one-on-one situations at home or in the preschool, adults often read books to children who sit on their laps or snuggle beside them. But story reading with larger groups can also be a warm and positive experience. After all, stories involve feelings, thoughts, and relationships. Hearing about and discussing these themes with a thoughtful, warm teacher supports bonds both among the children and between children and the teacher. For the preschool child, building attachment to this larger world of people is an appropriate and important social and emotional goal.

Support Understanding of Other People

Story characters have thoughts, feelings, goals, and motivations, and they act in response to their own current mental state and what they perceive as the mental states of others. For example, characters cry, write letters, notice interesting things on a walk, and build roads, all of which are motivated by something.

Preschoolers learn a great deal about the world, including the minds of others, just from overhearing others talk about different people's mental states (Gola 2012). Stories present a wonderful context in which this happens very frequently. The text, illustrations, and a teacher's comments provide some of this information; a discussion following a reading provides more; and a teacher's responses to children's questions add still more (Mills et al. 2012).

Build Knowledge About Emotions and Model Strategies for Regulating Them

Teachers often comment about emotions as they read a story, and emotions come up again when teachers and children discuss a story after each of its readings that span a week or more. This experience helps children develop not only an understanding of emotions but also a language for talking about them (Taumoepeau & Ruffman 2006, 2008). A broad vocabulary learned from stories helps children understand a story's characters and regulate their own behavior in emotionally charged situations (Campos, Frankel, & Camras 2004). This vocabulary includes words such as *sad, astonished, distraught, remembering, wondering,* and *wishing.*

The ability to regulate emotions affects learning because it allows children to allocate more mental resources to it (Copple 2012; Raver 2002). In other words, because cognition and emotion are intertwined, children learn better when they are less occupied with intense emotions (Bell & Wolfe 2004; Cole, Martin, & Dennis 2004; Tamouepeau & Ruffman 2008).

In addition to teaching about identifying and understanding emotions, stories also model some effective strategies for coping with them. One strategy, **cognitive reframing**, involves turning a negative situation into a positive one (Morris et al. 2011). The resolution of the central problem in many stories involves this strategy. For example, Ernst, the main character in *The Puddle Pail,* by Elisa Kleven, cognitively reframed his strong desire to collect puddle reflections (i.e., they disappeared once placed in his pail) by deciding to paint the reflections he had collected in puddles. This idea allowed Ernst to keep the reflections he had seen, though not in their original puddle form.

Support Language Development

Story reading fosters all aspects of language development, including vocabulary (Neuman & Kaefer 2018; Wasik, Hindman, & Snell 2016).

Vocabulary development from stories. Stories expose children to a range of words, both common (i.e., heard in everyday talk) and sophisticated (i.e., rarely heard in daily conversation). Read alouds provide exposure to most of the sophisticated words that young children hear. When it comes to sophisticated word knowledge, children need both breadth (i.e., a lot of words known at least minimally) and depth (i.e., some words known deeply) in their vocabulary (Coyne et al. 2009; Dickinson et al. 2019).

Story reading introduces children to many new words (breadth) as well as subtle variations in word meanings, using the same word in different contexts (depth). For example, in the story *Possum's Harvest Moon,* by Anne Hunter, children are exposed to new meanings of *great* (i.e., large) and *grew* (i.e., to become). In *Mouse Paint,* by Ellen Stoll Walsh, the word *cried* is used to mean shouted rather than produce tears.

Some depth in vocabulary knowledge helps children comprehend stories during their preschool years and later on when they read challenging texts independently (Ouellette 2006). A broad vocabulary allows children to understand more during their preschool years when listening to books or engaging in conversation. As discussed in Chapter 1, a broad vocabulary also seems to support the development of a child's phonological awareness (Chambre, Ehri, & Nest 2020; Metsala 1997).

Also discussed in Chapter 1 was how a larger receptive vocabulary acquired in the preschool years contributes to skill in reading words and in comprehension in later years (Dickinson & Porche 2011; Storch & Whitehurst 2002). This, no doubt, is because learning words minimally early on provides a starting point for children to learn more about them when they read those words again and again later on. This early vocabulary foundation, upon which deeper meanings are built, benefits reading comprehension as books become more challenging, especially from fourth grade on (Lesaux & Kieffer 2010; Ouellette 2006). Although technical language used in content areas, such as biology, earth science, geography, and history, can be learned best as children study these areas (Nagy & Townsend 2012), preschoolers do learn initial meanings for some content-specific vocabulary in stories. These meanings can be deepened when preschool, kindergarten, and primary grade teachers read informational books and provide hands-on experiences related to the topics covered by these books. (See Chapter 4.)

Support for understanding the complexity of language. Reading and discussing books also helps preschoolers understand

> *Syntax,* or word order in sentences
> *Grammar,* or how sentences are constructed and how various words change depending on their position and the features of other words in the sentence
> *Pragmatics,* or the effect of context on language

High-quality stories also help children learn sophisticated language structures because they expose children repeatedly to many varied sentences. For example, consider the complex language in *Possum's Harvest Moon*, a story about a possum who wants to celebrate the waning days of the season with a party but encounters disinterest from animal friends who want to work or sleep: "'How could they work on such a beautiful night?' Possum asked himself. 'How can they think of sleep in such moonlight?' He put on his hat and sat alone, looking up at the great harvest moon."

As Possum asks these *how* questions, children hear language that reveals Possum's thoughts about other characters' motivations. This information prompts engagement in contrastive thinking (i.e., Possum's rationale for a party and other animals' disinterest). The modifying phrase "looking up at the great harvest moon" is considerably more nuanced than simply saying, "He put on his hat and looked at the moon." Later, when hearing "It was a moon that made them dream of dancing, of eating and singing," children learn causal detail from embedded clauses (e.g., "that made them dream . . . ") and are exposed to an ellipsis, a literary device to indicate omitted words, assumed to be understood and indicated in a read-aloud setting by the adult's short pause.

Finally, inferential thinking is fostered by the structure of the language in high-quality stories. In "The mice danced until the crickets played every jig twice, and the frogs grew hoarse from singing," children must infer that the party and dancing lasted so long that the crickets ran out of original songs and the frogs sang a lot. Putting this all together, a child can conclude that everyone ultimately enjoyed the party. The adult reader can also help the children draw these conclusions through commentary.

Storybook reading also develops understanding of language *use* across different social contexts. For example, stories model how children talk to friends versus adults, how feelings and different points of view are expressed, and how language use depends on the speakers and the situation.

For example, people speak softly in libraries but yell and squeal loudly when on the playground. Children raise their hands to take turns offering comments during group time, a context in which a system of mutual participation is beneficial.

Of course, even extensive opportunities to listen to stories and participate in discussions about them cannot provide all of the support that preschoolers need to develop language. Adults must talk with children in a variety of situations throughout the day. Children also need opportunities to play and talk with peers.

Children with less language skill benefit from classmates with more (Justice et al. 2011; Mashburn et al. 2009). The effect of the more skilled peers' language on children with less initial skill probably occurs indirectly through the influence on teachers because teachers might talk more and use a wider range of language with children who have more language skill, and other children listen in. Children also learn more language from interactions with more highly skilled peers.

Multilingual children also benefit from many opportunities to play and talk with monolingual English-speaking peers. These opportunities occur most frequently in early learning settings that have a variety of languages represented; in early learning settings comprised mostly of children who speak a common language other than English, those children mostly interact with one another. Of course, the few children who speak only English in such settings benefit greatly from exposure to the language used by the other children because, in today's world, knowing two or three languages is an advantage. (See Box 3.2.)

Box 3.2. Peer Effects on Children's Language Learning

The authors' experiences with multilingual early learning settings are varied. Some included nine or 10 children out of 18 who spoke a language other than English, with as many as six or seven different languages represented. English was the language of instruction and of play among the children because the multilingual children typically had no home language peers. Other early learning settings served fairly large numbers of children who spoke primarily one language other than English (e.g., Portuguese, Spanish, Mandarin, Vietnamese, Somali), and just a few children who spoke only English. English was the language of instruction in these early learning settings as well, although one teacher in each was usually bilingual (i.e., knew the home language of the children who were also learning English).

Because our own competence in languages other than English was always quite limited, we never collected detailed case data on any of the monolingual children's use of a second language in play situations with peers. Thus, the example of peer interaction provided here is of a 3-year-old dual language learner, JK, who began preschool as a monolingual speaker of Korean.

According to Wong Fillmore (1976, 1991), multilingual learners use several strategies to engage with monolingual peers: (1) join in and act like they know what's going on, (2) use a small number of well-selected words from the shared language, and (3) don't worry about details at first. López and Páez (2021) write about the importance of peer interaction for multilingual children and about the negative consequences of social isolation among children who attend English immersion preschools.

Box 3.2. Peer Effects on Children's Language Learning (continued)

In the early learning setting from which our data were collected, the educators supported peer interactions and offered a program rich in play opportunities. They also maintained a consistent daily schedule and used established routines to manage transitions. The language of instruction was English, and English was the first language of about two-thirds of the children. The remaining six or seven children spoke a language other than English at home (e.g., Arabic, Farsi, Greek, Hebrew, Hindi, Italian, Korean, Mandarin, Russian, Spanish), and some were trilingual (e.g., Arabic, Farsi, English; Hindi, Russian, English).

September–October

1. At snack time (late September), JK took a Cheerio from a friend's supply, held it up to her eye, peeked at her friend through the hole, and said, "Gi!" (first syllable in the friend's name).

2. One week later during center time, JK said "Come here" in Korean to a friend as she motioned with a wave.

3. In mid-October, JK said "triangle" when referring to a shape on a peer's geoboard.

4. A week later, JK said, "Sit down, please" to a child who was standing up in the car she had made with blocks.

During this period, JK engaged with peers in play or conversation by using children's names, Korean sentences, one-word English labels, or formulaic English utterances, usually accompanied by gesture (e.g., hand motions) or other nonverbal behavior (e.g., smiling and shared eye gaze).

November–December

1. JK said, "Meeting time, Gabrielle. Stop!" when a classmate continued playing after the teacher dimmed the lights (the cleanup signal). The peer responded by sitting down on the floor where morning meeting was always held after center time.

2. After a peer knocked over a block structure, JK turned to the child and said, "Shhh! Baby sleeping!" The child she shushed looked at her from the pile of toppled blocks.

3. JK said, "Baby head! Baby head!" as she handed a baby doll to a peer in the house play area. The peer accepted the doll carefully by cradling its head.

During this period, JK used English with peers more frequently and with increasing skill. JK now used multiword utterances, similar to a monolingual's telegraphic speech (e.g., "meeting time" and "stop" rather than "It is meeting time"). Like other multilingual learners, JK also picked up the language of classroom rules and routines and "tried it out" (López & Páez 2021). In example 2, JK used the -ing form of the main verb (*sleep*) but omitted the auxiliary verb (*is*). In example 3, she omitted the possessive morpheme (-'*s*), which is also typical morphological development of monolingual children (Brown 1973). In example 2, JK's directions to a peer indicated a play role that JK had adopted. This prosocial mechanism invites peers into play. In example 3, JK appeared knowledgeable as she offered guidance about holding a baby. This characteristic, which makes play interesting and moves it forward, increased JK's appeal and status as a play partner.

January–March

1. On the snowy playground, JK asked, "What doing?" as a peer cleaned snow off the playhouse roof.

2. At the water table, JK initiated a pretend scenario by saying, "Misha, here's your juice," and offering a cup of colored water.

3. At the end of the song "Everybody Wash" at circle time, JK laughed, turned to peers seated nearby, and said, "That's funny."

4. JK shouted, "Hey! Who eat ice cream?" to a peer walking by the doorway of the playground playhouse.

By now, JK used some full English sentences, including wh-questions and contracted verbs (e.g., "Here's your juice" and "That's funny"). Her strategies supported a variety of social purposes: (1) asking questions about peers' ideas in ongoing play, (2) making bids to others within pretend play roles, (3) telling others her opinion, and (4) inviting peers to play without breaking her role. JK's central desire was always to engage in play with peers.

April–June

1. JK said, "I'm help you" as she began to fasten a bike helmet's snaps for a peer.

2. In the block area, JK said, "Yes, there are four children here" to a child who wanted to know if the limit for this play area (four) had been reached.

3. Directing a peer's attention to the garden on the playground, JK pointed to a plant and said, "Look, that's growing!"

4. When scooping goop at the water table, JK initiated a conversation with a peer by exclaiming, "Hailey, look at my hands!"

By year's end, JK used English fluently throughout her play with peers to offer help, confirm limits in a center, comment about growth of the vegetables in the garden, and initiate conversations about play.

Together, these examples demonstrate how an early learning setting, rich in opportunities for play, provides varied opportunities for multilingual learners to use language with monolingual peers and other multilingual children. Strong teacher support for play, a consistent daily schedule, and routines are also important.

Another critical element that is not evident in the specific excerpts is direct teacher support during children's play. By joining in play with multilingual learners, teachers serve as magnets that draw other children in. From this position, teachers coach children about play and model strategies when occupying a role. Of course, teachers move in and out as needed to leave plenty of room for the children to play and talk with one another on their own.

Young multilingual learners acquire considerable language from interacting with monolingual English-speaking peers, although more than just these interactions is needed for the development of the academic language that is so necessary for later success in school. A balanced preschool program provides plenty of time for play that's supported and facilitated by the teacher, as well as for teacher-led group activities in which English technical vocabulary and grammatical structure and other literacy-related learning are supported directly and explicitly.

Build General Knowledge

Even though informational books, not stories, are designed specifically to convey information, narratives also provide some information about a wide range of topics (Neuman & Kaefer 2018). For example, *Dreams,* by Ezra Jack Keats, and *The Puddle Pail* provide information about shadows and reflections, respectively. Similarly, children learn about bats, mammals, and fish versus amphibians from *Stellaluna,* by Janell Cannon; *Amos and Boris,* by William Steig; and *Fish Is Fish,* by Leo Lionni, respectively. Of course, the primary purpose of these stories is to inform about friendship, separation, adapting to circumstances, solving problems, and accepting one's limitations. Yet, some content knowledge is also conveyed.

Whole Group Story Reading

Preschool teachers read to children in multiple contexts that allow varied grouping. For example, during center time, teachers can read to children individually or in small groups of two or three. It is also common for preschool teachers to read daily to the whole group. Here is an overview of a few issues that teachers typically consider when reading in this context.

Seating for Whole Group Story Reading

All children must be able to see the teacher and the book's illustrations. When reading to the whole group, a teacher holds the book up, facing outward, and makes sure that children can see exactly where they are pointing at an illustration.

Several rows of children a few feet in front of the teacher work better than one big circle that places some children too far back from the teacher and others too close (see also Paciga et al. 2022). When organized into two to three rows in front of the teacher, taller children are placed in the back and shorter ones in the front, with seating positions staggered to prevent children from blocking views of others. Quite soon, children take a place in the row where initially assigned out of consideration for others in the group.

Teachers also consider carefully where to sit. Sitting on the floor rarely makes a book's pages visible to all children in a large group. Additionally, when teachers sit on the floor in this context, the physical conditions can unintentionally invite children sitting closer to the teacher to approach the book, thus blocking other children's view or encouraging them to get up too. In contrast, sitting on a chair sends a clear message that children should remain seated instead of approaching the book to look at or touch it. Sometimes, story time turns into a negative experience, rather than one of joy and delight, as teachers devote considerable time to managing children's behavior. It is better to sit in a location (i.e., on a chair) that helps children show respect to others in the group rather than send mixed messages.

Appropriate Book Size and Format for a Whole Group

Illustrations work with the storybook's text to convey story meaning (Temple, Martinez, & Yokota 2019). Illustrations also help support vocabulary learning because many items referred to by name in a story's text appear in its illustrations (e.g., *overalls* and *escalator* in *Corduroy*, by Don Freeman; *slug*, *swallowtail butterfly*, *skink*, and *sparrow* in *Some Smug Slug*).

Because "big books" make pictures more visible, many teachers use them rather than standard format books. Large-size books, however, can draw too much of a child's attention to pictures and divert them from listening as the teacher reads the text (Beck & McKeown 2001; Schickedanz & Collins 2012). Big books are also rather unwieldy to hold and turn pages, even when positioned on a stand or easel. When teachers select standard-size books carefully (i.e., illustrations that are reasonably easy to see from a distance), they can support children to achieve a balance between listening to the text and looking at the illustrations. Children can look more closely at illustrations in storybooks in the book area, where storybooks should be placed after they have been read aloud a time or two.

Of course, teachers also consider specific children in the group. For example, children with visual or hearing impairments or delayed language often need more picture support. Teachers sometimes provide an individual standard-format book for some children to hold, while other children in the group focus on the standard-format book the teacher holds and reads. When available, a teaching assistant can help an individual child by pointing to pictures that relate to the text read by the teacher and whispering to provide verbal support.

The use of SMART boards in early learning programs should be considered carefully and with attention to guidance for digital media use. (For more, see Box 3.7 later in this chapter.) The enlarged display for pictures can help children with visual impairments, but the digital format of a SMART board results in losing some of the comprehension supports that a physical book offers. With a print book, for example, teachers can flip back to earlier pages for simultaneous comparison or use features of a physical book's design (e.g., foldouts), techniques that offer children meaning-making opportunities to handle and navigate stories.

Some teachers also use big books or SMART board versions of stories to teach print concepts. For example, they underline print from left to right or ask children to find specific letters or words. While research shows that children *can* learn about print from storybooks when adults focus on it while reading (Justice & Ezell 2002), this does not mean adults *should* focus on print at this time. In the authors' view, it is wiser to have children focus primarily on the meaning of stories rather than on print. Many other contexts can be used to support print-related learning, while only the story-reading context can support meaning directly. Moreover, many predictable books are more appropriate than complex stories for teaching print concepts. (See Chapter 5.)

Thinking of the Group, Not Just Individuals

Each child brings to the group unique experiences with stories and different content knowledge. In this context, a teacher cannot always respond at length to an individual child's questions, nor can a teacher linger on pages to have an extended discussion of one child's ideas. Teachers learn to respond to individual children, even while taking more than an individual child's needs and interests into account.

Comprehension: Supporting Meaning

The most important goal when children listen to a story is to comprehend it. Comprehension requires understanding characters' feelings, motivations, and goals, as well as how these are connected to characters' actions. Story comprehension also sometimes requires understandings about the physical, biological, and social worlds; for example, what happens to hair or clothing in a rainstorm, why animals run away if approached, or why people should not go outside in a bad thunderstorm. Finally, because a story's author never tells everything, story comprehension requires reasoning to fill in a multitude of gaps. (See Table 1.1 in Chapter 1 for an illustration of the gaps in the story *One Dark Night,* by Hazel Hutchins.)

To provide the help that preschoolers need to comprehend good stories fully, adults can use several strategies: (1) introduce each story; (2) use voice, gesture, pacing, gaze, and expression when reading; (3) point to illustrations; (4) provide comprehension asides; (5) respond to children's comments and questions; and (6) engage children in thoughtful discussions after the story reading. Teachers can also read a story multiple times, over a week or more, to give children the time they need to think about its many facets (Martinez & Roser 1985; Morrow 1985; Yaden 1988).

Story Introductions

Because the problem in a story is not always explicitly stated (Paris & Paris 2003), young children often miss it. If they do not understand the story's problem early enough in the reading, children can't judge well the significance of story events or characters' actions and motivations (Benson 1997). Preschoolers might also have trouble identifying characters or settings, especially early in a story. A good introduction helps to prevent these problems (McGee & Schickedanz 2007).

When introducing a story for its first reading, start by reading the title and the names of the author and illustrator, and then introduce the main characters. Next, situate the story in its setting and state the story's problem. An introduction can end with a comment that beckons curiosity and leads right into the reading (e.g., "Let's find out what the slug does one day when out for a walk"). (See Table 3.1 for examples.)

While reading the title and author and illustrator names during the introduction, a teacher shows the book's front cover and underlines the print, using good speech-to-print matching. The cover is also in view as characters are introduced if they are pictured. The back cover, end pages, and title page are sometimes used to support the story problem, characters, or setting (McGee & Schickedanz 2007).

Introductions should not be used to query children about the book (i.e., to make predictions) or to conduct a picture walk. These approaches distract children from focusing on relevant information for constructing meaning (see Serafini 2011).

Table 3.1. Introducing a Story for a First Reading

Inch by Inch, by Leo Lionni	
Reading the title and the name(s) of the author(s) and illustrator(s)	"I have a new book to read today. Its title is *Inch by Inch*. The author of this story is Leo Lionni. Mr. Lionni also made the illustrations for this story."
Introducing the main character(s)	"Here on the cover, we see the main character—a little inchworm." (*Points to the inchworm.*) "He's a little caterpillar who got the name 'inchworm' because he's about one inch long. Several birds are also characters in this story, but they aren't pictured on the cover. We'll meet them as we read the story."
Stating the story's problem	"In this story, the little inchworm was busy, one day, eating leaves and grass, when a hungry robin spotted him. The robin thought, 'Oh, what a nice lunch you would make.' Birds like to eat worms and insects." (*Raises eyebrows, opens eyes wide*.) "But, of course, the little inchworm did not want the robin to eat him."
Transition language	"Let's read the story and find out what that little inchworm did."

Swimmy, by Leo Lionni	
Reading the title and the name(s) of the author(s) and illustrator(s)	"Our new book today is *Swimmy*. Leo Lionni is also the author of this book. Remember, we just read another book that was written by Mr. Lionni—*Inch by Inch*. Mr. Lionni wrote the words and made the illustrations for this story, just like he did for *Inch by Inch*."
Introducing the main character(s)	"We see the main character of this story, a little fish, right here on the cover." (*Points to the fish.*) "His name is Swimmy."
Stating the story's problem	"Swimmy is a brave and smart little fish, and it's a good thing, because, one day, in the big ocean where Swimmy and his brothers and sisters lived, something very bad happened. After this bad thing happened, Swimmy had to figure out what to do about it."
Transition language	"You'll see what I mean when we read the story. Let's begin."

Some Smug Slug, by Pamela Duncan Edwards, illustrated by Henry Cole	
Reading the title and the name(s) of the author(s) and illustrator(s)	"Our new book today is *Some Smug Slug*. The author is Pamela Duncan Edwards, and the illustrator is Henry Cole."
Introducing the main character(s)	"Mr. Cole, the illustrator, made a very big picture of the main character in this story—a slug—right here." (*Points to the slug.*) "A slug is an animal that is very similar to a snail, except that slugs do not have a shell. There are other animals in this story, but they are not shown on the book's cover. We'll meet them as we read the story."
Stating the story's problem	"In this story, the slug goes for a walk and climbs up a slope—a hill—and is in for a very big surprise—something happened that he did not expect."
Transition language	"Let's read the story and find out what happened."

Voice, Gesture, Gaze, and Pacing

The volume, pitch, and pace of the reader's voice, along with gestures, gaze, and facial expression, all convey meaning beyond what children can glean from just hearing the written text read aloud. For example, when reading *Possum and the Peeper,* by Anne Hunter, to help convey the bear's sleepy state and the meaning of *blearily,* you might speak the words that the bear utters very slowly, close your eyes, and yawn. Opening your eyes wide and rolling them quickly suggests that something is nonsensical. Squinting can convey a character's state of mind or the meaning of their actions. Likewise, a reader's own reactions to the story can be expressed; for example, raising your eyebrows can imply surprise, curiosity, or even skepticism.

Meaning is also conveyed by reading dialogue with appropriate intonation. For example, throughout the story *Farmer Duck,* by Martin Waddell, illustrated by Helen Oxenbury, the farmer asks his hardworking duck, "How goes the work?" The duck utters a consistent response, "Quack!" with waning enthusiasm and energy, indicating increasing fatigue. To remedy the

Box 3.3. Story Misunderstanding and Adult Response

Although adults might think that children understand a story fairly well after hearing it the first time, their comments often indicate otherwise. When misunderstandings arise, adults have opportunities to clarify each specific meaning and to help children learn to use relevant sources of information.

In the first example, which occurred during a second reading of *Max's Dragon Shirt,* by Rosemary Wells, the teacher discovers that some of the children do not understand one of the characters. Before reading the text, the teacher points to two rabbit characters.

Teacher: Who do we see here?

Children (all): Max and Ruby.

Hannah: Ruby is Max's mother.

Teacher: Is Ruby Max's mother or his sister?

Children (several): His mother.

Children (others): His sister.

Teacher: I think the book tells us some information about that. (*Reads from the book.*) "Max loved his old blue pants more than anything. 'Those pants are disgusting, Max,' said his *sister,* Ruby."

In this story, Ruby behaves much like Max's mother (i.e., takes him shopping for new pants at a department store and dresses up as an adult might for the trip). The rabbit children's mother never appears in the book's illustrations, nor does she enter directly into the text. For these reasons, a preschooler has no contrasting depiction of the mother. Furthermore, Ruby's identity is provided only a few times, and indirectly at that (e.g., at the end of one sentence the author writes "said his sister, Ruby").

duck's plight, the duck's farm animal friends roust the farmer out of bed and chase him away. When the unknowing duck encounters his friends as they return, he says "Quack?" By reading, "Quack?" with the appropriate rise in intonation, the reader indicates that the duck is now *asking* about the situation. The reader's intonation conveys the different meanings of "Quack!" which is used throughout most of the story, and "Quack?" which is used near the end.

Referring to Illustrations

Because text and illustrations work together in storybooks to convey meaning, teachers often refer to the illustrations by pointing to them. For example, when reading *Swimmy*, by Leo Lionni, a teacher might point to the little black fish among the many red ones to help children understand the text: "A happy school of little fish lived in a corner of the sea somewhere. They were all red. Only one of them was as black as a mussel shell."

The teacher is appropriately direct in leading children to the critical information. Although the children had heard the text during the story's first reading, they apparently missed some details. This is not too surprising given the children's likely attention to other picture details and to the salient part of the text in which Ruby tells Max his pants are "disgusting."

In a second example that occurred during the fourth reading of *A Hat for Minerva Louise*, by Janet Morgan Stoeke, the teacher's behavior and the illustration design both probably contributed to the children's misunderstandings.

> **Teacher:** (*Reads from the book.*) "Her friends didn't like them one . . ." (*Pauses at end of the sentence.*)
>
> **Children (several):** Two, three, four!
>
> **Teacher:** (*Reads the correct word from the book.*) ". . . bit."

In response to the teacher's pausing, the children deployed a familiar counting routine, which indicated a lack of understanding of the story and an inability to link the meaning of text on one page ("Minerva Louise liked snowy mornings") to the meaning of text on a following page. Furthermore, the details of the illustrations showing the ideas in the text (that some hens are sleeping, some have their heads tucked under wings, and some are watching Minerva Louise leave) are not prominent enough to gain children's attention and help them infer the contrast of Minerva Louise liking something that the other hens do not.

In this example, it would have been wise to read the entire phrase in the text, "They didn't like them one bit," and then follow with a brief explanation of "not one bit." The teacher might then have focused on the consequence of the hens' decision by saying, "Those other hens didn't like snowy days *at all*, not even a little bit." Then, the teacher might have asked, "What did they do all day while Minerva Louise went out to explore the snow?" to help children focus on the hens' whereabouts (i.e., in the henhouse with heads tucked under their wings).

Similarly, pointing to the slug near the toad's mouth on a page of *Some Smug Slug* prompts children to notice information that is related to what has happened when they see the toad licking his lips on the next page. On the last page of this story, the teacher can point to the toad's tongue while commenting, "I don't see the slug anywhere, but I see the toad licking his lips. Oh, my. What do you think happened to the slug?" (This question prompts the discussion that follows the story reading.)

Pointing also helps to fill in actions mentioned in the text but not illustrated. For example, the text in *Whistle for Willie*, by Ezra Jack Keats, says that Peter jumps up off his shadow and then lands back on top of it, although the illustration only shows Peter suspended above the shadow, not landing. A teacher's finger can move from Peter in midair down to the shadow on the sidewalk to demonstrate the action.

Research on visual literacy explores how children interpret illustrations of various kinds to derive meaning (Duke et al. 2010). Visual literacy, however, is not purely visual because it requires background knowledge, attention to text information, and reasoning (Schickedanz & Collins 2012). Thus, when helping young children understand the story, adults must take account of not only what and how something is pictured in an illustration, but also how young children might interpret and use illustrations.

For example, when reading *A Hat for Minerva Louise*, by Janet Morgan Stoeke, a teacher read the text that refers to Minerva Louise's less adventurous hen friends: "They stayed inside all day with their heads tucked under their wings." The next spread shows Minerva Louise venturing out (on the left page) and sitting on the fence (on the right page). Misinterpreting the second illustration of Minerva Louise as another hen, a 4-year-old announced, "There's another one!"

Not surprisingly, preschoolers often misinterpret illustrations in storybooks, in part because they do not understand that these are creative art, not realistic representations of the world, and in part because they quickly apply their own personal experiences without taking critical illustration details into account. Understanding the various sources of confusion that contribute to young children's story misunderstandings can guide a teacher's response. (See Box 3.3.)

Comprehension Asides

A teacher's comments during story reading, or **comprehension asides**, serve several purposes. They sometimes are intended to make a character's emotional state clear. For example, after reading the text on the post-party scene in *Possum's Harvest Moon*, the adult reader might say, "The frogs' voices were worn out from singing so much, so they must have had a good time." At other times, comments might be made to explain an illustration or indicate what various characters do and do not know.

These comprehension asides not only call children's attention to critical information, but also model how to reason using the information. For example, in *Peter's Chair*, Peter's mother does not know that Willie knocked over the block building. Here's how a teacher might help children understand this situation:

Teacher: We know what Peter's mother said to him, but we don't see her in the room with Peter. She is in another room, where she's taking care of Peter's baby sister, Susie. (*Draws inference using information from the illustration—mother is not shown.*)

Teacher: She thinks Peter knocked the blocks over. She wasn't there, so she doesn't know that Willie did it. I think Peter's feelings are hurt. Look at his face. (*Makes emotions explicit and indicates information that is used to draw this specific inference.*)

Teacher: Peter probably *did* remember the new baby (*Infers a character's knowledge.*) and tried to stay quiet (*Infers a character's intentions.*), but his mom didn't know that. (*Infers a character's knowledge.*)

Teacher: Let's read more and see what happens. (*Transitions back to the reading.*)

Story understanding develops more through learning from modeling than through asking children, "Who knows why _____?" because preschoolers usually don't know the answer. Even infants and toddlers learn by observing what happens in the world and listening to what people say and do (Gola 2012; Horner 2004). Preschoolers also learn a lot by listening in to what others say (Mills et al. 2012), including a teacher's comments and explanations.

Responding to Children's Comments and Questions During a Story

Responding to comments and questions supports children's comprehension, although in a whole group setting, a teacher sometimes cannot respond immediately. If a question indicates that a child has missed something critical, answer fully but as briefly as possible before continuing the reading. Turning the child's question into a discussion during the story causes a long break in the story reading, and long breaks in the first reading make it hard for young children to hold onto their understanding so far. Moreover, they don't like these breaks in the story reading because they want to know what is going to happen next.

If the answer to a child's question is provided later in the story, a teacher can say, "I think we'll find out about that pretty soon." This response acknowledges the child and alerts all of the children in the group about important information to come. When an answer is revealed on the very next page, a teacher can use eye contact and a head nod to indicate "I hear you, and we'll find out *very* soon," then finish the current page and move immediately to read the next one. After reaching the relevant portion of the text and reading it, the teacher can comment in a way that links the information read to the child's previous question.

Guiding Discussion

Guiding a good discussion *after* a story reading deepens the basic understanding that children have built *during* a story. Saving actual discussion until after the story reading maintains the story's flow and also gives children considerable information to draw upon (e.g., text information, illustration information, information from the teacher's comprehension asides). The read-aloud experience is also more enjoyable for children when they have deep understanding and information to use in a discussion.

Good discussions follow from questions that focus on something that is important to the story as well as to the children and that foster thinking. These discussions are conversations in which educators model complex language with children and engage in multiple exchanges about cognitively stimulating topics. They are paramount to children's linguistic and cognitive development (Collins 2016; Rowe, Romero, & Leech 2023).

A topic for discussion after a first reading might explore the story problem and its resolution (Collins 2023; McGee & Schickedanz 2007). Discussion questions are typically one of two kinds. *Literal* questions seek factual information from the story's text and illustrations (e.g., "What piece of baby furniture did Peter at first think he would save?") and require only the mental process of recall. In contrast, the answers to *inferential* questions are not provided explicitly in the text or the illustrations (e.g., "Why did Peter change his mind about his little chair?").

Box 3.4. Strategic Use of Literal Questions: *Peter's Chair*

In this example, a teacher uses literal questions to help children focus on story information needed to answer an inferential question.

Teacher: (*Asks after reading the last page.*) Why did Peter decide that Susie should have his little blue chair? (*Shows page 19.*) What did Peter find out about his little chair when he tried to sit in it?

Child 1: It didn't fit.

Child 2: It was too little.

Child 3: Peter was too big.

Teacher: Yes, Peter found out that he could no longer fit in his little chair. I guess he hadn't sat in his chair for quite a while, because he tried to sit in it as if he thought he could. Maybe he's not so interested in keeping the chair for himself now that he knows it's too little. (*Shows page 20.*) What did Peter's mother say to Peter here?

Child 1: You should eat lunch and come back in the house.

Child 2: She said she made a special lunch for him.

Teacher: Yes, and she was talking very nicely to Peter, wasn't she? She called him "dear." People talk like that to someone they love. Maybe Peter noticed that his mother spoke nicely to him. It looks like he's thinking pretty deeply here. (*Points to Peter's face.*) What do you think he might be thinking about?

Child 1: He's sad because he can't sit in it.

Child 2: He doesn't want it anymore, because, because he doesn't.

Thus, to answer inferential questions, children must integrate and reason about information in both the text and illustrations, as well as use background knowledge (Collins 2023; Walsh & Hodge 2018).

Preschoolers are quite good at acquiring literal facts from hearing a story read two or three times. In contrast, without help from adults, children do not obtain understandings that require reasoning (Collins 2016; van Kleeck, Vander Woude, & Hammett 2006). Thus, it is best to spend precious story time on inferential, not literal, questions.

Sometimes, though, children do need help in noticing and recalling specific information that different parts of a story provide (i.e., literal facts) before they can answer an inferential question. Thus, literal questions have a place in story time discussions, as long as the ultimate goal for asking them is to support children in drawing inferences.

As the example in Box 3.4 illustrates, the teacher's explicit guidance helps children identify relevant information and learn how to use it in drawing inferences. The teacher guides the discussion by clarifying and connecting responses offered by a number of children.

Child 3: He's going to give it to his baby.

Teacher: Maybe Peter is sad but maybe not. Maybe he's thinking that he doesn't need his little chair anymore, after all, because he can't sit in it, and he's thinking about giving it to his baby sister.

Teacher: (*Shows page 25.*) Do you remember what kind of chair Peter was sitting in here?

Child 1: A big one!

Teacher: Yes, he sat in a grown-up chair because he is big enough now. Look at his face and how he is sitting all the way back in that chair. (*Points.*) And look at Peter's father's arm. (*Pointing to arm around Peter.*) I think Peter might have realized here that his father loves him still. And what else was he probably thinking about?

Child 1: His chair?

Child 2: He wanted to paint it, and he had to ask about that.

Teacher: Yes, he was probably thinking about his chair and about asking if he could help paint it because this is when he asked his father about that.

Child 1: He said, "Could we paint it?"

Teacher: Yes, he wanted to help. He said, "Let's paint it for Susie."

Teacher: (*Summarizes.*) So, Peter changed his mind about keeping his chair, because he realized he couldn't fit into it anymore, and probably because he felt a little better about what was happening to his baby chair after his parents were so kind to him and gave him some attention.

Doing so helps children to understand what information is important, where it fits into the inferential question, and where the group's current thinking about the question is going.

Because discussion time after reading a story is often limited, it is important to keep focused on topics that help children think analytically about the story's events and the characters' thoughts and feelings. Personal affect questions (e.g., "What did you like about the story?" or "What was your favorite part?") do not deepen children's story understandings to any extent (Walsh & Hodge 2018). For this reason, rather than exploring them during discussion time, they should be saved for conversations at mealtimes or at the end of the day, when a teacher can spend more time talking with an individual child. Teachers should also avoid letting a discussion get off track. (See Table 3.2.)

Table 3.2. Avoiding Discussion Pitfalls

Avoid this pitfall . . .	Because . . .	Instead . . .
Asking children to retell the story	This taps only memory for story events and characters, not analytical thinking or reasoning. Moreover, retelling does not constitute a discussion.	Use specific events and literal questions as a means to establish facts needed when analyzing and synthesizing story events to answer inferential questions.
Forgetting the topic or specific questions to use in a story's discussion	Opportunities to execute a carefully planned and thoughtful discussion are missed.	Jot the question down on a sticky note and attach it to the book's back cover, until you are comfortable with remembering the language for your discussion prompts.
Letting a child's tangential comment redirect the discussion (e.g., "I played in the snow one day . . . and I got snow in my boots")	These personal experience comments often divert a teacher from pursuing a more beneficial discussion question, such as "What do you think Peter and his friend from across the hall might do in the snow when they go out to play on this day?"	Reframe the response to address the question you are pursuing (e.g., "Oh, that must have felt cold, but we are talking about what we think Peter and his friend might do in the snow. Do you have an idea about that to share?").
Using low-level (i.e., literal) questioning for a lot of the discussion (e.g., "And then what happened?")	Literal questions do not require children to reason about cause and effect, consider characters' motives, or make informed predictions. Unless children learn to think in these ways, they will not comprehend stories very well.	Create a discussion that includes questions and statements that prompt examination (e.g., "What did Peter learn about the snow after playing in it?" Use examples from the text to support children as they engage in thinking about the question.

Avoid this pitfall . . .	Because . . .	Instead . . .
Using discussion time as a "question and answer" session	It feels drill-like and performance-oriented and doesn't prompt higher-level thinking. The goal of a discussion is not for children to perform or demonstrate their knowledge; rather it is to foster their learning about how to reason and draw inferences.	Conduct the discussion as a conversation. Intersperse key questions with your comments, and add short embedded vignettes that are related to a point. Clarify what children say, and explain why and how a child's comment is or is not related to a point.
Asking children to relate the story to a personal experience (e.g., "Tell me about a time when you received a birthday present you really liked")	These questions pull the discussion away from the story content, which usually needs discussion if children are to reach a deeper understanding. They also reduce opportunities for the teacher to use and explain some key vocabulary words, as is possible during a more story-based discussion.	Solicit accounts of personal experience *sparingly* after several rounds of discussion have solidified basic comprehension of story content and when children are poised to make thoughtful connections between text and their own lives. Pose a question that requires thinking, not just "Have you ever . . . ?" (e.g., "What do you think you might add to your snow person, if you made one?").
Relying on just generic open-ended questions (e.g., "Can you tell me more about that?" or "Why do you think so?")	The aim of story discussion is not simply to prompt children to produce language. What they talk about matters. To meet goals for a discussion, a teacher often must scaffold children's thinking by suggesting relevant information to consider or by asking fairly specific questions. If a child says just a little bit in response to a question and has more to say or if they should provide evidence, specific follow-up questions are desirable.	Craft detailed questions to elicit the information children need to understand. When responding to children's questions, use specific language to indicate what you understand about their thinking or to ask for more clarification (e.g., "Are you asking about why the Peeper's throat is puffed out like a balloon?").
Telling children the correct answers	Children must learn to consider information in the text and illustrations and to engage in reasoning to sort out confusions. If teachers simply provide correct information without revealing its sources or how it is used in reasoning, children will not learn how to use sources or to reason about information.	Refer children to sources of helpful information, such as illustrations, text, and what you think they already know (i.e., prior knowledge). Model thinking and offer explanations about why children's thinking seemed accurate to them but was not because some information was not considered.

Supporting Vocabulary

Children acquire the meanings of a few new words just from listening to a story multiple times. But children's learning of new word meanings can be increased when teachers identify key vocabulary in each story and use specific strategies to support children's learning (Biemiller & Boote 2006; Bus, van IJzendoorn, & Pellegrini 1995).

Identify Key Words

The first step comes before reading a story to children: identifying and selecting sophisticated words (Dickinson & Porche 2011; Weizman & Snow 2001). Teachers might use the tiered system suggested by Beck, McKeown, and Kucan (2002) to guide this selection. **Tier 1** includes words that children hear almost every day (e.g., *car, walking, red, dog*). **Tier 2** words (e.g., *industrious, vehicle, reflection*), on the other hand, are less common and more important for comprehending texts, not only in preschool but also later on. Tier 2 words are used across many topics or fields of study (e.g., science, math, social studies), which makes knowing them especially useful. Beck, McKeown, and Kucan suggest that teachers select mostly Tier 2 words for explicit support during story reading. (See Nagy & Hiebert 2011 for a more detailed discussion of word selection.)

Of course, when a book has an abundance of Tier 2 words, teachers select those that are likely to increase children's comprehension of the story the most. For example, in *Possum and the Peeper*, which is about hibernating animals who were awakened at spring, the words *clamor, crest, burrows, glorious, overheard, speck, proclaimed, deny, swamp, reeds, pond, din, muskrat,* and *grumbling* are used. From among these, a teacher might select *din, clamor, reeds, overheard, proclaimed, deny,* and *grumbling* to support explicitly.

Finally, a teacher decides whether to include sophisticated words in their commentary about the story that are not used in the text. For example, in *Whistle for Willie*, Peter spun around so fast that lights in a traffic signal seemed to move out of their sockets. Even though the text does not

use the word *dizzy* to label Peter's mental state, a teacher can use it in a comment that explains what is going on. Similarly, if reading *Henny Penny*, by Paul Galdone, a teacher can use *sly, sneaky,* and *gullible* even though they are not in the text. For example, the teacher might say, "I'm so surprised that none of these birds is asking Henny Penny why she thinks the sky is falling. I'm thinking these birds are a bit *gullible*—just believe everything they are told. I hope she knows what she's talking about."

Using Illustrations, Explanations, Gesture, and Voice

Pointing to illustrations in storybooks helps children learn key word meanings (Collins 2010), especially nouns. In a process called ***fast mapping*** (Carey 1978), young children link the meaning of a new word to its referent (i.e., the actual object a word names) after only one or two exposures if they can see the named item in the immediate physical environment or pointed to in a book's illustration.

Even though children still have much to learn about a word (Justice, Meier, & Walpole 2005), fast mapping gives them a quick *start* in learning many words. A teacher follows up with explicit support in subsequent book readings and other activities and strategies outside the book (Wasik, Hindman, & Snell 2016). (See Chapter 4.)

Although a teacher usually points to the illustration almost simultaneously with reading the word in the text, this need not be done if the teacher feels that concentrating on pointing will disrupt the flow of reading. If you feel distracted by pointing to illustrations while reading key words in the text, finish reading the sentence, and then say, "Oh, here's the *hedge* at the edge of the lawn, right here," while pointing to the hedge in the illustration. Although this approach stops the reading briefly, it is preferred over reading a sentence awkwardly or losing phrasing or good intonation. The teacher should provide a brief definition to support a word's meaning when they point to the relevant illustration at this time and use the key term in their comments.

Gestures that model meaning are helpful, especially for verbs. For example, a teacher can convey the meaning of *inhale* by deliberately breathing in to demonstrate. When demonstrations might be missed or misinterpreted, teachers can call attention to them by making eye contact with children while making the gesture or, occasionally, prefacing it with "Like this." Limiting gestures to what you can show while seated avoids distracting children from the story reading. For example, a teacher would not get up to demonstrate *dashing,* but they could use a hand gesture to indicate very fast movement.

Onomatopoeia—the use of sound or pronunciation to convey a word's meaning—is a perfect strategy for some words, such as *peep,* which can be read in a high-pitched, staccato tone. Other words (e.g., *murmur, snarl, mumble, whisper, whine, sputter*) also lend themselves to onomatopoeic renderings.

Synonyms (e.g., "*Chilly* means cool") or ***brief definitions*** (e.g., "*Clamor* means a loud noise") also support vocabulary development. Synonyms can be tucked into the reading (e.g., when reading the following line from *Rabbits and Raindrops,* by Jim Arnosky: "*Baby rabbits can become soaked—very wet—and catch cold*"), but tucking in longer explanations (e.g., "—soaked means that their fur would get very, very wet—") can make it difficult for a young child to grasp the entire sentence, especially if they are a multilingual learner. It is better to read the sentence in the text with a very brief explanation of *soaked* (e.g., "—very wet—") or, if a longer explanation is preferred, wait until after reading the sentence to add, "*Soaked* means that the baby rabbits' fur would become very, very wet."

Box 3.5. Questions About Supporting Key Word Understanding in Storybooks

1. Should I simplify words or substitute an easier word for a sophisticated word?

No. Use the sophisticated word and multiple exposures, both within the book context and in other settings. Simpler synonyms for the sophisticated word can be used to explain the sophisticated word in a story's first reading. Brief explanations (i.e., child-friendly definitions) can be used to give more information about each sophisticated word in later readings.

Sometimes, if a book has very long sentences and many new words, the amount of text can be simplified temporarily without harming the plot. For example, in a first reading, you might skip some clauses, phrases, or words or even whole sentences. The same strategies for word support apply to new words that remain. In a second reading, the teacher reads more or all of the text that is present on the pages. All of the original text can be read by the third or fourth reading. This method eases children into a more complex and word-rich text, over several readings.

2. How should I adapt my reading and word support for multilingual learners?

Provide the same quality and frequency of exposure to words and discussions as for other children. Standards and expectations for learning are the same, but supports for learning can and should vary.

› Multiple exposures to words are especially important for multilingual learners. Use key words from the book in teacher commentary and in the discussion.

› Explain some Tier 1 vocabulary; don't confine key word selection to just Tier 2 words.

› Read in small groups in addition to the whole group. This offers a comfortable setting for producing English (or any other second language).

› Recognize that engagement and rapt attention are marked by nonverbal behavior (e.g., eye gaze, facial expression). Although a silent period is common during the first few months of exposure to a new language (López & Páez 2021), receptive language is being cultivated even if young multilingual children do not produce the second language (English).

› As you would for all children, pronounce words clearly.

› In story discussions, simplify the language used, but not the question. For example, change "Why did Henry frown?" to "Henry frowned. Why?" Repeating the question a time or two is important for all children, especially multilingual learners.

› Accept word production warmly, interpret what is said, and repeat the word with an accurate pronunciation in a genuine response (e.g., "Yes, that is a *porcupine*. See all those quills—these long things in its fur that have sharp pointed ends?").

› During the discussion, expand and rephrase children's responses. If the child says, "Henry not like it. He chocolate," the teacher can say, "Yes, Henry did not want vanilla frosting because he liked chocolate frosting better."

> If books can be translated or are available in the child's home language or if families read English, send books home for reading and discussing (Roberts 2008). Remember that older children can read to their preschool sibling and can also benefit from the experience.

> Guard against thinking about storybook reading as primarily a language production opportunity because this can undermine a focus on comprehension. Red flags for this include: (1) a steady diet of predictable texts, which limits exposure to varied language structures and vocabulary and typically encourages imitation without much understanding; and (2) the use of low-level prompts (e.g., "What's this?") to elicit labeling only without supporting inferential thinking.

3. Should I present (teach) key words before I start reading the book?

Teaching words before reading the story removes context and results in very didactic instruction. A good story introduction is more important. Picture walks—going through the book, page by page, before its first reading to show illustrations and comment about each one without reading any of the text—also take illustrations out of their print-related context and can preempt attention to the necessary order in which important details unfold. Picture walks can ruin suspense and intrigue, which decreases children's attention to the story during the reading. Children can also become impatient for the story while the talk, talk, talk and quiz, quiz, quiz drag on. When teachers are strategic with their word support and comprehension asides during reading, story time remains a delightful experience.

4. Should I ask children to provide word meanings?

No. Asking preschoolers for the meanings of words requires a full stop and a long break. It is also not terribly effective because preschoolers cannot easily use a teacher-provided correct explanation after they have heard two or more incorrect meanings from their peers. In cognitive science parlance, preschoolers, unlike older children and adults, do not delete or revise their mental files very well to take account of new information. In addition, children are confused when kind and warm teachers acknowledge all meanings offered (e.g., "Okay, thanks for sharing that *good* idea. Who has another *good* idea?"), but then provide a correct one that contradicts all of the ideas that children have proposed.

With age, mental flexibility increases, and children develop organized knowledge frameworks. For example, they realize that roots, stems, leaves, buds, and flowers are related because all are parts of a plant. With these stores of knowledge and new cognitive capacities, children begin to filter incoming information (Willingham 2009) and judge the word meanings they hear. However, it is wise to remember that preschoolers are just beginning to acquire organized frameworks of knowledge.

A final difficulty with asking children for word meanings is that it can dominate the focus of story reading. Although vocabulary provides strong support for comprehension, learning to integrate background knowledge and storybook information and to draw inferences are also important. Furthermore, learning to use these supports for comprehension *must* take place during book reading, while vocabulary can and should be supported in many other contexts in the preschool classroom (Nagy & Townsend 2012; Schickedanz & Collins 2012; Schickedanz & McGee 2010).

Of course, when a word is hard to explain, a teacher should not try during the story reading. For example, a verbal explanation of *edge* in *Rabbits and Raindrops* would become far too wordy and complicated. It is best to support this word simply by pointing to the lawn's edge in the illustration while reading, then using the word later in other contexts, such as at the art table (e.g., "You are smearing the finger paint all over your paper, all the way to its edges").

During a first reading, skilled teachers use verbal support (i.e., synonyms or brief explanations) that is connected to the text (e.g., "*Soaked* means that the baby rabbits' fur would become very, very wet"), not decontextualized meanings (e.g., "*Soaked* means something is very, very wet, like how wet we got on the playground last week when it started to rain before we could come

Box 3.6. Supporting Key Vocabulary from Stories During Other Parts of the School Day

During center time, vocabulary is supported best when adults talk with children about ongoing activities. Some specific vocabulary materials can also be used to support children in reviewing vocabulary from storybooks or other teacher-guided activities. The meanings of key vocabulary words from storybooks can also be deepened if children are engaged in playing word games during circle time.

Materials for Supporting Vocabulary During Center Time

A teacher can make lotto cards using pictures of key vocabulary from stories. When playing, children have opportunities to use the names of items pictured (Figure 3.2). A teacher can also include items that are not from storybooks, along with those that are.

Figure 3.2. Labeled picture lotto board and tiles.

If teachers prepare pictures for lotto games for each unit of study, they will soon have a fairly large collection to use in a variety of ways. For example, picture sets can be organized around categories, such as animals, plants, vehicles, furniture, clothing, or cooking utensils. Make a background board with two columns, and then label each column with a category name (e.g., Animals/Plants, Vehicles/Furniture). Children play with six or seven pictures that are examples of items belonging to each category designated by a column heading, placing each picture into the column where it belongs. If the background boards are laminated without designated category names, create category labels (also laminated) that can be removed and replaced with new ones, using masking tape or pieces of Velcro.

inside"). A brief definition teaches the meaning of the word and anchors to the text, whereas decontextualized definitions during the reading have the potential to distract children with another context.

We authors also agree with literacy experts who suggest that teachers should not ask preschoolers what *soaked* means (Beck, McKeown, & Kucan 2002), even though others advise this practice (e.g., Christ & Wang 2012). Teachers usually plan one or two strategies to use for a first exposure and then plan other strategies when the word comes up a second time in the first reading, the discussion, or a subsequent reading. (See Box 3.5.)

A category focus helps children think more about individual words than does simple matching of pictures to identical twins as when playing with lotto cards. In addition, children understand more about new items they encounter if they have category labels and know basic features required for membership in a category (Gelman & Coley 1990). For example, if children have never seen a praying mantis and one appears in a storybook, they would know something about it if the teacher said, "It's a kind of insect." If children do not know category labels, a teacher's use of them won't advance a child's learning. Some examples of developing category-level knowledge about insects are provided in Chapter 4.

Knowing some details about human-made items, such as their functions, also helps children learn and retain new words (Booth 2009; Nelson, O'Neil, & Asher 2008).

A Word Clue Game for Circle Time

In this game, which uses key vocabulary from storybooks, a teacher starts by telling children they are going to hear clues about some words from specific storybooks. On any one occasion of playing, the teacher selects words to support from just one or two storybooks, showing the books' covers to start the game.

The teacher uses a category clue first, along with a few specific details (e.g., "This is a *toy* that is small, round, and made of glass. Children play games with these small round toys"). If children do not guess the item's name (marbles) from the first two clues, the teacher provides a story-related clue (e.g., "Noisy Nora's sister had some of these little, round, glass toys, and Nora spilled them onto the floor on purpose"). Because story-related clues usually lead children quickly to the item's name, using these first removes the opportunity for children to use a category clue. This is why it is recommended to first use the category clue.

To provide a good first clue for *bat* (a key word in the story *Stellaluna*) a teacher might say, "This is the name of an animal that is a mammal. But this mammal flies, and other mammals do not." This clue uses two category names—animal and mammal.

Other Opportunities to Expose Children to a Word

Repeated exposure to the same word aids learning (Nagy & Townsend 2012; Wasik, Hindman, & Snell 2016). Beyond the exposure to a word in the text during a book's first reading, teachers can use it in comments (e.g., "The rabbits' fur looks darker here because it is *soaked*") and during the story discussion (e.g., "Some animals might not mind getting *soaked* in a rainstorm. Let's take a look"). A thoughtful teacher also sometimes reuses one key word when explaining other key words that are encountered later in the story. For example, when reading *Rabbits and Raindrops*, a teacher might reuse the word *lawn*, explained earlier in the text, when supporting the meaning of *hedge* later.

Teachers can also reuse words, both from the story's text and their commentaries, in the story's discussion. For example, in discussing *Henny Penny*, a teacher can find ways to reuse *sly* or *gullible* (e.g., "I know we were worrying about how *gullible* those birds were, as we read the story. And, yes, that *sly* fox knew how to get those birds into trouble, for sure").

Some exposure to key words from storybooks can and should occur outside the book, such as during center time activities and in activities that are planned for small groups. For example, in *The Little Red Hen (Makes a Pizza),* by Philemon Sturges, illustrated by Amy Walrod, Hen uses numerous kitchen utensils and food items. To support children in learning the meanings of *colander* and *whisk,* teachers can offer these items for children to use in a cooking activity organized for a small group setting. Small group activities with these items help children comprehend and produce items' names, especially when teachers provide explicit support for the words in this context. Teachers can support the words more if the items are available for children's use at the water table or in the children's dramatic play in the house area. Teachers can also play a word meaning clue game during circle time, using key words from stories. (See Box 3.6)

Multiple Readings: Why Once Is Not Enough

From a first reading, children gain a basic understanding of a story and a beginning understanding of important vocabulary (McGee & Schickedanz 2007). Yet, hearing a story only once is not enough to support learning fully or to foster true love of a story. Additionally, because children bring more knowledge to second and third readings than to a first, each reading provides a unique opportunity for them to integrate knowledge and for a teacher to model inferential thinking and analytical talk and engage children in both (Collins 2023; Dickinson & Smith 1994).

For example, in one classroom, the book *Dreams* was part of a shadows and reflections unit. After the book's first reading, the children had opportunities to experiment with shadow creation, including changes in a shadow's size. During the book's second reading, one child commented, "Oh, it's not a monster! It's a shadow of that mouse, and it got bigger and bigger and bigger!" This comment indicated an increase in the child's understanding of the paper mouse shadow compared to the first reading, when some children seemed frightened for the dog who was scared of it as it grew larger and larger.

Introducing a Second or Third Reading

For a second reading, which typically occurs within a few days of the first, the story's problem is reviewed briefly and a critical event can be mentioned. For example, for the story *Swimmy*, a teacher might say, "We read this book on Tuesday, and you probably remember that it's about a little fish named Swimmy and what Swimmy does after something bad happens. We're going to read the story again today and talk about it some more."

Avoid asking a lot of questions before beginning a second reading because children often end up retelling most of the story, which is then followed by the teacher's reading and a discussion. Doing all of this can make story time last 35 to 45 minutes, which is far too long for children this age. One of the benefits of reading a story multiple times across several days is that story time need not last for more than 15 or 20 minutes.

The introduction to a story's third reading acknowledges again children's familiarity (e.g., "We've read this story two times already, and I know you know the title. Read it with me . . ."). The teacher can describe the children's role in the day's reading (e.g., "Today, you are going to help tell the story . . ."). The teacher can then turn to the first page and prompt children to begin reconstructing the story (e.g., "Here, when the story starts, where is Swimmy, and what is he doing?").

Strategies for supporting meaning and vocabulary in second and third readings.
Although the same story meanings and key vocabulary are supported in all readings, teachers can add more verbal explanations in second and third readings to deepen children's initial understandings (Justice, Meier, & Walpole 2005). Stopping now during the reading to insert synonyms or brief explanations is less likely to distract children from the story because children's knowledge from the first reading anchors their engagement. The teacher can ask a *few* questions in a second reading to prompt children to connect events and causes or to infer characters' motivations. The teacher also continues to use comprehension asides, but many will differ from those used in a first reading because children know more now and can benefit from somewhat different asides.

Children's familiarity with a story often prompts both more questions and comments during its second and third readings, and it also brings new cognitive challenges. For example, children learn things from a first reading that story characters will never know until the end of the story. However, children sometimes insist that characters do something, thinking that they too have learned the lessons the children did (e.g., the peddler in *Caps for Sale,* by Esphyr Slobodkina, should just throw down his hat and not go through all the other actions). A teacher might say, "Well, *we* know that because we heard all of the story, but the characters stay just the same in each part of the story every time we read it."

In a third reading, a few days or a week after the second, children are usually familiar enough with the story to retell its events. Teachers still provide asides that clarify or model reasoning after children retell parts (e.g., "You are right. The slug ignored the squirrel's warnings, too. I think the slug must have thought the bumps on the toad's back were pebbles on a road. He had no idea that he was walking up the bumpy back of a predator!").

Box 3.7. Sharing Digital Books

Kathleen A. Paciga

Digital books are presented to children on a screen, typically via a smartphone, tablet, or computer. Although they function in different ways from print books, and therefore offer new and important skills and literacies, educators and families must carefully consider when and how to share digital books with children. Pediatricians suggest that families who wish to introduce their older toddlers and preschoolers to digital books seek out carefully constructed, high-quality content that reinforces the child's understandings and/or provides exposure to new concepts that expand their knowledge. Common Sense Media (www.commonsensemedia.org/app-reviews) and the Association for Library Service to Children (www.ala.org/alsc/awardsgrants/notalists/ncdm) regularly provide reviews of digital media to help guide families and educators in selecting digital books that meet these criteria.

Research has documented some cases in which children older than 18 months demonstrated learning from digital books, video chatting, and other digital media designed for experimental trials (AAP Council on Communications and Media et al. 2016). Other studies indicate that preschoolers may learn new words from well-designed digital books, but their vocabulary learning and comprehension are enhanced when adults coview and extend the digital experience (Flynn & Richert 2015; Kirkorian, Choi, & Pempek 2016; Korat et al. 2014). The "new coviewing" (i.e., adults and children using digital media together) is just as important to learning from digital media as it is to television viewing (Takeuchi et al. 2011). Thus, when young children engage with digital media, high levels of interaction with an adult should always be a part of the experience (International Literacy Association 2019; NAEYC & Fred Rogers Center for Early Learning and Children's Media 2012).

Engaging Preschoolers with Digital Books

Young children encountering digital books for the first time may not understand their purpose. Children observe adults using their devices more commonly to communicate with others, engage with social media, stream video, and/or play games than for reading (Paciga, Lisy, & Teale 2013). When introducing digital books to children, there is a period of acclimation and learning about how they function. For 3- and 4-year-old children who are working toward autonomy, the ability to effectively operate a tablet or other device independently, plus the discoveries awaiting each tap and click, makes digital books highly interesting (Real & Correro 2015). Without adult support, or when the adult tries to control the device for the child, the child resorts to random clicking and exiting the reading platform or application unintentionally (Paciga & Quest 2017). In these instances, opportunities to expand knowledge and experience new content and stories are lost.

Although many digital books are designed for children to use independently, they can only promote language and cognitive development to the same extent as reading print books if adults scaffold digital books using similar practices. Therefore, adults should work to construct meaning with children as they reference illustrations and animation to label images with words, explain concepts and events presented in the text, connect the text to the child's experiences to make language more comprehensible, and ask questions to prompt the child's participation and language use (Hoffman & Paciga 2014; Salmon 2014).

Some studies on the effects of using digital books found them more effective than print books in promoting children's understanding of stories, especially their implicit features (e.g. character motivations) (Verhallen, Bus, & De Jong 2006), while other studies found that features of some digital books distract from story content and make them less effective (De Jong & Bus 2002).

Still other studies found that preschoolers benefited equally from digital and print books (De Jong & Bus 2004). A revealing finding is that different learning comes from different forms of book reading (Smith 2001), all of which can contribute to children's learning of multiple literacies.

Research has also emphasized that distracting features, such as irrelevant music, animation (De Jong & Bus 2002; Labbo & Kuhn 2000), and ongoing narration, discourage adults from reading and discussing the text (Kim & Anderson 2008). If adults are to use interactive reading strategies, digital books must (1) allow control over the pacing of the book sharing, rather than simply "play" continuously; and (2) provide narration turn off options that allow adults to read the text aloud (Labbo 2009). When the adult can control both the pace and reading of a digital text, patterns of adult and child talk are very similar to those found with print-based texts (Fisch et al. 2002), through which the adult and child construct meanings collaboratively (Labbo 2009).

The Changing Nature of Digital Texts

Many of the stories children are most familiar with were created and first published in print book format. CD-ROM technology began offering digital stories from the 1980s through the 2010s, when tablets and smartphones became more commonplace. As technology progressed, content developers integrated new elements into digital books, resulting in vastly different features (Paciga & Hoffman 2015).

Teamed with researchers, standalone digital book applications (apps) were designed to explore how presenting more or fewer hotspots (i.e., the points on the screen that are clicked, tapped, or otherwise manipulated by the viewer) and film-like, multimedia features (e.g., sound effects, musical accompaniment, animations) impacted young children's emergent literacy development. Interactive games and multimedia features incongruent (unrelated) to the storyline demonstrated negative impacts on vocabulary and story comprehension (Labbo & Kuhn 2000).

Meanwhile, interactive features congruent (related) to the book's plot may facilitate increases in children's vocabulary and word knowledge (e.g., Christ et al. 2019; López-Escribano, Valverde-Montesino, & García-Ortega 2021) or comprehension (Sari et al. 2019). Digital additions such as dictionaries, verbal explanations, and animations may contribute to learning the meaning of new words (Klop et al. 2018; Korat, Kozlov-Peretz, & Segal-Drori 2017; Leacox & Jackson 2014; Smeets & Bus 2014). Animations that visualize and highlight the print-tracking process support preschoolers' developing print awareness, phonological awareness, and decoding skills (Evaluation and Training Institute 2016; Guernsey & Levine 2015; Linebarger, Piotrowski, & Greenwood 2010). Research demonstrated, too, that digital books can effectively teach adults how to better support emergent literacy development in young children (Rvachew et al. 2017).

Technology is expensive and changes rapidly (Rideout & Robb 2020). Regardless of the form digital books take, they will continue to play an important role in young children's literacy development (Yokota & Teale 2014). Record numbers of K–12 schools have integrated digital and audiobook titles into their collections (OverDrive Education 2020) and few college bookstores stock print books. Ten years ago, podcasts and audiobooks were not included as examples of digital media appropriate for children, but with the increasing demand for audiobooks, the popularity of podcasts, the widespread use of smart speaker systems (e.g., Siri, Alexa, Nest), these media have made their way into homes, cars, and early childhood programs. At the same time, pediatricians continue to recommend limiting screen time for young children. Additional research is needed to explore how educators and families might implement these digital media into their contexts in ways that support literacy development in young children. Human ingenuity has propelled digital books forward. As the title of this box implies, *sharing* with informed and nurturing adults should be an abiding element of digital book use as children develop and learn.

In addition to teacher asides that focus on characters' thinking and causal explanations, prompts can now include a few *why* questions. These questions foster analytic talk, which can be supported by teachers scaffolding children's thinking and pointing to illustrations that contain relevant details (Collins 2023; McGee & Schickedanz 2007).

For example, while showing page 9 of *Max's Dragon Shirt,* by Rosemary Wells, a teacher might point to the hem of the yellow dress in the illustration and ask, "Why did Max think this person here was his sister?" Children would likely say, "Because he knew that Ruby was wearing a yellow dress." The teacher might then turn to the dressing room scene on page 8 and say, "Right. Max didn't notice that Ruby's yellow dress was still on a hook in the dressing room. He was asleep when she left while wearing a store dress to go find another to try on."

Discussion in multiple readings. A teacher keeps an open mind and pays attention to children's understanding in readings. Thus, questions for the second reading, and especially for the third, emerge not only from teacher planning but also from the children's spontaneous questions and comments. With study of a book and careful attention to children's comments and questions, teachers can generate a number of questions that are suitable for a story's discussion after each of its readings (Collins 2023).

After a second reading of *Peter's Chair*, a discussion might focus on personal things versus things that belong to the family (e.g., "Do you think Peter's parents would give some of his old toys to his baby sister, without asking him first, the way they did with his furniture?"). Exploring this topic helps children to distinguish between truly personal items from those that are "in the family and shared by all."

After a third or fourth reading of a story, a teacher might consider using an informational book as the basis for the story discussion. (See examples in Chapter 4.)

Use of Digital Books

Educators and families access stories in print and digital formats. Digital books have a place in the preschooler's life if the materials are carefully selected and used appropriately. A discussion of digital books and best practices for their use is provided in Box 3.7.

Concluding Thoughts

We are long past the era of thinking that we should "just read" to children. As this chapter explained, teachers must consider many things, including features of both individual books (e.g., story complexity, language richness, knowledge) and a year's collection (e.g., connections to units, diversity in universal themes) and interactions that can support meaning and language development. It takes considerable time to prepare story introductions, select strategies for explaining vocabulary, craft comprehension asides, and identify discussion topics and prompts for each storybook's multiple readings. But the time is worth the benefits that careful planning brings to young children.

The authors offer one caution about story reading in today's world. Now that policymakers, politicians, and educators understand the importance of the early years and have established high expectations for early learning, there is a danger that meeting these expectations will change preschool practices in ways that reduce children's enjoyment in listening to stories and in learning in general. For children, story reading must be as interesting and full of delight as ever, even as teachers make every effort to maximize the learning that children take from these experiences.

CHAPTER 4

SHARING INFORMATIONAL BOOKS WITH PRESCHOOLERS

Mr. Jacoby is sharing the story *Raccoon on His Own,* by Jim Arnosky, with his preschool class. After reading, "Mother found a crunchy crawfish," he points to that page's illustration and says, "Here's the crawfish. The mother raccoon is going to eat it for breakfast."

"Where is it?" a child asks. Mr. Jacoby points to the crawfish again and explains that its head is inside the mother raccoon's mouth. He tells the children he will bring in some books with pictures of crawfish the next day so they can see its head and talk about a crawfish's different body parts.

Situations like this occur frequently during story reading. Many characters and scenes pictured in stories are not explained, leaving children curious or puzzled about what they see. When this happens, Mr. Jacoby's approach is one all teachers can take: share informational books to help answer children's questions.

This chapter describes what informational books are and discusses the importance of sharing them with preschoolers. It also explains contexts for using informational books in the preschool learning setting, as well as effective strategies for reading them. Additionally, the chapter briefly overviews other nonbook informational materials that are appropriate to share with preschoolers.

Informational Book Features and Text Formats

There are several features that characterize informational books (Duke, Halvorsen, & Knight 2012). Informational books provide facts or explain processes (e.g., the number of legs that insects have, how whales breathe). They also have components that organize the content or provide supplemental information. These can include a table of contents that outlines the book's structure (e.g., chapters, section headings), an index, a glossary, timelines, author notes, and suggested resources for further reading and learning. All of these features allow readers to easily find specific information, which helps them use a book selectively. (This is discussed in more detail later in this chapter.) In contrast, because the parts of a narrative book work together, they must be read as a whole. Informational books also contain more technical vocabulary than stories, and they more frequently have realistic photographs, diagrams, and charts rather than creative art. The labels and captions often accompanying these illustrations provide explicit information that supports and enhances the text.

Informational books are written in a variety of styles (i.e., text structures): (1) informational, (2) informational narrative, and (3) informational poetic verse (Bintz & Ciercierski 2017; Duke 2000). *From Wheat to Bread,* by Stacy Taus-Bolstad, is an example of a book with an informational style. The text is straightforward ("Wheat seeds are called kernels. Trucks take the kernels to a factory"). Informational narrative style, on the other hand, weaves information within lyrical stories, as in *Honeybee: The Busy Life of* Apis Mellifera, by Candace Fleming, illustrated by Eric Rohmann ("At last, on the twenty-fifth day of her life—with the sun just rising and the dew still drying—she leaps from the next and . . . flies"). Informational poetic verse style, as found in *On the Wing,* by David Elliott, illustrated by Becca Stadtlander, offers facts about birds through playful, rhyming text ("Oh, good heavens! Oh, my word! The biggest bill of any bird"). There are also books that combine different elements from these three styles. For example, *A Beetle Is Shy,* by Dianna Hutts Aston, illustrated by Sylvia Long, is straightforward in its informational content ("The egg hatches into a wriggling larva . . .") and text features (e.g., labels, definitions, timelines) but poetic in its language and typography ("A beetle is shy. A newborn, soft and hungry, hurrying to seal itself into a cocoon, where it can be still and cozy until it becomes what it was meant to be").

Some informational books are organized around a guiding question or curiosity that explores a behavior or nuance about *many* animals, not just one. For example, there are books that explore how animals sleep (e.g., *Snooze-O-Rama: The Strange Ways That Animals Sleep,* by Maria Birmingham, illustrated by Kyle Reed), the sounds they make (e.g., *Can an Aardvark Bark?* by Melissa Stewart, illustrated by Steve Jenkins), and the reasons to love those with a bad reputation (e.g., *The Not BAD Animals,* by Sophie Corrigan).

Why Read Informational Books?

Teachers of young children typically devote more time to stories than to informational books and include more storybooks in early learning program book areas (Robinson 2020). One study broke down the genres of books preschool teachers used in their read alouds; storybooks were read 82 percent of the time, while mixed-genre and informational books were read 13 percent and 4 percent of the time, respectively (Pentimonti et al. 2010). These practices are based on beliefs, such as thinking that informational books are more difficult and less appealing for young children than stories. Interestingly, a small study found that teachers in the United States aligned with this perspective (i.e., narratives are easier and more appealing than informational books for preschoolers), while teachers in Korea held exactly the opposite view. Not surprisingly, the books these preschool teachers read aloud and included in their libraries in the early learning setting strongly reflected their attitudes (Lee et al. 2011).

The Common Core State Standards (National Governors Association Center for Best Practices, Council of Chief State School Officers 2010) require informational book use in the primary grades. This includes comparing, contrasting, and integrating knowledge and ideas through exposure to multiple texts on the same topic. Knowledge of informational text structure in primary grades is helpful to reading comprehension (Pyle et al. 2017). For children to successfully read and navigate informational books later in their schooling, it's important for preschool teachers to provide them with more experiences with informational books early. It is the authors' hope that teachers are helped toward this goal through attention to using informational books with young children in educator preparation programs, the ever-growing array of informational books, and the resources available for supporting teachers in this practice (Stewart & Correia 2021).

The following are just a few ways informational books benefit young children's learning.

Informational Books Are Interesting

The content of informational books is interesting to most preschoolers, and some young children like informational texts better than stories (Correia 2011; Robinson 2020). Having access to books that are preferred can affect a child's interest in books and in reading (Repaskey, Schumm, & Johnson 2017). Just as critical is having adults who are responsive to children's preferences.

This affective response is related to a child's reading success (Nevo et al. 2020; Parsons et al. 2018), which makes sense because children who are interested in books read more and develop greater reading skill. They also acquire more content knowledge and associated vocabulary (Conradi-Smith & Hiebert 2022). In fact, the majority of new vocabulary acquired during the school years (i.e., third grade and beyond) comes from the books that children read (Nagy, Anderson, & Herman 1987).

In the United States, around 42 percent of fourth graders read almost daily for fun, while 16 percent never or hardly ever read for fun. These figures reflect the lowest motivation to read for enjoyment since the mid-1980s (Schaeffer 2021). When preschool teachers read informational books and place some in the early learning setting's book area, more children have a chance to develop interest in books.

Informational Books Support Vocabulary Development

Informational books contain many sophisticated technical words and explain these words explicitly, so reading this kind of book helps children learn higher-level vocabulary (Young, Ricks, & MacKay 2023). In contrast, narratives contain fewer technical terms and provide very little explicit information about their meanings. This leaves children to infer the meanings of unfamiliar words when listening to stories or to learn them from information teachers or family members provide. (See Chapter 3.)

Crayfish, by Lola M. Schaefer, features the explicit explanations typically found in informational texts. One page states, "Crayfish are sea animals without bones. They are invertebrates." In this case, *invertebrates* is defined in the first sentence (i.e., "without bones"). Young children, however, do not always link information from two or more consecutive sentences, so teachers might also provide additional support for word meanings. A teacher's comments can broaden and deepen children's understanding of a word, including how it applies across different contexts. Children also learn related words, which increases their understanding of a story event that is related to the content of the informational book shared. Unlike the connected ideas and flow found in storybooks, many informational books are written with one fact or explanation per page. This structure makes it easy for the teacher to stop and comment after reading each one.

Revisiting the chapter's opening vignette, Mr. Jacoby and his preschool class went on to read *Raccoon on His Own* for a second time. They also explored some of the books about crawfish he told the children he would bring in, including *Crayfish*. Here is a glimpse of the discussion that followed:

> "Crayfish are sea animals without bones. They are invertebrates." After reading these lines from the first page of *Crayfish,* Mr. Jacoby says, "Many other animals have bones inside their body, which make up their skeleton. People have skeletons, and so do birds, snakes, and many other animals." Putting down the book, he holds up a poster that pictures human, bird, and snake skeletons. Then, he reaches for his left wrist with the fingers of his right hand, holding them up so the children can see. "Feel your wrist, like this. Animals with bones inside their bodies are called *vertebrates.* That's a great word. Say this great word with me." The children say the word with Mr. Jacoby. "Animals who do not have bones inside their bodies are called *invertebrates.* It was fairly easy for the mother raccoon in the story we read to chew up and eat the crayfish because it didn't have any hard bones inside." A child says, "A raccoon couldn't eat me because I have lots of hard bones." Mr. Jacoby agrees.

The illustrations in informational books also provide strong support for the meanings of technical vocabulary. For example, the photograph accompanying the text on page 5, "Crayfish have *jointed legs,*" shows very clearly a crayfish's jointed legs. Similarly, on page 21, which says, "Little crayfish come out of the eggs. They are called *instars,*" a photograph shows the instars.

> After reading the text on these pages, Mr. Jacoby points to the relevant part of each photograph and comments. For page 5, he says, "This is the joint of one of the crayfish's legs, and this line goes up from the joint to a label that says 'jointed leg.' The knees in our legs are joints, and they allow us to bend our legs. The joints in our arms are our elbows, and they allow us to bend our arms. We even have joints in our fingers." As the teacher talks, the children bend their legs, arms, and fingers along with the teacher.

Jointed legs and all other key vocabulary in *Crayfish* are in boldface print. Boldfacing key vocabulary, which is common in informational books, helps teachers know which words to support. It also makes the words easy for children to find, if interested, when looking at the books.

As discussed in Chapter 1, background knowledge supports deep understanding of vocabulary, which is critical for good reading comprehension (Duke, Ward, & Pearson 2021; Ouellette 2006). Because deep understanding of words depends on having related content knowledge (Nagy & Townsend 2012), children learn content and associated vocabulary best when they have access to both concrete experiences and informational books (Leung 2008).

Informational Books Help Children Acquire Content Knowledge

From abuelas to zucchini (and beyond!), informational books can expose children to new topics or deepen their understanding of familiar topics. Through books, children can learn about many things that are impossible or impracticable for them to experience for themselves. Even when firsthand access to information is possible, informational books allow children to see things they might not otherwise notice or think about. For example, while a child may have visited an airport or even flown on a plane before, books like *The Airport: The Inside Story,* by John Walton, illustrated by Hannah Abbo, introduces well-researched, detailed information about airport systems and structures.

Alternately, suppose children find a bee outside. Teachers might identify the bee by name, tell a little bit about it, and prompt children to observe some of the insect's physical features and behavior. The problem, though, is that children cannot safely approach some insects, and others fly away before children can observe them thoroughly. Informational books benefit learning, in part, because they make things "sit still" for examination in ways they often do not in the natural world. With access to books about insects, children can count the legs of various insects and learn that all have six. Children can also learn that insects are born as larvae, that larvae feed before turning into pupae, and that an adult insect emerges from a pupa after a few days or weeks. Children might also learn from informational books that, unlike insects, spiders have eight legs and babies look like tiny spiders when they hatch from their eggs and simply grow bigger as they mature.

Informational Books Expose Children to Dense and Abstract Language

Because informational books are packed densely with content words, their syntax differs from the syntax in narratives (Nagy & Townsend 2012). Informational books also contain verb forms that are timeless (e.g., "Crayfish are . . . "; "Crayfish live . . ."; "Rocks do not melt . . ."), rather than the mostly past tense verbs that are used in most narratives.

Thus, in addition to giving children access to vocabulary and content information, hearing informational books read aloud acquaints children with language of a specific kind. This familiarity helps all children comprehend content-area books they read later in school (e.g., science and social science textbooks), and it seems especially helpful to multilingual learners (Council of Chief State School Officers 2012; Kelly 2020).

Informational Books Help Children Understand Narratives

Although children do not need to understand *all* the facts in every story to enjoy and comprehend most of it, the more a child understands, the better. For example, a young child can enjoy *Raccoon on His Own* without knowing much about crawfish because they are not central to the story's problem or plot. Many stories are like this, but others are not. When understanding something is central to understanding the story itself, educators can help children acquire the content knowledge needed to aid their story comprehension.

Farfallina and Marcel, by Holly Keller, is a good example. Children will realize why Farfallina (a caterpillar when the story begins), does not return to her friend Marcel (a gosling) for such a long time only if they understand that the life cycle of a butterfly includes a metamorphosis from caterpillar to butterfly. Similarly, that same knowledge is what children need to realize that the butterfly that appears later in the story is still Farfallina, not a different creature from the caterpillar they met earlier. Table 4.1 contains a few examples of narrative books, as well as suggested informational books to provide content knowledge that will enhance children's understanding of each story.

When content knowledge is central to a story, it is a good idea to provide experiences from which young children can acquire the relevant information and concepts. These experiences should happen before children hear the story for the first time, or at least within the time taken for the recommended three readings of the book, which typically span a period of about a week or 10 days. This way, children have opportunities to integrate the content knowledge learned from their experiences with information provided in the story's text, which helps them draw inferences about story events and characters' behavior.

It takes time, of course, for children to acquire the full range of content knowledge that would inform all of the stories they hear. Although it is not possible for preschoolers to acquire vast stores of information, it is realistic for teachers to help them develop select content-area knowledge and then support their use of this knowledge to understand some of the stories they hear.

Contexts for Using Informational Books

Thus far, examples have illustrated how informational books can be used in conjunction with storybooks. The following section discusses this use further, and then explores other times and places in the preschool learning setting where teachers can use informational books.

As this section highlights, teachers should avoid relying too much on informational books to scaffold preschoolers' learning across all content areas. Carefully planned, hands-on activities must be central to young children's study of a topic, and these experiences must be integrated well with both storybooks and informational books. Books alone, no matter how well-designed or effectively used by teachers, are not sufficient to secure preschoolers' learning of many science concepts (Leung 2008). As with all learning, repeated exposure across a variety of experiences over a period of time is required.

Table 4.1. Examples of Using Informational Books to Enhance Story Understanding

Narrative book	Brief description of the story	Content knowledge supported by the narrative book	Informational books that offer additional content knowledge
Bear Has a Story to Tell, by Philip C. Stead, illustrated by Erin E. Stead	Bear desperately wants to share a story with his friends, but they all are too busy.	Animals prepare for winter in different ways.	• *Hiders Seekers Finders Keepers: How Animals Adapt in Winter,* by Jessica Kulekjian, illustrated by Salini Perera • *Over and Under the Snow,* by Kate Messner, illustrated by Christopher Silas Neal
Elmore, by Holly Hobbie	A lonely porcupine wants friends, but they are afraid of his quills.	Animals' behaviors or body parts protect them from predators. Porcupines have quills.	• *Porcupines,* by Amy McDonald • *Wildlife Anatomy: The Curious Lives and Features of Wild Animals Around the World,* by Julia Rothman, with Lisa Hiley
A House for Hermit Crab, by Eric Carle	In the underwater world, Hermit Crab meets interesting animals as he searches for a home.	Animals seek safe homes. Some might outgrow one home and move.	• *Animal Architects,* by Amy Cherrix, illustrated by Chris Sasaki • *Over and Under the Waves,* by Kate Messner, illustrated by Christopher Silas Neal
Make Way for Ducklings, by Robert McCloskey	A mallard family navigates the city of Boston to find a safe place to build their nest.	Mallard ducks need certain things to take care of their babies.	• *Feathers: Not Just for Flying,* by Melissa Stewart, illustrated by Sarah S. Brannen • *Just Ducks!* by Nicola Davies, illustrated by Salvatore Rubbino
Stellaluna, by Janell Cannon	A baby bat abruptly joins a nest of baby birds and discovers new ways of doing things.	Animals sleep in different ways.	• *The Magic of Sleep: A Fascinating Guide to the World of Slumber,* by Vicky Woodgate • *Snooze-O-Rama: The Strange Ways That Animals Sleep,* by Maria Birmingham, illustrated by Kyle Reed

Use Informational Books in Conjunction with Storybooks

The vignette on page 84 describes the use of an informational book in the discussion following a story's second reading to help explain something a child asked about during its first reading. In addition to using informational books to respond to something that arises spontaneously in a story, many educators plan for the coordinated use of narrative books and informational books within units of study (Pollard-Durodola et al. 2011; Stewart & Chelsey 2014). The authors have used and recommend this approach with children because it ensures more than one exposure to vocabulary in a story and allows children to build knowledge that supports their comprehension of the stories used in a unit.

It is not necessary to link every individual storybook within a unit of study to an informational book, nor must teachers use all informational books in the same way. Sometimes it makes sense to read a variety of storybooks, all of which are related to a major concept, and then use an informational book to address the concept. At other times, it is useful to read several informational books in conjunction with concrete experiences, and then read several stories. Keep in mind that preschoolers can enjoy many storybooks without understanding all the information and concepts they contain.

Use Informational Books to Introduce a Small Group Experience

Sometimes, informational books can orient children to a small group experience. For example, after children have explored magnets using trays of objects (e.g., paper clips, small wooden beads, bread twist ties, plastic discs), a teacher might organize a small group experience that focuses on some practical uses of magnets, such as in can openers and refrigerator doors.

Before demonstrating how a magnet in the can opener keeps the lid from falling into the can after it has been cut off or holds items up on refrigerator doors, a book like *Magnetic and Nonmagnetic,* by Angela Royston, can acquaint children with other uses for magnets, such as holding keys on a rack, connecting toy train cars, and holding pieces in place on a game board. The teacher would use only the pages that discuss practical uses of magnets and read only some of the text that explains each picture. They could also provide building materials that use magnets to hold pieces together.

Use Informational Books to Support Activities in Centers

Informational books placed in centers can support activities in current units of study. For example, books about flowers and gardens might be placed in a science center that is focused on the study of the plant life cycle. A unit on festivals and celebrations might touch on various cultures to give children a glimpse into traditions around the world or focus on your specific region to foster knowledge and appreciation of local history and customs. For example, books about marathons (*Ready, Set, Run! The Amazing New York City Marathon,* by Leslie Kimmelman, illustrated by Jessie Hartland), quilting (*The All-Together Quilt,* by Lizzy Rockwell), or food-related events (*Food Trucks!* by Mark Todd) help children learn more about the community they and their families are part of and share. These books, placed alongside photographs and other artifacts, can be placed in centers for reference or use during teacher-guided activities or independent exploration.

Similarly, if block building is related to a zoo or farm topic, books about the various animals can be placed in the center, along with wooden or plastic models of those animals. Children and teachers can use the books to learn about individual animals, and this information might be used to make small props for the play. For example, to support farm animal block play, grains of wheat or corn could be glued onto green construction paper for chickens to eat and pieces of blue paper could be laminated to make ponds on which small toy models of ducks and geese could swim.

Books can also support the use of math manipulatives in a center where both math and language and literacy materials are available. For example, after reading and discussing the book *More,* by I.C. Springman, illustrated by Brian Lies, a teacher can place the book in the manipulatives center along with concrete items for children's use in representing the quantity words (e.g., *more, a few, less, too much*) that are the focus of the book.

Including books in the writing center can support children as they explore facts for stories they write, compose ideas and organize writing on a page, or add details to pictures they draw. However, this might occur later in the preschool year, when children are experienced print users and not tempted to add marks to books. Positioning a couple of books on a nearby shelf or windowsill promotes ease of access without cluttering the writing surface, upstaging children's ideas, or squelching creativity.

A few pictorial examples of informational books in centers are provided in Figures 4.1, 4.2, and 4.3.

Of course, children can also use computers or tablets to access information online during small groups or center time. This is most beneficial with guidance and conversation with a teacher. An interesting example of using technology to support children's science learning is provided in Box 4.1.

Figure 4.1. As part of a unit on plants, a teacher provided books about flowers, with one clipped open to the relevant seed pages. Children used magnifying glasses to inspect seeds that had been glued onto a piece of poster board. Each group of seeds was labeled with the name of the flower that would grow from them, and a picture of the flower was also attached beside the seeds.

Figure 4.2. As part of a construction tool unit with 4-year-olds, the teacher provided a book with a page showing many different nails at the small table where the children could hammer nails into pieces of Styrofoam. (Note: Styrofoam can break down into small pieces that may pose a hazard. Use caution and supervision when using this material with young children.)

Figure 4.3. A teacher gathered books together to help organize a center about musical instruments. This activity, which focused on drums, was one of several about different kinds of musical instruments.

Box 4.1. Preschoolers Using Information Media and Technology

Children can also use computers or tablets during small groups or center time to access the vast amounts of information available online. To benefit most from this method of accessing information, children need guidance from and conversations with their teachers. Teachers can also use interactive whiteboards to display what is on a computer's screen to a large group of children.

The following vignette illustrates an interesting use of technology in the early learning setting to support children's science learning (in this case, about elephant seals).

Three children sit excitedly around the computer. Their teacher, Ms. Janirys, says, "I wonder what Ms. Liz and Ms. Alma have for us today." Ms. Liz and Ms. Alma are attending a conference in California, and they are posting photos of the different sights they see to their program-affiliated social media accounts. Ms. Janirys navigates to a picture of an elephant seal sleeping on the sand. Next to it is Ms. Liz's profile photo. Ms. Janirys clicks on a photo of Ms. Liz, and the children listen to an audio recording that explains what she's posted. Ms. Liz says, "This is an elephant seal. Elephant seals don't have any ears, and an elephant seal is so big, it could never fit in a family's car." Ms. Janirys asks the children, "Who would like to tell Ms. Liz something?" They all pounce at the chance.

Ms. Janirys helps Juanita type *What do elephant seals eat?* Thomas asks to record an audio message in reply and says, "An elephant seal won't fit into your grandma's or grandpa's or Aunt Bonnie's or Angelo's car." It's Shea's turn next. She says, "Why does an elephant seal have no ears? How can it hear with no ears? Because I can hear when I have ears."

The children leave and return to the other centers, knowing they can check back for their responses from Ms. Liz and Ms. Alma later in the day. They are excited to hear what their teachers have to say. That afternoon, they get their answers. Ms. Liz answers Juanita's question about what elephant seals eat and reaffirms that elephant seals would not fit in anyone's car, adding, "Elephant seals would weigh even more than the car." Ms. Alma explains that although elephant seals do not have external ears, they do have little holes on either side of their head, and the little holes are just like ears that allow them to hear.

Vignette adapted from V.B. Fantozzi, "Exploring Elephant Seals in New Jersey: Preschoolers Use Collaborative Multimedia Albums," *Young Children* 67, no. 3 (2012): 42.

Include Informational Books in the Book Area

Informational books should also be available in the early learning setting's book area. See Box 4.2 for information about other kinds of book to include, how many, and how to display them.

The informational books placed in the book area include those used recently with storybooks or to support small group activities because children almost always want to inspect their photographs and diagrams further and up close. For example, Mr. Jacoby placed the book he shared with the children (*Crayfish*) in the book area for children to examine, along with the skeleton poster.

Informational books that are not related to a current or previous unit of study can also be included in the book area to spark new interests or invite children with a specific interest to pursue it. Teachers also often include informational books that are related to experiences that commonly occur in children's lives—a new baby in the family, grandparents visiting from another country, or a broken arm.

To keep children's engagement high, it is important for educators to periodically rotate the books available in the book area (Vukelich et al. 2020). Though the frequency will vary depending on the specific children you teach, what you observe about their interest level, and the curriculum, the authors' general guidance is to rotate three to five books every seven to 10 days to provide children with exposure to a wide range of titles over the course of the year. This strikes a balance between a stale bookshelf and a revolving door of books that children do not have time to peruse. Keeping the selection of books regularly rotating also nurtures children's use of books in the book area, deepens content-area learning, and supports curricular connections. When books are used a few times, first in whole group settings and then in small group settings, before being placed on shelves for children's independent inspection, children have a chance to become familiar with them. Multiple exposures to a book are helpful to multilingual learners' confidence in choosing the book to look at independently.

Include Informational Books in a Lending Library

Book collections that are available for children to borrow and take home are an invaluable resource. If the early learning setting's book area collection is large enough (i.e., has multiple copies of each title), it can serve as a lending library. If not, other options might include the program library, a book collection shared among classrooms, or digital books downloaded to loanable tablets.

Children often have many questions about the illustrations in an informational book or about something they heard as the teacher read, but teachers do not always have time to address questions as fully as children would like. When children can take informational books home, a family member can read with the child. No matter their literacy level or home language, family members have considerable knowledge about things in the world. Children benefit enormously when an adult guides the children in looking at illustrations and talks with them about a book's topic when it's of interest to them.

Box 4.2. The Book Area

The book area or library houses a selected collection of books for the children's use. This area should accommodate four or five children comfortably without crowding.

Books to Include

A variety of books should be included in the early learning setting's library, including informational books, storybooks, concept books, and predictable books. Many of the books in this area are those read by teachers during story time, during circle time, or in content-focused small or whole group gatherings.

In addition to books from commercial publishers, teachers can incorporate books that children have made. These might include photo albums of the children in the learning setting, on a field trip, or at home, as well as books and albums that document long-term activities (e.g., a child-made alphabet book, plants growing from seed to maturity, the progression of a block structure). Teachers can also place illustrated copies of recipes that children have used in cooking projects in a binder to make them easy to browse in the book area.

How Many Books?

Experts suggest that a library include five to eight books per child to provide adequate choice (Vukelich et al. 2020). Depending on the amount of space and the number of display shelves available, this number must sometimes be decreased.

Shelving

Ideally, some of the shelving in the book area can display book covers (Figure 4.4); children are more likely to choose books when their covers, rather than just their spines, are visible (Martinez & Teale 1989, cited in Fractor et al. 1993). Front-facing bins (Figure 4.5) that showcase several books, perhaps all related to a topic, allow children to flip through books easily to make selections.

With preschoolers, it is preferable to use concrete approaches when studying authors, such as placing several books by the same author that the teacher has read to the children in a small basket in the book area. These book collections can include both storybooks and informational books, especially after children have used these in units of study. For example, a teacher might provide several books written by Dianna Hutts Aston and illustrated by Sylvia Long, such as *A Beetle Is Shy*, *An Egg Is Quiet*, and *A Rock Is Lively*. Similarly, books from Kate Messner and Christopher Silas Neal's *Over and Under* series, which explore animals and habitats with rich language and a wealth of information, might be grouped together.

Including Items Other than Books

Sometimes, a book area contains more than just books. These items might include a puppet theater and puppets, a flannel board and flannel pieces for a specific story, and bulletin boards that feature a specific author or children's dictated responses about a story they recently heard. If larger items (e.g., the puppet theater, the flannel board) crowd the book area or pull children away from looking at books, you might consider placing them in another area close by. (Also, have one or the other of these options available at one time, not both.) Some flannel piece sets can relate to informational books, such as the life cycle of a butterfly (e.g., *Butterfly,* by Mary Ling) or the sequence of events from planting a seed to its growth into a mature plant (e.g., *A Seed Grows,* by Antoinette Portis).

Educators might also gather together children's drawings or dictated responses to a specific story and make a class book for the book area. When in book form, rather than mounted on a bulletin board, the children have hands-on access and are more likely to share the experience with a friend. Reading or looking at books together is especially supportive of shy or nonverbal children's social opportunities.

If teachers want wall decorations in the book area, they can purchase book-related posters or draw large pictures of characters from stories recently read to children. In an early learning program the authors observed, the children loved seeing the story characters, and sometimes even talked to them! Teachers might also create attractive displays of plant and animal pictures related to a current unit of study on poster board and put the display on the wall.

Figure 4.4. Front-facing book shelving.

Figure 4.5. Front-facing book bin.

Many alphabet books that are also informational books make good candidates for a lending library. For example, books like *P Is for Pakistan,* by Shazia Razzak, photographs by Prodeepta Das, and *A Is for Africa,* by Ifeoma Onyefulu, contain a wealth of information about different countries. All of Jerry Pallotta's alphabet books are also content books (*The Frog Alphabet Book, The Yucky Reptile Alphabet Book, The Boat Alphabet Book,* etc.). And, of course, the classic book *Eating the Alphabet,* by Lois Ehlert, is a book about the many fruits and vegetables we eat.

Because these and many other alphabet books contain detailed illustrations and a great deal of information in their written text, they require one-on-one engagement with an adult to do them justice. It is difficult for teachers to find time to read and discuss these books with individual children during center time in the book area. Family members, including older siblings, can come to the rescue if books such as these are included in a lending library.

Strategies for Using Informational Books

Strategies for reading informational books depend on each book's features and on the specific purpose for and context in which a book is used.

Read Only Selected Parts

Teachers sometimes use selected portions of an informational book that are specifically relevant to the question at hand and are at a suitable level for preschoolers. For example, when one teacher's goal was to acquaint children with the idea that different birds have different beaks that can do different things, during a class discussion on the topic, she showed every picture in *Unbeatable Beaks,* by Stephen R. Swinburne, illustrated by Joan Paley, but read only the labels that name the birds pictured, not the main text. She then followed up with children who were especially interested by reading some or all of the main text in the book area during center time.

Read an Informational Book in Its Entirety

Using an entire informational book with a group of children is appropriate at times. For example, when an informational book is used in the context of a unit of study, rather than to follow up on a child's spontaneous question about a storybook, children bring knowledge to the book from firsthand experiences the teacher has provided. This knowledge often helps children engage well with the reading of an entire informational book. Additionally, hearing the book read, along with the teacher's comments inserted, extends the knowledge that children gain from their firsthand experiences. Other times, an informational book can be read in its entirety when ideas across the book cohere. For example, through the bold illustrations in *Hiders Seekers Finders Keepers: How Animals Adapt in Winter,* by Jessica Kulekjian, illustrated by Salini Perera, children learn not only information about how specific animals adapt in winter but also that groups of animals behave similarly and some, such as the chipmunk and the bumblebee, coexist during winter.

Model the Use of Informational Text Features

Young children learn how to use informational book features, such as its table of contents, index, diagrams, and glossary, as teachers model their specific uses. For example, if children spotted some ants on the playground and someone asked, "Where are they coming from? Where do they live?" a teacher might find a relevant book to answer the child's question by consulting its table of contents. The teacher would stop running their finger down the column of topics and reading them when an entry matching the information of interest is found. The teacher would then move their finger across to find the page number and comment, "This number tells us that information about where ants live is on page 5. Let's turn to page 5 and see what it says."

Children also learn how to use lines and arrows that link labels to their referents in diagrams and photographs when teachers explain their purpose and demonstrate their use, as Mr. Jacoby did when pointing out the joint in the crawfish's leg. In *Crayfish*, photographs always show the body of a crayfish with a line extending from a key vocabulary word boxed in the margin of the page. The key vocabulary word in the main text is also in boldface type (e.g., "Crayfish look like large bugs. They have two **eyestalks**"). If these words are pointed out and the line from a label to the illustration is traced, children will sometimes use these devices when looking at books independently. Some informational books organize text features in innovative ways to beckon curiosity. For example, teachers can explain what zombie worms are and where they attach to whale bones by referencing the insets in *Whale Fall: Exploring an Ocean-Floor Ecosystem,* by Melissa Stewart, illustrated by Rob Dunlavey.

Many informational books also have glossaries, which contain alphabetical lists of key terms used in the book. After reading a book, a teacher can use the glossary to review the book's key vocabulary and even flip back to relevant pages of the text, if useful.

Some informational books supplement the main text with additional material at the end of the book. For example, *Carry Me! Animal Babies on the Move,* by Susan Stockdale, provides more information about each animal that is discussed in the main text. Similarly, each book in the *About . . .* series, by Cathryn Sill, illustrated by John Sill, has small pictures of each animal in an afterword that correspond to their appearance in the main text. Each picture is paired with more detailed information about the featured animal. The more basic main text is suitable for reading to a whole group of children, while the additional information is more suitable for sharing with children who are interested when they are in the book area or a small group.

Exposing Children to Printed Information in Nonbook Form

Although the primary focus of this chapter is informational books, a considerable amount of printed information is also available in nonbook form. Children enjoy seeing and using many of these printed artifacts in their pretend play and other learning experiences.

Informational Print Artifacts

Many print artifacts (i.e., props) support children in playing out scripts that go with their roles in dramatic play. These artifacts include menus from restaurants, food containers from grocery store items, letters and flyers received in the mail, and package labels and advertisements from online retailers. Print artifacts also include store signage and receipts, food delivery orders and packaging, and items related to getting around, such as bus and subway schedules, parking garage tickets, and passports and travel itineraries.

Teachers can provide some real-life, print-based props for children to use in their dramatic play (e.g., grocery ads) and can make others (e.g., menus for a restaurant, an appointment book for a doctor's office). Children can also make some of their own play props using print artifacts from daily life as models (e.g., bus tickets, speeding ticket forms, order forms for wait staff in a restaurant).

Informational Magazines

Informational magazines for young children, such as *Click, Humpty Dumpty, High Five, National Geographic Little Kids, Ranger Rick Jr., Your Big Backyard,* and *Zootles,* can be included in the book area and, after they have been in the book area for several weeks, in the lending library. Several are available in digital and print formats, some are bilingual, and many can be accessed at no cost through a library digital service (e.g., Libby, Overdrive). Magazines can also serve as props in dramatic play; for example, as the reading material in the waiting room of a pretend doctor's, dentist's, or veterinarian's office. These waiting rooms can also have brochures or booklets about eating healthy foods, brushing teeth, and taking good care of pets.

Figure 4.6. Parts of a chart about the source of crayons' color names.

Informational Displays

Displays like charts and posters can also be placed on the walls (Roskos & Neuman 2011) or on an easel during small group activities. A large illustrated recipe chart used in teacher-led cooking projects, for example, allows the children and teacher to work together to select ingredients and read information about how to prepare, measure, and combine them. An illustrated chart of steps to follow in planting seeds or bulbs can also be helpful for an individual child or a small group of children engaged in planting seeds or bulbs.

Another example of an informative display that a teacher placed on a wall for children's use during center time, in the context of a unit on color, included paper crayon wrappings mounted on poster board to display their printed names in English, Spanish, and French (e.g., *dandelion, diente de león, pissenlit*).

Box 4.3. Using a Calendar to Keep Track of a Butterfly's Development

During circle time, the teacher started by attaching a small picture of a caterpillar on the monthly chart mounted on a classroom wall to mark the arrival date of some caterpillars that were ordered a few weeks earlier. The children expected their arrival because the teacher had talked with them about the upcoming unit of study and showed them the form used to order the caterpillars. At that time, the teacher also used an informational book (*Butterfly,* by Mary Ling) to review the life cycle of a butterfly.

Of course, once the caterpillars arrived, the children fed them and watched them grow. When they began to form their chrysalises, the teacher marked this date on the monthly chart using a picture tile of a caterpillar partially enclosed in a chrysalis. On this day at circle time, the teacher also told the children that it would take quite a long time for the caterpillars to change into butterflies and that the current month posted on the classroom wall would be all used up before the butterflies emerged.

She showed the children a calendar that was in booklet form and located the current month (May). Then, she turned to the next month (June) in the calendar booklet, read its name, and marked a date on this page with a butterfly sticker. She told the children that the butterflies would emerge from the chrysalises during this month, on about this date. She explained to the children that once the monthly poster chart on the wall was changed to the new month, she would put a sticker picture of a butterfly on it too to give the children some idea of how much longer they must wait for the butterflies to emerge.

In the meantime, the teacher placed the calendar booklet in the book area. She had written children's names on their birth dates on the calendar booklet. The children were accustomed to seeing a new month's name posted on the wall chart and looking at dates marked on it to indicate children's birthdays, school holidays, and any expected classroom visitors. Now they could search the entire calendar booklet to find their own birth date and the birth date of friends. And, of course, children with summer birthdays, who usually did not get to see their birth dates marked on the classroom monthly chart, could find theirs too!

After the butterflies emerged from their chrysalises, the children observed them for a few days in a net cage, and then took the cage outside to set them free. This day was marked on the monthly poster and in the calendar booklet, which remained in the early learning setting's book area.

The English version of each color name was provided in larger print above each crayon wrapping, and a picture of the item (e.g., dandelions) that inspired each color name was placed below the crayon wrapping. Two examples are shown in Figure 4.6, one for the crayon color named *asparagus,* the other for the crayon color named *dandelion.*

Other displays might include one that shows steps for good handwashing. These can be obtained from your local public health department and mounted on the walls near bathroom and classroom sinks. Still others could contrast pictures of healthy and less healthy foods.

Calendars

Calendar time (i.e., days, weeks, months) is beyond the capacity of preschoolers to understand (Beneke, Ostrosky, & Katz 2008); therefore, daily exercises in reciting the days of the week or the current month and year are a waste of time. However, calendars can be used with children for their intended purpose: marking and keeping track of important events. Children become somewhat familiar with calendars that family members and teachers use to note appointments and special occasions. They often enjoy having a calendar booklet in the dramatic play area for noting appointments for themselves or their dolls, and they also like smaller calendars, such as those with months for the entire year printed on a small card, for the wallets and purses they use when pretending they are adults.

Teachers can also use calendars to support some units of study that require keeping track of the passage of days or weeks. Box 4.3 describes one teacher's use of a calendar in booklet form, in conjunction with the monthly poster in her classroom, to help children anticipate and record events during a unit of study on the development of butterflies.

Concluding Thoughts

Young children can use informational books to answer questions that arise during story reading and in other contexts. Informational books extend children's knowledge beyond what they learn from hands-on experiences. Moreover, early experience with informational books supports children later in comprehending content-area textbooks because they augment children's vocabularies and familiarize them with the specific language structures found in these books. Printed information that is in nonbook form is also of great interest to preschoolers. They can use print artifacts and magazines in their pretend play and displays in some small group activities that take place during center time. Preschoolers can also learn about calendars in authentic ways.

Experience with informational books helps to prevent a cascading barrage of barriers to good comprehension—a lack of interest in books, lower levels of academic vocabulary, lack of content knowledge, and limited experience with some written language structures. One early literacy expert has even suggested that a content knowledge gap is responsible for much of the achievement gap (Neuman & Celano 2013). The authors' recent work with a colleague makes the same case. In a book devoted to preschoolers' thinking (Schickedanz, Collins, & Marchant 2022), classroom data illustrates that preschoolers engage in drawing inferences and can think at high levels; however, they often arrive at the wrong conclusion because they lack background knowledge. Preschool teachers are uniquely positioned to help close the achievement gap by using informational books in the ways this chapter explored.

CHAPTER 5

YOUNG CHILDREN AND LITERACY SKILLS DEVELOPMENT

Twenty-six-month-old Chara pushes a play stroller to give her doll a ride. She stops while strolling through the kitchen to remove the magnetic letter *C* from the set of letters on the refrigerator door. Chara holds and admires it for a moment, then gently places it in her doll's lap and continues on.

A few days later, Chara is at the playground with her babysitter. When the babysitter takes out some chalk from her pocket, Chara says "Chara," "mommy," and "music," indicating the words she wants the babysitter to write. She listens and watches as the babysitter names the letters needed to write each word on the sidewalk. When it is her turn, Chara makes 10 short lines while reciting the names of letters in her name.

At 28 months, when Chara scribbles on paper, she sometimes asks her mom to join in. Often, her mom writes Chara's name and *mommy*; Chara then scribbles over and around these words. Sometimes, Chara's mom writes names of familiar foods, such as *cheese* and *chocolate* (Figure 5.1).

At 33 months, Chara snips pieces from thin strips of paper and notices a strip on the table lying across the end of another. "*T* for Tricia," she announces with authority and delight. (Her aunt's name is Tricia.) At this age, Chara can also

Figure 5.1. Chara's scribbles with the letter *C* and her mom's words.

Figure 5.2. Chara's scribble drawing with the letter *C*.

Figure 5.3. Chara's grocery list.

identify many uppercase letters and is aware that several letters are used together to make words. She routinely includes *C*-like marks in her scribble drawings (Figure 5.2) and starts writing grocery lists, using wavy lines that she arranges horizontally (Figure 5.3).

Although most young children experience literacy at home during their early years, the onset, frequency, and focus of these experiences differ across families. Some children's families cover a wide range of activities, including many that focus specifically on print and how it works, while other children's experiences are both limited in range and more general (Purcell-Gates 1996; Taylor & Dorsey-Gaines 1988; Teale 1986).

As discussed in Chapter 1, print-focused experiences support the acquisition of literacy skills, while book reading and conversation support the development of oral language and content knowledge (Grolig 2020; Hood, Conlon, & Andrews 2008; Montag, Jones, & Smith 2015). Much of Chara's early years were spent engaging in book reading; outings to farms, vegetable stands, and playgrounds; and conversation. Her alphabet and word experiences are highlighted here to illustrate that some children begin to learn—and find delight in acquiring—print-related skills at home before they are 3 years old (Baghban 1984; Schickedanz 1990).

This chapter focuses on three areas of understanding and skill: (1) alphabet letter-name knowledge, (2) phonological awareness, and (3) print conventions and functions. Because complete alphabet knowledge includes the understanding that letters in printed words represent sounds in spoken words, alphabet knowledge and phonological awareness are discussed in the same section before print concepts and functions.

Alphabet Letter-Name Knowledge

There was a time when no one expected preschoolers to learn the names of alphabet letters, but researchers and early childhood educators now know that preschoolers do have the capacity to learn this information (Piasta 2023). While there was concern that adding literacy learning to preschool programs would displace other important experiences (see Copeland et al. 2012; Milteer, Ginsburg, & Mulligan 2012), learning frameworks in most states currently stipulate alphabet and phonological awareness teaching, demonstrating that it is both possible and necessary to support literacy skills learning while maintaining a wide variety of other experiences.

By the end of a year of a literacy-rich preschool program, a typical older 4-year-old can often name at least 18 to 19 uppercase letters and 16 to 17 lowercase letters. Some older preschoolers learn the uppercase and lowercase forms of all 26 letters (Piasta, Petscher, & Justice 2012).

While it might seem like a lot for preschoolers to learn some lowercase as well as uppercase letters, many lowercase letters are relatively easy to learn because they closely resemble their uppercase forms (e.g., *Ff, Mm, Oo, Pp, Ss, Tt, Yy, Zz*). The words in books that children will later read contain mostly lowercase letters, so it is important to get a good start in learning both uppercase and lowercase letters during the preschool years.

Using Children's Names

Research has not determined any best order for teaching alphabet letters, nor has it found any advantage to exposing preschoolers to just one or two letters at a time. The one fairly definitive finding is an "own name advantage," meaning that a child is more motivated to learn the first letter in their own name and in the names of family members before learning other letters (Justice et al. 2006; Treiman et al. 2007). For example, Chara linked *C* to Chara, *M* to mommy, and *T* to her Aunt Tricia.

Children's motivation for learning must always be a major priority (Berhenke et al. 2011; Nevo et al. 2020). With 18 to 20 preschoolers in an early learning setting, there's enormous potential for more letter name learning using the variety of first letters in children's names. Of course, some first letters will be the same, but those that differ will provide exposure to many new letter names.

Do not worry about exposing children to many letters all at once. Children already see many letters in their everyday environment (e.g., street signs, license plates, building signs). Furthermore, the accurate naming of letters rests on good letter discrimination, which requires active comparison of letters (Gibson 1975). If children's exposure is restricted to one letter a week, or even to two or three, opportunities to compare and contrast letters are reduced. (See Box 5.1 for an illustration of how exposure to multiple letters aids learning to distinguish among them.)

Box 5.1. Three-Year-Old Sara Learns About *A* and *H*

At the end of a morning of preschool, 3-year-old Sara occupies herself by writing on a sheet of paper with a thin marker. First, she creates two lines of letters in the upper-left quadrant of her paper. The student teacher watches, commenting, "You have written some *A*s and *H*s." Sara glances at the student teacher but does not smile.

Sara begins writing again, this time in the upper-right quadrant of her paper. After pausing, the student teacher again comments about the *A*s and *H*s that Sara has written. When Sara glances up this time, it is clearer that she is not happy. The student teacher is puzzled about Sara's negative responses. As she and her supervisor discuss the situation, the supervisor wonders, "Might Sara have considered all of her marks *A*s?"

The next day, when Sara plays with an uppercase alphabet puzzle, one of her teachers discovers that she knows the letters *S*, *R*, and *A*, but not others—including *H*! This explains Sara's negative reaction to the student teacher's comments—it stemmed from having been misunderstood. She was writing only *A*s.

The teacher then names *H* and other letters in the puzzle, commenting that *H* is a lot like the letter *A* in Sara's name. She goes on to describe how the bottom of *A* is always open and its top is always closed, while both the top and bottom of *H* are open. From that day on, Sara always closes the tops of her *A*s, even if she has to accomplish this by adding a short line.

Because many letters vary from one another minimally, knowing the configuration of one letter often depends on knowing another similar letter. When a child does not know the other letter that contains an important contrast, the child might unknowingly vary the known letter in a way that moves it into the "territory" of an unknown letter. Sara seemed very glad to know about *H* and wanted to make sure that her *A* was never again confused with it!

At just 3 to 4 months old, young children can detect very small differences in the configuration and orientation of lines (Cohen & Younger 1984; Fantz 1963). Infants begin to develop visually based categories late in their first year of life (Spriet et al. 2022). Thus, when they encounter alphabet letters as older toddlers or young preschoolers, they respond with expectations that apply to most categories in the world. In other words, they group together letters that are similar in features, thinking they are different variations of the same letter (e.g., *E/F, O/Q, M/W*).

Preschoolers are fully capable of detecting small differences that distinguish one letter from others. At first, they may be unaware of the significance of minor variations; in some cases, letter differences are much subtler than the differences between the examples in other categories they've seen up to this point. For example, despite the wide variations found among forks, all pronged eating utensils are called *fork*, whether they have two, three, or five prongs. Different kinds of forks are indicated by adding a modifier (e.g., pickle fork, salad fork, pitchfork). In contrast, if just one more line is added to *F* it becomes the letter *E*.

With exposure to a substantial number of letters, children realize that each letter is its own category, which can vary somewhat across fonts, but not in other ways.

Of course, simply putting children's names around the classroom is not enough. Although children will notice their names and might even begin to recognize them in stable locations on cubbies or an attendance chart, they will not learn letter names or how print works unless letter names are used intentionally and named explicitly in routines and other contexts (Masonheimer, Drum, & Ehri 1984; Rowe, Shimuzu, & Davis 2022). For example, when reviewing assignments on the classroom helper chart (Figure 5.4), a teacher can name the first letter in a child's name and underline the name, rather than just read it while pointing quickly at its middle.

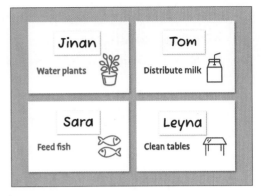

Figure 5.4. Classroom helper chart.

Similarly, teachers can point out and name the first letter of each child's name on a name card when holding these up to send children to wash their hands for lunch or go to their cubbies and begin putting on their jackets for playing outside (i.e., in transitions). Or, when helping children find their places at breakfast (i.e., find their name card on the table), a teacher can locate a child's name, point to and name its first letter, and then underline and read it.

After a month of reviewing names on a helper chart during a morning meeting, a teacher can place the name cards on the chart before children's arrival and then ask children to check whether they have a job. After this amount of time, children are familiar with the first letters in their names and know to look at the uppercase letter at each name's left end.

Of course, children whose names have the same first letter (e.g., Juan, Junko, and Jamila) will probably need help figuring out whether a *J* they see in a name posted is theirs or a peer's. As a matter of fact, preschoolers often treat the first letter in someone's name as if it belongs to that person, sometimes going as far as saying something like "*K* is Kumiko's" or "*D* is Danielle's" (Ferreiro 1986; McGee & Richgels 1989). This mindset reveals that a child does not yet know that each letter is used to write many words, not just one. Asking children to check a helper chart for their names provides additional opportunities for a teacher to help children learn letter names and increase their understanding that the letters in their names are used in other words.

For example, if Juan points to Junko's name card and calls out, "Hey, is this me?" his teacher can read the name to him and explain, "Both your name and Junko's start with the letter *J*. (*Points to letter.*) Then, both of your names have a lowercase *u*. (*Points to letter.*) But, after that, Junko's name has a lowercase *n* and yours has a lowercase *a*. That's how we know that it's Junko's turn to water the plants today. Maybe you will have a job tomorrow." (See Box 5.2 for information about designing and using helper and attendance charts.)

After about two months of preschool, a teacher might also begin to play a name game at circle time. This requires letter tiles and a binder of the children's name cards organized alphabetically for easy reference. One uppercase letter tile is held up at a time, as the teacher says, "If your name starts with the letter ____, raise your hand." When confirming each child's raised hand, the teacher might say, "Yes, Kieran, your name does begin with the letter *K*." If a child whose name starts with the letter does not raise their hand, the teacher can pull that child's name card from the binder and point to and name its first letter (e.g., "Mirabel, your name also starts with the letter *M*. You may raise your hand").

Box 5.2. Maximizing Learning from Helper and Attendance Charts

The design of both helper and attendance charts affects the opportunities they provide for letter learning. The teacher's use of these charts also affects children's learning. For example, as already discussed, in addition to the teacher's specific attention to first letters when reviewing helpers for the day, assigning jobs daily rather than weekly gives children more opportunities to interact with the names. This greater frequency aids children in learning letter names and recognizing classmates' names.

Many preschool teachers use an attendance chart with name cards organized alphabetically. To increase children's focus on the print, names should be printed clearly in a single color, font style, and font size. Only children's names should be featured on the chart, not photos or other decorations, which can distract children from inspecting the print. (See Figure 5.5.)

Some teachers start the year using name cards with a picture of each child and then change to name cards with names only after the first month of school. At this time, children can usually find their name cards based on print features, such as their name's first letter. While children soon learn the physical location of their name and stop looking at the name text, learning to navigate alphabetical order provides children with the opportunity to develop and use knowledge of this organization method in a meaningful context. Later in the year, when children have even more print knowledge, you can change the order of names to engage and delight children in a search that adds more challenge.

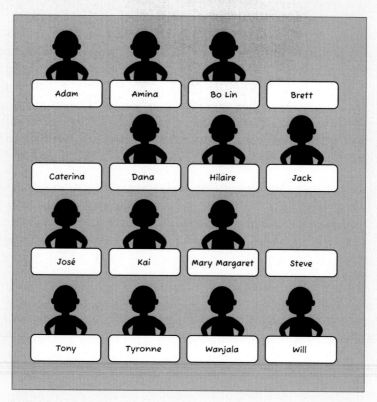

Figure 5.5. Attendance chart.

So Much More than the ABCs: The Early Phases of Reading and Writing, Revised Edition

Alternately, you might transition to providing name cards in small containers, such as a shoe box or basket. Whether organized alphabetically or randomly, this method requires children to inspect the print of their peers' names to find their own, which supports a lot of letter learning.

Instead of creating a separate helper chart, some teachers post children's jobs directly on the attendance chart (Figure 5.6). In this approach, small squares of Velcro are placed on each child's attendance chart pocket and on the back of each job title.

Figure 5.6. Attendance chart with pockets designed for posting classroom jobs.

Combining attendance and helper charts reduces the wall space needed, but there is a disadvantage for literacy skill learning—children can see immediately whether they have a job without inspecting the print. However, if children are provided with multiple other opportunities to inspect their names daily (e.g., names are used in circle time literacy activities and in transitions), a teacher might judge that a combination chart would work fine.

Teacher comments can extend the learning about alphabet letters and written words that happens when children engage with name cards. For example, as a child identifies their name, the teacher might say, "Yes, that name card is yours. It says Victoria—*V-i-c-t-o-r-i-a*" (*Points to each letter as they name it.*), or "Yes, that is your name, Oliver. I noticed the other day that your name has a *V* in the middle and that Victoria's name has a *V* at the beginning. You are the only children in our class who have the letter *V* in your names."

At about this time of the year, one preschool teacher also used children's names in a small group activity (making a bookmark) that was related to a paperback book each child was given to keep. Children were asked to arrange letter tiles for their names on the table. A teacher checked each child's letter series, naming and pointing to each letter, and then either confirmed the order or assisted in rearranging letters to spell the child's name correctly. The child's name card was used as a reference. (For children with longer names, this happened quite frequently.) Each child then used a glue stick to attach the letters to one side of the bookmark, which was made from a narrow rectangle of poster board. Children also received a printed conventional form of their name (i.e., first letter capitalized; others in lowercase) to glue to the bookmark's other side. Last, children glued a nameplate inside their book's front cover (*This book belongs to _____*) and wrote their names on its blank line. Any form of the name the child produced was accepted, and a teacher assisted any child who said, "I can't. I need help."

Additional Letter Materials

Even though a teacher uses only the first letters from children's names at the start of a year, other letter materials are introduced shortly thereafter. For example, in small group sessions, a teacher might use letter Bingo, letter Memory, and letter-matching materials that include highly confusable letters. (See the example in Figure 5.7.)

Teachers can also use letter-matching materials that show letters in different fonts. Several letters are written on the left side of a board. For each letter, there are three or four corresponding letter tiles featuring the same letter but in different fonts. Children arrange the corresponding letter tiles in the space on the right side of the board.

After their introduction in small groups, some of these letter-matching materials are made available for children's independent use during center time.

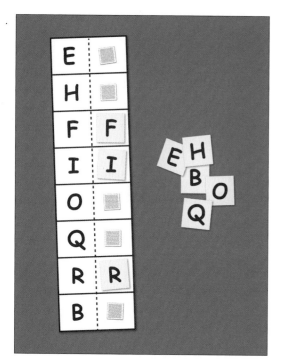

Figure 5.7. Letter-matching manipulative with highly confusable letters.

Teachers also provide alphabet puzzles. The kind of puzzle that helps children best to distinguish among letters has a separate space in the background frame for each letter. In contrast, alphabet puzzles in jigsaw form have pictures of letters on irregularly shaped pieces. To assemble these puzzles, children must attend to the shape of the puzzle pieces, not to letter shapes. Alphabet puzzles should expose children to uppercase and lowercase letters, but not all in the same puzzle. Younger preschoolers, especially, become quite overwhelmed when trying to assemble a puzzle that has all 52 letters! Using puzzles that have either uppercase or lowercase letters, not both, provides a more manageable experience.

A teacher might also start using a Letter Clue Game at circle time. (See Box 5.3.) Of course, letter names come up in writing contexts from the very beginning of the school year. Chapters 7 and 8 discuss ways to support letter-name knowledge and other literacy skills.

Phonological Awareness

Phonological awareness refers to skill in detecting and manipulating sound in spoken words while setting aside word meanings. It can be thought of as a kind of play with the sound structure of words. Children must acquire this skill to understand how letters function in printed words. This section discusses (1) speech units, (2) manipulations of speech units in phonological awareness tasks, (3) expectations for phonological awareness during the preschool years, and (4) instructional strategies that help preschoolers develop phonological awareness.

Box 5.3. The Letter Clue Game and Its Benefits to Young Children

This game helps children realize that two very similar letters can differ physically in only one small way. When children first begin to learn about alphabet letters, they apply to some letters (e.g., *E/F; T/L; N/Z*) what they have learned when comparing items that belong to a category (like dogs)—ignore small differences and focus on shared features. In other words, children at first think *E* and *F* are two different versions of the same letter, not two different letters, because they have learned to ignore differences far greater than these when learning about other categories (e.g., cats, automobiles, chairs). Exposure to letters, especially in this game, helps children begin to realize they must instead focus on small differences and ignore shared features when they are distinguishing among letters.

How to Play

> Tell children that you are thinking of a letter. Write just one part of it at a time, as clues. For example, if *P* is the target letter, draw a long vertical line on a piece of chart paper, then pause to give children a chance to guess which letter it might be.

> Children might guess *T, L,* or *M.* For each letter guessed, say, "I see what you are thinking," and then form that letter. When responding to *T,* you might say, "We do start with a long vertical line when writing *T* (*Write it.*), and then we use a short horizontal line across its top. (*Write it.*) *T* was a good guess because it does have a long vertical line, but *T* is not the letter in my mind." You can respond to guesses of *M* and *L* in the same way.

> Provide a second clue: "This line starts at the top of the long vertical line, then moves to the right, and then moves back to the vertical line's middle, like this. At this point, several children might guess *P.* Confirm that this is the letter.

Next Steps

> If the letter formed is similar to yet another, you can keep going! For instance, *P* could lead to either *R* or *B.* You could say, "Now, I'm thinking of another letter that is very similar to *P.* I'll write another *P* (*Write it.*), and then add a line to it. I'm going to add a little diagonal line down here (*Write it.*)." A child or two usually calls out *R.* Confirm that the new letter is *R,* and comment that the only difference between *P* and *R* is one small diagonal line, pointing to it.

> Consider following up this game with others that reinforce the concept. Matching games using tiles of letters in several different fonts also help children to understand that each letter may vary somewhat (e.g., E, E, ɛ, $\mathcal{E}$), as long as a variation does not turn the letter into a different one.

Speech Units in Words

Syllables are the largest sound units in words (e.g., ba-by, ba-na-na). In turn, syllables can be divided into two parts—an onset and a rime. All of the sounds before the vowel comprise a syllable's **onset**. A syllable's **rime** includes the vowel and any sounds that follow it. For example, in *bed*, /b/ is the onset and /ed/ is the rime; in *string*, /str/ is the onset and /ing/ is the rime; in *tea*, /t/ is the onset and /ea/ is the rime. A word can also be divided into even smaller sound units called **phonemes**. The word *bed* has three phonemes (i.e., /b/, /e/, and /d/). *Plate* has four (i.e., /p/, /l/, /a/, and /t/).

Box 5.4. How Different Writing Systems Work

If creating a written language for a society without one, the first step is to decide what kind of writing system would represent the oral language. You could create a logography (i.e., each symbol represents one word), a syllabary (i.e., each symbol represents one syllable, used across many words), or an alphabet (i.e., each symbol represents one phoneme, used across many words).

Characteristics of Different Writing Systems

Learning a logography requires linking a particular symbol to the object, action, or idea it represents (for example, Chinese). It is a direct writing system, meaning each symbol directly corresponds to the word it represents. In a syllabary, on the other hand, syllables are combined in various ways to create all of the words in the language (for example, in Japanese). Syllabaries are abstract systems with a code that intervenes between symbols and their meanings. Languages with alphabets use symbols that represent the individual sounds in spoken and written words. They too are abstract and code based. Different alphabetic languages may use different letters; for example, English uses letters in the Latin alphabet and Russian uses letters in the Russian alphabet. In any alphabetic language, symbols are combined in a multitude of ways to spell all of the words in that language.

A logographic system is easy to understand, but a child must learn several thousand characters (Cahill 2023). Writing systems that are sound based require a child to learn fewer basic symbols, but because they are abstract and code based, they are harder for children to fathom at first. Because syllables are easier to detect than phonemes are in spoken words, syllable-based writing systems are easier to learn than alphabetic systems. However, even though phonemes are difficult for children to detect in spoken words, phoneme-based writing systems have the advantage of requiring knowledge of relatively few symbols.

Phonological Awareness in Multilingual Learners

If a child's home language is based on an alphabetic system, when learning English, they can transfer phonological awareness skills from English to their home language and vice versa (Dickinson et al. 2004; Hammer et al. 2014). These skills transfer very well from one alphabetic language to another. The critical feature of effective phonological awareness instruction is explicitness and adequacy of exposure (Hammer, Scarpino, & Davison 2011).

Speech changes at the boundaries between syllables, and between onsets and rimes, in ways people hear, even though we don't notice these boundaries when communicating with others. Phonemes, on the other hand, are not distinct, but instead run right into one another in spoken words. Not surprisingly, syllable and onset-rime units are relatively easy for children to learn to detect, while phonemes are harder. ***Phonemic awareness*** is the ability to identify and manipulate individual sounds in words, and it is the most difficult level of phonological awareness for children to achieve. It is also the level most closely related to reading and writing because alphabet letters represent speech at the phoneme level.

On the other hand, if a child's home language uses a logographic system or a syllabic system, when learning English, they would at first find it strange that each alphabet symbol (letter) represents an individual sound in a spoken word, not a whole word or a syllable, respectively.

Luckily, for most preschoolers learning English, these differences in writing systems are not terribly confusing because they have not yet learned to read or write in their home language. They often learn to read and write in both languages at the same time, whether at preschool, at home, or in both contexts. As with most other things, they simply think, *Well, this is how reading and writing work in Chinese (Korean, Japanese), and this is how they work in English.* Some advantages to multilingualism are that children become more flexible and creative in their language use (Bialystok 2015; López & Páez 2021) and may show faster development of executive functioning as well as other cognitive skills (e.g., planning, attention, inhibitory control) when compared to their monolingual peers (White & Greenfield 2017).

Children who are new to English often forget the less familiar English words a teacher provides as targets in phonological awareness tasks and have trouble generating matches to a target (e.g., other words that begin with the same sound or rhyme with the target word) because they have relatively few English vocabulary words from which to draw (see Yesil-Dagli 2011). It makes little sense to spend an inordinate amount of time on phonological awareness tasks in English, thinking that multilingual learners are performing poorly because they lack specific phonological awareness skills, when the issue is likely the child's small English vocabulary. Multilingual children perform better on phonological awareness tasks with known words—that is, words in their home language vocabulary— than they do on unknown words (Paciga & Cassano 2023). Moreover, because phonological awareness learned in one language can transfer to another alphabetic language (Hammer et al. 2014), words in tasks can be known words from either language.

In addition to providing some phonological awareness tasks in the child's home language, teachers can use children's first names, English words that are becoming familiar (e.g., blocks, paint, jacket, milk), and key words from storybooks. Teachers can also use pictures of target words so that children are better able to keep the target words in mind. Of course, all the while, teachers are supporting children in learning English vocabulary using a wide variety of contexts in preschool.

There are other writing systems used throughout the world with symbols or characters that represent syllables or whole words and concepts instead of phonemes. Multilingual learners might learn writing systems that differ in the unit of sound they represent; for example, a child learning Chinese and English, or another learning Japanese and Spanish. Children who are becoming multilingual in alphabetic languages (e.g., English, French, Italian) are learning languages that do not differ in the level of sound represented in their writing systems because all of these languages use letters to represent phonemes. (See Box 5.4 for more discussion about different writing systems.)

When children use language for communication, *conscious* phonemic analysis is not required (i.e., children have no difficulty distinguishing between the words *bat* and *bag* or *silly* and *Willy*). But when learning to read and write, conscious awareness of sound units is needed. Teachers engage children in a variety of tasks to develop their conscious awareness of different sound units in words, including phonemes. (See Chapter 8 for information about helping children develop phonological awareness in writing contexts.)

A teacher can ask children to manipulate any size speech unit in a variety of ways. For example, children might create a word by **blending** sounds the teacher provides (e.g., "I'm going to say some sounds. Hold up your hand if you know what word they make when we put the sounds together: /s/, /n/, /a/, /k/"). Or, children might **segment** (i.e., break apart) the sounds in a word if the teacher provides its syllables or phonemes (e.g., "Say *baby* in two parts"). Alternately, they might be asked to **delete** or **substitute** a sound unit in a word (e.g., "Say *fin* without the /f/ sound") or **generate** words that rhyme or begin with the same sound (e.g., "Let's think of some words that begin with the same sound as *boat*—/b/oat").

The Course of Phonological Awareness Acquisition

Children can detect syllable segments first, then onset and rime segments, and, finally, phonemes. But assessment of a child's level of phonological awareness also includes consideration of the manipulations that they are asked to conduct with a sound unit.

Blending is easier than segmenting, and segmenting is easier than deleting or substituting. Tasks requiring the deletion or substitution of speech sounds are quite difficult because they involve more than one manipulation. For example, if asked to say *sand* without its /s/ sound, a child must segment /s/ from *sand*, delete it, and say *and*. Or, if asked to substitute the sound at the beginning of their own names with /d/, children must first segment and delete a sound (e.g., /s/ in *Sue*), and then put /d/ in its place (e.g., *due*).

Generating words with the same first sound or rime also requires several steps: (1) holding a target word and a sound in mind (e.g., "Can you think of other words that begin with /b/ like *boat*?"), (2) searching their vocabulary store for possible matches (e.g., *ball, bib, baby*), and (3) comparing each selected word to the target word. Generating words for phonological tasks is especially difficult for younger children who do not yet have substantial vocabulary stores from which to draw words to analyze and for multilingual children (see Box 5.4).

Where to Start with Phonological Awareness

If exposed to texts written in verse, children will enjoy their rhythmic quality and their emphasis on rhyming and alliteration (i.e., words beginning with the same sound). As explained in Chapter 3 (specifically, see Box 3.1), books written in verse are often described as predictable books because their repeated features (e.g., refrains, cumulative text, stable sentence frames) help children to remember them.

Although experience with verse by itself will not develop conscious phonological awareness, nothing is better as a basic experience for exposing children to language in a form that is enjoyable because sounds in words are highlighted and sentences flow musically. Additionally, children love to "read" these books by themselves in the library area, and doing this can enhance alphabet knowledge, letter-sound association knowledge, and print knowledge (see Box 5.5). Experiences with verse can be provided daily throughout the year.

Box 5.5. Finger Point Reading of Predictable Books

Finger point reading entails matching a book's printed words to a verbal recitation of its text that children have memorized after they have heard the book read aloud multiple times. Children who can finger point read memorized books have higher levels of alphabet knowledge and phonological awareness than children who cannot. Children without these specific literacy skills engage more globally with print in the books they have memorized; that is, they run their finger under print, not under specific words, as children do when finger point reading them (Ehri & Sweet 1991).

Finger point reading may help a child increase their literacy skills. For example, scanning from left to right and top to bottom becomes more automatic, sight recognition of some repeatedly encountered common words increases, and children consolidate information about how specific letters or letter pairs represent sounds in spoken words. Some children actually move into conventional reading through repeated use of finger point reading, probably because it requires the integration of literacy skills to locate specific printed words, and reading unfamiliar text also requires similar integration.

The increase in explicit literacy skill teaching in today's preschool settings may allow more children to finger point read familiar predictable books. Although predictable books do not contribute as much to vocabulary development as narratives and informational books do and do not involve reasoning of the kind required by narratives, they are useful in their own right because they expose children to beautiful, literary language and contribute to children's interest in books and reading. Moreover, as suggested here, they can contribute to literacy skill development if children take letter knowledge and skill in phonological awareness to these books as they "read" them.

Teachers can also use books that play with language to draw children's attention to interesting sounding words. For example, clusters of words on the pages of *Roadwork,* by Sally Sutton, illustrated by Brian Lovelock, provide information about the sounds that construction vehicles make (e.g., *screech, boom, whoosh, splat*). Words like these are fun for children to say and play with. *Salsa Lullaby,* by Jen Arena, illustrated by Erika Meza, and *Beep Beep/Piip piip,* by Petr Horacek, are bilingual books that play with sounds common in familiar experiences, such as bedtime or things that go. *Bee-Bim Bop!* by Linda Sue Park, illustrated by Ho Baek Lee, and *Mamá Goose,* by Alma Flor Ada and Isabel Campoy, illustrated by Maribel Suárez, delight with rhyming and alliteration, while *Wombat,* by Philip Bunting, plays with word parts.

With respect to specific phonological awareness tasks, teachers usually start with those requiring the blending and segmenting of syllables and then move to tasks in which these same manipulations are used with smaller units of sound. Teachers usually save deletion, substitution, and generation tasks for later.

Research indicates, however, that children need not master lower levels of awareness (i.e., syllable tasks) before they can benefit from experiences with higher levels (i.e., onset-rime and phoneme tasks). In other words, the acquisition of phonological awareness does *not* occur in distinct stages, one after the other, but is instead quasi-developmental (i.e., skills develop in an overlapping fashion) (Anthony et al. 2003; Lonigan 2006).

Researchers have also discovered that experience with syllable tasks are not necessary as a foundation for skill in detecting and manipulating onsets, rimes, and phonemes (Ukrainetz et al. 2011), as many early educators had assumed based on earlier research that allowed multiple interpretations (Lundberg, Frost, & Petersen 1988). Syllables are certainly the easiest and most accessible speech unit for children to blend and segment, but it makes no sense to linger for several months on a speech unit that children can detect and learn to manipulate so easily when research suggests that this might interfere with children's progress in detecting and manipulating smaller speech units (Ehri 2022).

Early childhood educators should start with tasks involving syllables (e.g., blending and segmenting) because, up to this point, children have been using language for communication—focusing on meaning—which causes difficulty when children first transition to focusing only on sound. For example, when first asked to think of other words that begin with the same sound as *cake,* a young child might say "birthday" or "chocolate." These responses focus on meaning rather than sound.

In the face of such puzzlement, phonological awareness tasks using larger sound segments (i.e., syllables) introduce children to the general idea of playing with sounds in words. But because this is perhaps the only advantage of starting with syllables, it is probably wise for teachers to use this sound unit for only a few weeks before moving on to smaller speech units (i.e., onsets, rimes, and phonemes).

Syllable blending and segmenting tasks. If children's names are used in syllable tasks, the sound units are more accessible to children, and the tasks are more enjoyable. For example, as a game during circle time or for a transition, a teacher can ask children to listen carefully as they say the parts (i.e., syllables) of each child's name. The teacher explains, "If you think the parts I say are for your name, raise your hand and say your name 'the right way.'" The teacher might first model the process using names of characters from a familiar story, teachers' names, or the names of children who are absent. When presenting names, repeat the series of syllable segments that comprise a child's name two or three times, pausing very briefly in between each presentation. The repetitions give children a chance to hear and process the syllables presented.

Turns for children whose first names have just one syllable (e.g., Cho, Sue, Juan) might use their last names if these have more than one syllable. For children whose last names also have just one syllable, the teacher can display three pictures of familiar objects at a time (e.g., cray-on, ea-sel, ba-na-na, um-brel-la), and then present the syllable segments for the name of just one after designating whose turn it is. After the first child's turn, the focus picture card is removed from the chart stand and the syllable segments for the name of the object pictured next are presented to the next child. (Display no more than three pictures at once to limit cognitive load for each child's turn.)

After using this blending syllable task on a few occasions, a teacher might say each child's name naturally and ask children to join them in saying each name in parts, providing a segmenting task. After using this teacher-supported task on several occasions, children can take turns saying a classmate's name in a funny way for the teacher, who is now in the role of guessing whose name it is and saying it "the right way."

Children need not clap the syllables in names or report their number in these face-to-face experiences with a teacher. They can simply listen to and say the sound segments, marking the "beats" of their names with verbal emphasis and synchronized head nods. There is no point in making the task more complicated for children by asking them to clap when a teacher can listen and watch to obtain information about children's understanding. With some digital-based phonological awareness tasks, asking children to count phonemes is appropriate where phoneme segmentation is part of a game (e.g., the child's game piece moves when the child has correctly counted phonemes in the words presented).

Next Steps in Phonological Awareness Instruction

After using syllable tasks for a few weeks, teachers move next to blending and segmenting onset and rime units, as well as phonemes. These tasks can be used with the whole group during circle time or in daily transitions. Again, a teacher starts with children's names but focuses on first sounds. By now, children should be somewhat familiar with the first letters in their names from repeated exposure and activities like those explored earlier in this chapter, and they will enjoy a new game with a first-sound focus.

Before starting the game, explain that it focuses on sounds in their names, not letters (e.g., "Instead of looking at letters I hold up, today you will listen for me to say the first *sound* in your name"). Provide some examples, perhaps using teachers' names (e.g., "When I say, 'If your name starts with /t/, raise your hand,' then Ms. Tanya would raise her hand because her name starts with the /t/ sound. Listen—/t/, /t/, Tanya"). Use a second example before beginning to present the first sounds in children's first names.

In each instance, the teacher says the target sound two or three times (e.g., "If your name starts with the sound /d/, /d/, /d/, raise your hand") and provides detailed feedback when a child raises their hand (e.g., "Yes, Devone, your name starts with /d/—Devone," or "Your name starts with /t/, Tanika, not /d/. I'll say the /t/ sound pretty soon. Put your hand down for now"). If a child does not raise their hand when the relevant sound is presented, the teacher again provides informative feedback (e.g., "Dante, your name also starts with the /d/ sound—Dante. You can raise your hand too"). See Box 5.6 for a discussion of some interesting consequences for children due to their participation in games that focus on both the first letter and the first sound in their name. After playing the first sound name game multiple times across several weeks, other tasks can also be used (one each day). For example, words beginning with the same sounds as the children's names can be presented.

Educators can also use poems, songs, and predictable books that children help recite as a jumping off point for phonological awareness tasks because they usually contain both rhyming words and alliteration. (See Table 5.1 for examples of phonological awareness tasks, some of which are based on words from predictable books.)

Using phonological awareness manipulative materials during center time. Materials that offer children opportunities to practice phonological awareness skills can be provided for their use during center time. Decks of picture cards are the basic materials used. The example in Figure 5.8 focuses on the beginning sounds in words. A target picture appears on a background board; tiles to match have pictures of objects beginning with the same sound as the target pictures' names.

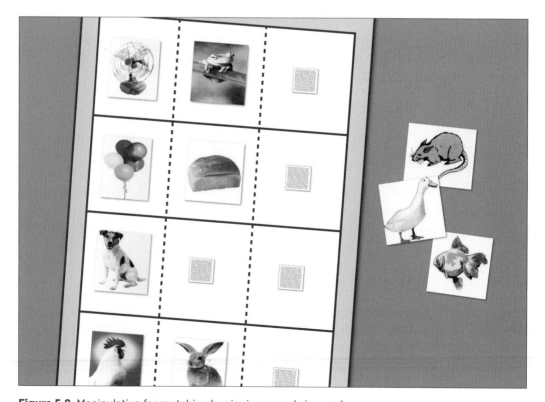

Figure 5.8. Manipulative for matching beginning sounds in words.

Box 5.6. Interesting Learning from First Letter Versus First Sound Name Games

By using children's names in phonological awareness tasks, teachers expose children to some interesting information about English spelling. For example, based on their experience with the first letter name game, children might think they should also raise their hand for the first sound name game alongside the same children. In other words, they assume that if the first letter of their names is the same, the first sound must also be. Some children, however, discover that they raise their hand with a different child or two when focusing on the first sound.

For example, Gordon, Gustav, and Giovanna raise their hands together for the first letter name game; however, when playing the first sound name game, Giovanna learns that she raises her hand when Jamilla does, not when Gordon and Gustav do. The first time playing the first sound name game, when Giovanna raises her hand after she sees Gordon and Gustav raise theirs, the teacher explains to Giovanna that she should raise her hand for the /j/ sound, just like Jamilla. Gordon and Gustav might say, "Hey, she's like us, not like Jamilla!" This is a wonderful opening for the teacher to say, "You are right that both of you and Giovanna have names that start with the same *letter*—with *G*—but your names start with different *sounds*. Giovanna's name starts with /j/—Giovanna; yours start with /g/—Gordon and Gustav. So, in the sound game, you and Giovanna raise your hands at different times."

Preschool children accept these irregularities and often become quite interested in them. For example, once, after a preschool teacher introduced Ms. Judy (one of the authors) to her class, 4-year-old Giovanna approached Judy and asked, "Are you a *J* or *G*?" Her teacher smiled broadly and said, "She wants to know whether your name starts with *J* or *G* because she knows that her name and Jamilla's have the same first sound but different first letters."

Multilingual children might have knowledge of some alphabet letters and their sounds in other languages. Instruction like in the above games leverages that knowledge to clarify sound differences between languages. For example, *W* represents /v/ in Polish and German; *V* represents /b/ at the beginning of words in Spanish; and *J* represents the /j/ sound in English (e.g., *judge*), the /h/ sound in Spanish (e.g., *jugo*), and the /zh/ sound in Portuguese (e.g, *beijo*).

Another irregularity within the English language that sparks interest among children are **digraphs,** or the combination of two letters that make a single sound (i.e., *Ch, Sh, Th, Wh*). When teachers include digraphs among their set of single letter tiles for use in name games, children learn that Chauntise's name begins with *Ch*, not *C*; that Shawn's name begins with *Sh*, not *S;* and that Theodore's name begins with *Th,* not *T*.

Knowing these truths about English spelling is likely to pay off when children are learning to read. Children from early learning programs where names starting with digraphs were highlighted are less likely to focus on *T* alone, when approaching words such as *the, this,* and *they*. Instead, they are likely to respond to the *Th* letter pair, which is what they must do to read these words accurately.

Table 5.1. Circle Time Beginning Sound and Rhyming Word Activities

Activity	Feedback	Presentation
Tasks that use songs, poems, and predictable books		
Sing songs, recite poems and rhymes, and read predictable books	• Sing songs, recite poems, and read books, using good expression to capture the natural rhythm. • Repeat the same songs, poems, and predictable books over weeks and months. • Encourage children to join in as they learn the verses.	• Vary pace to allow children to recite, sing, or read along. • Use eye contact and facial expressions to connect with children.
Teacher identifies rhyming words or words that begin with the same sound in familiar nursery rhymes, poems, songs, or predictable books	• After using a rhyme, poem, song, or predictable book several times across two to three weeks, comment that some of its words sound alike. For example, for the poem "Little Bird," say, "I noticed that both *hop* and *stop* have /op/ as their second part—h/op/ and st/op/. Those two words rhyme." • After identifying the second pair of rhyming words (e.g., *do* and *flew*) in the poem, present each word's onset and rime parts (i.e., d/o/ and fl/ew/). • Proceed similarly over the first three or four months with a variety of poems, songs, and predictable books as they become familiar.	• Comment that it is interesting to find rhyming words (or words that begin with the same sound) in poems and songs. Then move on to the next circle time activity. • If children repeat the words after you say them, comment, "Yes, *hop* and *stop* rhyme."
Children identify rhyming words or words that begin with the same sound in familiar nursery rhymes, poems, songs, and predictable books	• After three or four months, recite a poem or sing a song as usual, then ask children to listen for rhyming words or words that begin with the same sound as you recite some verses again. • Ask children to raise their hand if they hear words that rhyme (or start with the same sound, if this task is the day's focus). • Ask a child called on to say the words that rhyme (or begin with the same sound, if this is the focus). Provide detailed feedback.	• Use detailed responses, such as, "Yes, the words, *rocks* and *box,* do rhyme. Their last parts sound alike—r/ocks/ and b/ox/." • Avoid saying, "Yes, Jonas. Those two words rhyme. Good job!" (See the section "Constructive Teacher Feedback" in this chapter.)

Activity	Feedback	Presentation
Blending and segmenting tasks		
Teacher presents phonemes for children to blend into familiar words	• Explain that to play a new game with sounds, you will say the name of something in a funny way—in little pieces—and then a child can say it "the right way" when called on. • Use a few picture cards, one at a time, to provide some examples (e.g., "If I said /d/-/o/-/g/, then one of you could say to me, 'You were saying dog'"). • After two to three examples, display three pictures at a time, name the items pictured (e.g., *dog, cat, hat;* or *sock, cup, spoon;* or *gate, coat, tree*), and then present sounds for the name of just one of them (e.g., /k/-/a/-/t/; /k/- /a/-/t/). Call on a child to respond. Provide feedback. • Set up and name three more pictures. Present the individual phonemes for one item, as before, and let children guess. Provide detailed feedback. • Continue through three to four sets of pictures to present the sounds for three to four different words.	• After children respond, say the word again as presented ("Yes, /k/-/a/-/t/ are the sounds for the word *cat*"). • If a child says the name of another object pictured, such as "hat" instead of "cat," say, "Let me say the sounds again: /k/-/a/-/t/; /k/-/a/-/t/. What do you think?"
Teacher presents words in pairs or in triplets and asks children to judge words that rhyme or begin with the same sounds	• Tell children that you will say some words and they should tell you whether they do or do not start with the same sound (or do or do not rhyme, if that is the day's focus). • Provide a few examples (e.g., *boat* and *girl*, with feedback; then *doll* and *dig*, with feedback). • Continue with pairs of words for children to judge and provide feedback. • After a month or two, present three words and ask children which two rhyme (or begin with the same sound, if that is the day's focus). Say the three words twice. Provide detailed feedback.	• "Right. *Boat* and *girl* don't start with the same sound. *Boat* starts with /b/ and *girl* starts with /g/. Yes, *doll* and *dig* both begin with /d/—/d/oll and /d/ig." • For incorrect responses (e.g., says that *top* and *boat* rhyme), say, "Mmm, /t/op, /b/oat. Their last parts—/op/ and /oat/—do not sound the same. They do not rhyme."
Teacher asks children to help think of words that begin with the same sound or that rhyme	• Provide a target word and ask children to think of words that begin with the same sound (or rhyme with it, if that is the day's focus). • Provide examples to start: "*Boat, bat*, and *bug* begin with the same sound—/b/—/b/oat, /b/at, /b/ug." • Provide a target word and ask children to think of other words that begin with the same sound: "*Sink* starts with /s/, /s/ink. Can you think of other words that start with /s/ like /s/ink?"	• Provide examples if children do not respond. For example, say, "Do you think /s/oap starts with /s/ like /s/ink?" • Provide detailed feedback: "Yes, *sun* begins with /s/ like *sink*—/s/un."

Teachers can use many sets of materials with the same instructional purpose but with different pictures. The specific focus of the phonological awareness task can also vary over time. For example, later in the year, the task might focus on ending sounds in words, rather than on beginning sounds.

For the manipulative materials to be effective learning tools, the items pictured should be very familiar to children; this helps children label the items as intended. A teacher need not place printed labels for the pictures on the background board or tiles. This sometimes shifts the teacher's—and thus the child's—focus from sound (phonological awareness) to letters.

Many digital applications are available to help children learn about letters and the sound or sounds that each letter can represent in words. A few examples are discussed in Box 5.7. Studies indicate that children from families or school districts with fewer resources have less access to computers, as well as to apps that are designed to support learning, compared to children from families or school districts with more resources (Common Sense Media 2011). Experience in preschool can help reduce this "app gap," while also keeping screen time within the recommended range (AAP Council on Communications and Media et al. 2016).

Using writing to support phonological awareness. Phonological awareness is also supported in writing activities, and each child's progress can be observed in these contexts. Although phonological awareness is an oral language skill that can be developed without reference to print, research indicates that embedding phonological awareness instruction in writing is highly effective (Ball & Blachman 1991; Ehri 2022). Chapter 8 discusses the use of writing to support preschoolers in acquiring phonological awareness.

Constructive Teacher Feedback

Often, just a few children in a preschool group can identify words that rhyme or have the same beginning sound. Children who do not respond probably *are* listening, but they do not respond because they do not yet understand what to do in a specific task or cannot yet detect the sound unit on which the teacher has focused.

Sometimes teachers respond to correct answers with only a general comment, such as, "Yes, you are right. *Rocks* and *box* rhyme." Informative feedback, in contrast, makes the features of a correct response obvious to *all* children in the group. For example, a teacher might say, "Yes, both *sand* and *sun* do begin with /s/. Okay, I'll read some more lines of this poem, and you can raise your hand when I stop if you think you've heard any words that begin with the same sound." When children respond correctly, a teacher avoids praise that is not informative, such as "Good job!" or "You are such a good listener." Instructional language, on the other hand, provides specific information that helps children learn.

Phonological awareness tasks are opportunities for instruction, not quizzes or tests. Asking, "Who can tell me which words rhyme (or begin with the same sound)?" or "Who knows which words rhyme?" can suggest that children should already know. To set these up as opportunities to learn, a teacher can address task information to the whole group (e.g., "I'm going to recite this poem that all of you know, a few lines at a time. I'll stop and ask if anyone heard words that begin with the same sound. Please raise your hand if you think you heard any").

Box 5.7. Using Educational Technology to Support Literacy Skills Acquisition

Kathleen A. Paciga

Technology motivates and engages children. Devices like tablets and smartphones are intuitive and portable enough to add to the early literacy environment. High-quality content may be accessible online or via downloadable apps. The technology provides a variety of options to support children as they acquire early literacy skills (International Literacy Association 2019).

The focus here is on apps and software that support early literacy skills such as

> Letter-sound knowledge, providing children with practice identifying, writing, and connecting sounds to letters

> Phonemic awareness, helping older preschoolers and kindergarteners with segmenting and counting phonemes

> Phonics, integrating word identification and spelling into gameplay activities

The examples highlighted represent only a small selection of what is available, but they illustrate the diverse ways game designers create high-quality experiences for practicing early literacy skills. Many are related to familiar characters from TV programs or movies, while others introduce original characters.

Elmo Loves ABCs, Duolingo ABC, and Starfall ABCs focus on letter knowledge. Children play letter identification games, trace and write letters, listen to alphabet songs, and view videos or color pictures of things with names that begin with the sound each letter represents. For example, in Elmo Loves ABCs, the child clicks Z, traces it with a finger, and watches Elmo sing, "/Z/, /z/, /z/, /z/, /z/. Zebra is a word that starts with Z." Children can also play a hidden picture game (i.e., move balloons around the screen with their fingers to uncover the zipper, zucchini, and zebra). Other letters show clips from Sesame Street that include animals and objects (e.g., Murray and a child pretending to be a rocket serves as a video about the letter R). This app can extend traditional letter exploration, while also serving as a vehicle for growing preschoolers' vocabulary and content knowledge.

Apps such as Elkonin Boxes or Teach Your Monster to Read serve as examples of the ways these skills can be developed through digital games. In Elkonin Boxes, children view photos of objects, hear the name of the object, practice hearing the phonemes, and then tap one box below the photo for each sound they hear in the word. The boxes enlarge and change from yellow to green as children tap. There are two practice modes and a quiz mode in the application. In the first practice mode, each phoneme is produced as the boxes are touched. In the second practice mode, a simple one-note tone replaces the phoneme. The number of boxes aligns to the number of phonemes in each word in both practice modes, whereas in quiz mode, each photo has five boxes, and the child has to tap the correct number of boxes corresponding with the number of phonemes in each word (see Figure 5.9). The Space Race game in Teach Your Monster to Read invites children to focus on blending and segmenting phonemes in a set of words.

Box 5.7. Using Educational Technology to Support Literacy Skills Acquisition (continued)

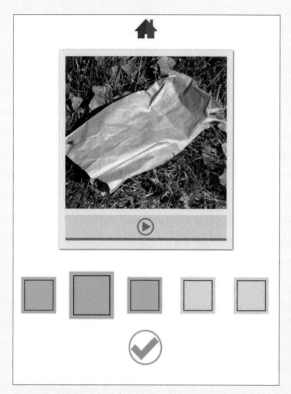

Figure 5.9. Children tap a box for each phoneme in *bag*.

From *Elkonin Boxes: A Literacy Tool for Beginning Readers*, copyright © 2015 by Ross McNamara. Used by permission of Ross McNamara.

Prompts such as "Find each of the sounds in the word *fan*" establish the task for children. Children must listen carefully to each of the three options provided for each prompt and select the correct phoneme.

Apps such as Princess Presto's Spectacular Spelling Play or those by Bob Books (e.g., Reading Magic, Spin and Spell) ask children to apply what they know about letters and sounds to decode words presented on the screen. In Dora's ABCs Vol. 3: Reading, the child helps Dora and Boots cross the lily pads by first listening to the sounds in a word, blending the sounds together, and then identifying an image that corresponds to the word constructed from the sounds they blended (i.e., "What picture goes with this word?"). Afterward, the child manipulates the beginning or ending sound of the word, placing a new letter at the beginning or end of a word following a prompt; for example, "Change *rug* into *hug*. Touch the letters on top to hear their sounds."

Many comprehensive subscription-based early learning apps are also available. Examples include ABCMouse, HOMER Learn and Grow, Khan Academy Kids, Noggin, Waterford Upstart (for homes), and Waterford Reading Academy (for schools). These integrate a variety of games designed to foster the development of the range of early literacy skills alongside activities and games that focus on numeracy, art, music, and/or read-aloud activities. Family and teacher dashboards track children's progress and use.

Not all children or early learning programs will have access to these apps or the devices they require (Pila et al. 2019). Availability varies across device types, but that is just one factor. While some public libraries may provide access to tablets (e.g., Playaway Launchpad) preloaded with a range of early literacy learning apps, this is not a resource that is available in all communities. Technology is expensive and changes rapidly (Rideout & Robb 2020), but ensuring equitable access to these tools provides opportunities children may need to succeed and thrive later in school and society.

Print Conventions and Functions

As discussed in Chapter 1, print conventions are rules for organizing and using print. These rules specify that print is read from a page in a specific direction and that spaces separate printed words in a sentence. Print conventions also include rules for the use of uppercase letters, lowercase letters, and punctuation.

Children observe and learn about the convention for reading print from left to right as teachers underline the titles of poems, songs, and books; when they read signs or lists to children; and when they write with children. The titles of some books and the information on some charts also provide opportunities to model sweeping back to the left to read multiple lines of print.

Table 5.2. Strategies for Underlining Titles

Underlining technique	Effectiveness
A general, "sweeping" gesture, aimed at a title. Uses no underlining.	Ineffective—only conveys the general idea that the teacher is reading the print.
Points to the middle of each word. Uses no underlining.	Ineffective—only conveys the general idea that the teacher is reading the print.
Underlines each word from left to right, as it is read. Reading is quite fast, as an adult might read when not in an instructional setting. Reading sometimes ends before the title has been completely underlined, or vice versa.	Reasonably effective—models the tracking of print from left to right, which helps children learn in which direction print is accessed. Useful for preschoolers who have little alphabet knowledge or phonological awareness (perhaps at the start of the school year).
Underlines each word from left to right, and at a slower pace than an adult normally reads when not in an instructional situation. Underlining coordinates print and the teacher's speech fairly well, although some mismatches exist.	More effective—allows children to observe a line of print more closely and may lead them to notice space between clusters of letters (i.e., words) the teacher reads. Suitable for the middle months of a preschool year.
The teacher's finger lingers under the first letter of each word, as it is translated into sound, then underlines the remaining letters as the rest of the word is read. Underlining coordinates print almost perfectly with the teacher's speech. The title is read more fluently a second time, with underlining of each word without lingering on its first letter.	Most effective—specific, and can be used during the last three or four months of a preschool year when children know many letter names and have some phonological awareness. Some children will read along as a teacher uses this approach. Rereading the title a second time, after the more deliberate first reading, gives children another chance to read the title along with the teacher and allows children to focus on its meaning.

Because books and poems or song charts are used daily, their titles can be used in circle time or story time for teaching some print conventions. It is important to use effective strategies when underlining titles and to change these over the course of a year as children's literacy skills increase. This table outlines some underlining techniques and their varying effectiveness in helping children acquire specific literacy skills.

Table 5.3. Print Uses in a Preschool Classroom

Lists	
Turns lists in centers	• Children write their names as best they can on turns lists available on clipboards in each center. • When a child asks, "When is it my turn?" the teacher might say, "Helen is using the easel now, and then Tyronne's name is next on the turns list. Your name follows his." • Children cross off their names after taking their turn and can notify the child whose name is next.
Shopping lists	• As children and teachers notice that snacks or other supplies are running low, they add items to the shopping list. • Children can attempt to write an item's name using words on a printed list of typical supplies the teacher provides, or the teacher helps them spell the words.
Field trip item list	• The teacher can review the list of items they take along—class list with the day's attendees checked, first-aid kit, bottle of water, and cups. • Though the teacher's responsibility, reading the list to children and pointing out each item teaches children about the required items and that lists are used for such purposes.
List-related props for dramatic play	• Emergency numbers (e.g., police, doctor, fire personnel) can be posted on the play refrigerator. • Include common items needed from the grocery store. Children can use these when preparing to go shopping. • Include examination items (e.g., blood pressure cuff, thermometer, stethoscope, scale) for doctor's office play. • Add food carton lists for children to take home when items are needed for grocery store play.
Labels	
	• Place children's names on cubbies. Use uppercase for the first letter and lowercase for the rest. • Place names of items on both their containers and the shelves to help children know where items can be found and put away. • Write children's names on strips of paper to accompany artwork posted on bulletin boards.

- Use signs to indicate limits in areas (e.g., asking children to "whisper please" in the book area or to "walk please" down a hall).
- Create signs with the children to greet, welcome, and inform visitors (e.g., "Hello, Mr. Juarez. Rainbow classroom is this way").
- Help children create signs for the departments in a play grocery store (Figure 5.10), for "daily specials" in a play restaurant, and a sign saying "receptionist" for a play doctor's office.

Figure 5.10. A sign for a play grocery store.

Print use in play and on play materials

- Miniature commercial road signs for streets and highways made with blocks
- Child-created road and street signs (e.g., detour, caution, children playing)
- Commercial wooden "toppers" for block buildings (Hospital, Post Office, Gas Station)
- Child-created block signs for neighborhood spots (Milo's Subs, Johnny's Neighborhood Market, Ana's Burritos)
- Commercial community figures (e.g., mail carrier's bag is labeled US Mail) for block play
- Commercial vehicles with labels (e.g., taxi, police, fire truck, ice cream truck, ambulance)
- Road sign puzzles
- Storybook and nursery rhyme puzzles with titles the puzzle pieces depict
- Food cartons and grocery store ads from newspapers in house play area
- Children's books, magazines, and pamphlets (e.g., brushing teeth, eating healthy food, wearing seat belts) in doctor's office play area
- Cookbooks for chefs (teacher-created, laminated pages) and menus in restaurant play area
- Maps or an atlas, travel brochures, and a poster with arrival and departure times for train station or airport play area

Preschool teachers can use print for a variety of purposes to expose children to its many functions and forms.

Teachers need not underline the lines of print on poem and song charts or in predictable books as they recite, sing, or read. Children should hear the beauty of the language in these forms, and underlining often distorts its natural rhythm and flow. If teachers underline all titles of the items used daily and the directions on charts they use in small groups (e.g., planting a seed, making a food item), children will have adequate exposure to print conventions. Strategies for underlining titles, signs, and lists to help children learn both the direction in which print is accessed and about print and speech mapping are discussed in Table 5.2.

Print functions refer to the many uses of print. In addition to learning about uses, children also learn that print is arranged differently in different contexts of use. For example, the headings on a menu do not resemble headings found in informational books, street signs differ from lists, and a storybook differs from a cookbook.

Print (referred to as *text* in this context from this point on to avoid confusion) in digital formats is also organized differently from print formats. In apps, for example, text is arranged according to procedural (e.g., previous/next, go/play, exit, logoff) or content functions. Procedural text is usually located on the perimeter of a screen in a static task bar or near arrows that provide navigational support. In contrast, placement of content text varies according to the digital format's focus (e.g., book, game) and topic, and it is featured more prominently in the center of screens or in salient places among digital images. Digital text experiences provide opportunities for young children's expression of ideas, especially those still acquiring the physical skill to manipulate writing tools. Use good judgment in offering digital text experiences that foster engagement in the topic as well as cultivate media literacy (Rogow 2022). This includes avoiding replacing opportunities for children to write or simply adopting digital experiences for mere technology exposure.

Preschoolers become familiar with many print functions as they observe print used for a variety of purposes in many different contexts (e.g., observe signs and charts in the early learning setting, make cards for a family member or friend, add items to a teacher's list, make and use print props in dramatic play). (See Table 5.3.)

Concluding Thoughts

This chapter overviewed literacy skills that are important for children's later success in learning to read and write, along with many suggestions for activities and instructional strategies that preschool teachers can use to help children acquire these literacy skills.

It is important for teachers to do everything they possibly can to develop children's interest in literacy activities. Without opportunities to use literacy skills as children acquire them, children's skill learning will be diminished, and their interest in literacy skills is likely to decline. Chapters 7 and 8 provide many examples of children's use of their developing literacy skills in play and other learning contexts.

Although literacy skills are important for children's later success in learning to read and write, always remember that children's long-term success depends not only on literacy skills but also on general oral language and content learning. (See Chapters 3 and 4.) It is vital that preschool programs provide a good balance among literacy skills, oral language, and content knowledge in the instruction they provide.

PART TWO
BUILDING A FOUNDATION FOR WRITING

CHAPTER 6

WHAT'S INVOLVED IN WRITING?

Many of the understandings and skills foundational to reading are needed when learning to write. Additional knowledge and abilities also come into play because the physical act of writing challenges a young child's fine motor skills. This chapter provides a brief overview of the two main processes involved in writing—generating and organizing ideas (composing) and meaningfully representing these ideas. It also describes milestones of writing development through adolescence and discusses issues related to writing in preschool, kindergarten, and the early primary grades. These include the importance of striking a balance between code-related skills and meaning, where drawing and talking fit into writing for a preschooler, and how much attention to give handwriting.

Creating Messages

Before writing a message, writers think about—and sometimes even talk through—what they want to communicate. This meaning-creation part of writing is called ***composing***. Composing draws on the writer's knowledge of the physical, biological, and social worlds; their understanding of different genres (e.g., fiction, nonfiction, lab report, friendly letter, note, sign); and their language and cognitive skills. Planning is part of the composing process, and more experienced writers often prepare an outline before they start.

The degree of challenge involved in composing depends in part on the message and its purpose. For example, a short note to a friend about an upcoming meeting is far easier to compose than a short story or a persuasive essay. When the message is fairly complex (i.e., a story, an essay, a newspaper column), writers usually rework their message several times before it fluently expresses what they intended. The reworking of drafts is called *revising*.

When revising, writers scrutinize a draft for accuracy (i.e., "Am I conveying the information correctly?"), adequacy (i.e., "Is the information sufficiently detailed?"), clarity (i.e., "Will a reader understand what I mean?"), and appeal (i.e., "Will my intended audience like this?"). Revision by experienced writers is a complex process because they look for problems in meaning, sentence structure, and spelling. Once found, the problems are repaired. Evaluating the meaning in drafts is especially important for expert adult writers. It requires some of the same skills that readers use to comprehend text (Hayes 2000).

Representing Messages

Of course, as writers compose a message, they represent it in some way. Some older preschoolers, and all school-age children and adults, use written words, which requires knowing how to create and arrange symbols (i.e., alphabet letters/graphemes) to spell specific words. Language skills (i.e., syntactic and grammatical knowledge) then guide the writer in arranging words into sentences. By the primary grades, children are also expected to place words on a writing surface, such as paper or a white board, according to established conventions (e.g., from left to right and from top to bottom; leaving space in between words; using uppercase and lowercase letters; inserting punctuation appropriately).

Younger emergent writers (i.e., preschoolers, kindergartners) usually do not check if spelling is correct (Adams 1990). For one thing, they are not yet reading, which is how children inspect words and become aware of conventional spellings. Though unconventional, some young writers' spellings show that they know some of the basic spelling rules of their language—or languages, in the case of multilingual children.

Figure 6.1. A note written by a kindergartner, which reads, *Dear Amanda, I hope you are feeling better. Are you? Love, Adam.*

For example, refer to the note written by a kindergartner to his friend late in the year (Figure 6.1). In writing the word *dear,* he placed two vowels in the middle, an acceptable representation for tense vowel phonemes in some word contexts, but he used the wrong pair (*ee* rather than *ea*). Similarly, in the grammatical morpheme in *feeling*, the child placed a vowel before *ng* but used a more literal spelling (*feeleang*) than the standard *I*. Specifically, he chose two letters that are an acceptable representation for the tense vowel in this spot in some other words (e.g., peat, meat, seat), not the standard spelling for the same sound in this word context.

Likewise, he spelled *better* with just one *T,* not two. He did include the *E* between *T* and *R,* which indicates an understanding of the requirement that each syllable must have a vowel. Or, if he did not know this specific English spelling rule, he knew that he had never seen the consonants *tr* in this sequence at the end of a word but had seen another kind of letter (vowel) in between them. He might have guessed which one to use. The words *I, you, are,* and *love* were all spelled correctly, which illustrates that young children learn many standard spellings from seeing words frequently, especially when learning to read.

Phases of Writing Development

Children's writing development can be thought of in terms of three major phases: (1) emergent, (2) beginning conventional, and (3) more mature conventional. Developing skill in writing takes years. The timeframes for these phases are rough approximations, not sharply delineated stages. There is also considerable development *within* each phase.

Emergent Writing

The emergent period of writing can be divided into three subphases:

1. **Pre-representational,** in which marks are not intended to convey a message (see Chapter 7).

2. **Intentional representation with multiple symbol systems,** in which marks convey meaning. Linear, wavy, or looped scribble or mock words are added to "help" represent meaning, but children convey much of their meaning verbally because neither drawing nor writing conveys as much as they wish to express (see Chapter 8).

3. **Intentional representation with more balanced symbol systems,** in which children convey more of their meaning. Marks intended as writing are more letter-like in form, and spellings that children invent for words are often readable. Even with these improvements, talking about drawings and writing to explain what they say is still extremely important for older preschoolers, kindergartners, and even first-graders because their full meaning is sometimes hard to convey with only drawing and writing. By late in the preschool years, many children can represent some simpler meanings by writing marks or mock words alone, but in these instances, children's meanings are often single words or simple messages, such as *I love you* (see Chapter 8).

The emergent phase starts around 1 year old, continues through kindergarten, and extends into first grade. Naturally, there is a world of difference between an emergent writer who is a toddler versus one in preschool; between one in preschool versus one in kindergarten; and between one in kindergarten versus one in first grade. For example, infants and toddlers make marks just to explore marking and the tools used for their own sake, not to represent messages (Figure 6.2). In contrast, preschoolers and kindergartners draw and label pictures that represent objects and events, write their names, and use scribble writing and **mock words** (i.e., letter strings that look like words but are not actual words) to create grocery lists, notes to friends, and signs for block buildings. An older first-grader spells more words correctly, invents others that closely resemble their conventional spelling (Figures 6.3 and 6.4), and separates words with spaces (Figure 6.4).

When comparing less experienced emergent writers to more experienced ones, there are also major differences in the complexity of messages created. Although older toddlers sometimes name scribble drawings after creating them, they have relatively little to say beyond the label. In contrast, by 4 years old, children typically set out to draw with intention (i.e., to represent something), and they use details that help convey their meanings. They also use oral language to relate much of their meaning, and an adult sometimes writes down what they say.

Figure 6.2. Seventeen-month-old's scribble.

Figure 6.3. Picture with writing (*This kind of dinosaur feeds on trees*). The convention of using space in between words is not used.

Figure 6.4. Older first-grader's thank-you note to his father with spaces separating words.

Beginning Conventional Writing

From kindergarten through third grade, writing and drawing are almost always intentional. Children in kindergarten and the primary grades also create more complex messages than preschoolers and begin to use features that distinguish one genre from another (e.g., stories versus informational text) (Duke & Kays 1998). Compared to preschoolers and kindergartners, first-graders also begin thinking more about the content of their writing, and they often use sentence forms and content from familiar books (Dahl & Freppon 1995).

Yet, first grade writers are still quite spontaneous—they do not engage in extensive planning before beginning to write (Graves 1981). They talk a bit about what they are going to write and talk *as* they write and draw (Cioffi 1984). Moreover, if a message includes several ideas, first-graders formulate each in the moment as an "add-on," rather than revising the whole as they think of new ideas.

The first grade child forms alphabet letters fairly well, but it still takes some deliberate effort. Handwriting skill increases over the primary years and becomes more automatic. First- and second-graders develop considerable skill in spelling and acquire more knowledge about punctuation and the appropriate uses of uppercase and lowercase letters. Much of this learning comes from observing these print conventions while reading books.

As children gain skill and automaticity in these writing mechanics, they can devote more time and energy to thinking about what they will write. Even though first- and second-graders have considerable skill in creating written words, they still use drawings to represent some of their meanings. Moreover, kindergartners and first-graders, in particular, still need to use oral language to communicate much of their meaning.

More Mature Conventional Writing

As language facility, knowledge, spelling, and other technical skills increase, a writer's messages increase in length and depth, and the words used to convey messages increase in specificity. In fact, a good vocabulary is as important for writing as it is for reading, if not more so (Johnson 2000). Good instructional support for writing also includes vocabulary development (Kelley et al. 2010). When reviewing a draft of an autobiography with a second-grader, the teacher might discuss using one higher-level word to replace several words the child used to capture a specific meaning. For example, a teacher might say, "Right here, you've written, *I like soccer better than baseball, basketball, or hockey. I like soccer more than any other sport.* For that second sentence, you could instead say, *Soccer is my favorite sport.* The word *favorite* by itself would express the same idea as *more than any other sport.*"

As children progress through school, they craft sentences to express increasingly complex relationships, and they write more clearly and with more coherence. They also think more specifically about the intended audience and gradually develop skill in writing for a wider range of purposes. Children make progress in their writing when they share it with teachers and peers and receive helpful feedback from them.

Effective Early Childhood Practices

Unfortunately, research shows that the majority of high school students in the United States are not proficient writers (NCES 2003, 2008, 2012). One misstep in US education followed from the publication of a report of the National Reading Panel (NICHD 2000). Research on writing did not clearly show the effects on reading skill development, and the panel's report did not recommend writing practices as a strategy for supporting reading development. As schools tried to make language arts instruction "scientifically based," writing was often neglected.

The Common Core State Standards for the English Language Arts (National Governors Association Center for Best Practices, Council of Chief State School Officers 2010) now include writing, and many states have adopted these standards or have set their own to communicate the importance of early writing experiences. Recent research reports encouraging changes as well as obvious needs (Gerde & Bingham 2023). For example, teachers acknowledge the importance of young children's access to writing materials and provide up to an hour of daily access to them; however, some teachers do not provide dedicated writing centers in their classrooms, lack knowledge about using materials to foster children's writing beyond developing fine motor skills, and do not provide writing materials across multiple learning centers. Findings illuminate the need for professional learning on instruction that underpins meaningful early writing experiences.

There are many things that early childhood educators can do to help children get off to a good start. This section highlights some of the ways to help, along with some pitfalls to avoid. Chapters 7 and 8 will discuss specific writing-related information and strategies more fully.

Read to Young Children

Reading to children, starting in infancy, helps them develop language and become familiar with different forms of written discourse. Children also learn a lot about people and the natural world from books, especially when adults engage children in conversation about the books that adults read and discuss with them. (See Chapters 3 and 4.)

Expose Children to a Range of Purposes for Writing

Young children benefit from seeing writing used for a wide variety of purposes (e.g., menus, signs, stories, recipes, instructions). They can use scribble writing and mock letters and words for many of these purposes in house pretend play (e.g., making a grocery list, leaving a note for a babysitter), in block area play (e.g., signs for buildings and streets), and when making a card for an absent friend or creating a drawing and note for a teacher at the writing center.

Using writing for these purposes is highly motivating to young children no matter their level of skill (e.g., scribble, mock letters, mock words). Confining preschoolers' writing to set tasks, such as alphabet letter and name writing, stifles their motivation to write and severely limits their opportunities to compose messages.

Provide Mark-Making Experiences Early

Early mark-making experiences gradually lead to the creation of pictures and scribble writing to which children attribute meaning. Because the physical form of a young child's representations does not give others access to its meaning, very young children relate meanings orally. Early marking provides a wonderful opportunity for adults to talk with children about their meanings.

Talk with Children About Their Writing and Drawing

As adults talk with young children about their drawings and writing, the children learn not only about oral language but also about message creation (e.g., how much detail to include, how to organize messages). When adults prompt children to tell more, they are helping children develop their narrative skills (Peterson & McCabe 1994).

Keep the Focus on Meaning

Preschoolers also begin to learn how to form alphabet letters, link letters to sounds, and use various print conventions. However, if code-based skills, handwriting, and print conventions are the primary focus in the early years while meaning is given little attention, children are not served well in the long run. It is important for early childhood educators to keep the primary focus of writing on meaning and on providing support for children to communicate that meaning. In short, experiences in the early years must be balanced.

Understanding the Young Child's Approach to Representing Meaning

Young children, including first- and second-graders, have several well-established ways of conveying meaning before they can use writing well for this purpose (Dyson 2000; Genishi & Dyson 2009). For example, they engage in pretend play, draw, use gestures, and talk. Young children are more comfortable using these forms over writing to convey their meanings. Although it takes years for children to develop skill in handwriting and spelling, they try to express complex meanings very early in life. It's important to keep meaning afloat in these early years; do not focus narrowly on requiring children to represent ideas only in writing or include writing with all of their pictures. For example, when a 3-year-old boy drew a fairly detailed picture of a lady in a green hat, he told a lot about it but did not add writing to the picture. His teacher accepted his verbal commentary and did not ask him to add any writing (Figure 6.5).

Figure 6.5. "This is a lady with a green hat and polka dot eyes and nose and a mouth."

The challenge for early childhood educators is to help children acquire skill in using written forms of communication, while also maintaining and nurturing their skill in communicating meanings through pretend play, drawing, and talking. As a start, teachers can do more than ask children to label their drawings (e.g., "What is it?") and then move quickly to saying, "Let me write that down." Learning that what is said can be written down is easy for children to understand and fairly trivial in the grand scheme of things, especially when the teacher elicits only a few labels. If a teacher asks a child first to "Tell me about your picture" and they say, "It's a bird's nest," the teacher can ask, "Did you see a bird's nest somewhere?" to prompt the child to provide more information. If the child seems interested, a teacher can then ask another follow-up question after the child responds to keep the conversation going.

It's far better for the child in the long run to talk more about what they mean and worry less about writing it down. Far better too if the teacher writes down messages for young children, rather than expect them to write complex meanings by themselves. While there is a time and a place for expecting independence in action, pushing independence too soon in some realms stifles what children are willing to think and say because representing it by themselves is overwhelming.

Concluding Thoughts

Early childhood educators can open up various means of symbolizing and communicating for young children if they provide ample opportunities for pretend play and block building, as well as for drawing, painting, and writing. Notably, the Common Core State Standards for the English Language Arts (National Governors Association Center for Best Practices, Council of Chief State School Officers 2010) recognize the importance of drawing and dictating messages in the kindergarten-level writing standards. Preschool teachers can certainly follow suit.

Good preschool programs nurture a balance, tipped at first toward the development of meaning and the use of multiple symbolic strategies (i.e., drawing, talking, and writing) to represent them. To nurture young children's writing, teachers and families must provide many opportunities and sufficient time, interacting and assisting in numerous ways all the while. Chapters 7 and 8 provide many examples of how early childhood educators and families might do this.

CHAPTER 7

INFANTS AND TODDLERS LEAVE THEIR MARK

When Adam is 12 months old, his mother touches the tip of a washable, nontoxic black marker to a piece of paper she taped to his high chair tray. She then hands Adam the marker, and he is fascinated by it. Adam's mother is inspired to provide her child with these materials because of something she observed him doing earlier that week: he dipped his fingers into the pureed peas and carrots he was meant to be eating and made marks on his high chair tray.

For about five minutes, Adam makes marks and inspects them. He touches the marker's tip with his index finger and looks astonished when he sees a dot of ink. Next, he turns the marker around to try its other end. After turning it again to test its tip, he turns to its other end again. Upon finding no trace on the paper left by the marker's nonwriting end the two times he tests it, he returns to using only the tip. Adam also makes a few marks with a brown crayon. His mother watches closely, concerned that he might take a bite of it, but he does not, probably because the visual effects he creates hold his attention (Figure 7.1).

A Rationale for Early Mark-Making Experiences

Figure 7.1. Adam's marks on paper.

Recent research on mark-making opportunities reveals very young children's avid interest in writing activities, the influence of well-supplied early writing environments, and the impacts of educators' early writing instruction on children's writing engagement and literacy skills (Gerde & Bingham 2023; Rowe, Shimuzu, & Davis 2022; Rowe et al. 2024). Recommendations for play materials for children younger than 3 years old include paintbrushes, water-based paints, washable markers, and crayons. Although children's fine motor skills are still developing and they do not use these materials for representation, toddlers can explore the materials and learn from their discoveries. Adults talk to babies who cannot yet understand what they say, knowing that language understanding and skill emerge only out of this experience. Adults also encourage children to stand up and cruise while holding onto furniture before they can walk without support. The same principle applies to mark making—a toddler's fine motor skills are good enough to make marks with tools and to learn from the process.

A whole world of learning about movement and its effects on tools is possible long before infants and toddlers ever use marks to represent something specific. Consider also that most infants begin exploring a spoon at mealtimes a few months before their first birthday (Gesell & Ilg 1937). Although *skilled* spoon use comes many months later, infants quickly start taking account of the effects of their actions on a spoon and constantly adapt to make it work better (Connolly & Dalgleish 1989). Mark making provides a unique opportunity for learning because, unlike other object exploration, it creates permanent visual effects.

This chapter focuses on mark making in children from about 10 to 30 months old. It chronicles physical mark making (i.e., what shows up on the paper) and the emergence of the child's understanding that lines and designs can represent ideas (i.e., convey meaning). The vast amount of learning that takes place during infancy and toddlerhood is also overviewed. This learning comprises the cognitive, social, emotional, and language foundations that affect the content of young children's drawing and writing for years to come. Alongside this information is featured the original work of young children in full color, which gives early paintings and drawings the attention and respect they deserve.

Infants' Actions on Objects and the Use of Mark-Making Tools

Early mark making is a motor, visual, and tactile delight, and infants also take account of the effects of their movements. Indeed, physical actions and thinking are closely intertwined in the young child (Bartlett 1958). Before describing the very young child's mark-making behavior, this section summarizes some research about infants' learning from their manipulation of physical objects. It illustrates how much infants observe about objects and their properties and how they vary their actions in response to what they notice when manipulating these objects. This influences how they adapt exploration to new objects in the future (Marcinowski et al. 2019). The information provides some background about the knowledge and skill that very young children bring to mark making and indicates the contributions of mark making to early learning.

What the Infant and Toddler Bring to These Experiences

Throughout much of the first year, infants handle objects and adapt their behavior in response to feedback the objects provide. Here are some examples:

> **At 4 months,** the infant moves objects they hold toward their mouth more and more if the object fits in their mouth. If objects do not fit, they mouth them less (Rochat 1989).

> **At 6 months,** the infant begins to adapt their actions on objects based on the objects' surface features. For example, they use their hands more to feel bumpy objects and mouth them less, but they do the opposite with smooth objects (Ruff 1984). The infant also mouths objects more if they don't make sound and less if they do (Morgante & Keen 2008; Palmer 1989). They bang objects more on a bare table or floor than they do on a padded, carpeted, or liquid surface (Bourgeois et al. 2005; Morgante & Keen 2008; Palmer 1989).

> **From 8 to 9 months,** the infant bangs rigid objects more and squeezes them less while squeezing pliable objects more and banging them less (Bushnell & Boudreau 1993).

> **From 6 to 12 months,** the infant decreases their mouthing of objects they hold, instead looking at and manipulating them more (Rochat 1989).

Mark Making Provides a New Context for Learning

Infants and toddlers learn a lot about mark-making tools and substances. For example, they discover that crayons must be applied with relatively more pressure than soft-graphite pencils or ballpoint pens. Markers leave wet marks with only a soft touch of their tip, while chalk is dry, smears on paper, and leaves dust on fingers. A paintbrush must be dipped into paint, which is unlike other writing tools that have some writing substance already loaded inside of them (e.g., graphite in a pencil, ink in markers).

Young children could injure themselves with a pencil or pen if they are permitted to walk around with them. Moreover, they certainly will decorate walls and furniture with any mark-making tool if given the chance. For these reasons, educators and families provide safe contexts and supervise young children as they explore these tools (see Figure 7.2). That said, they are ready to begin.

Early Mark-Making Phases

Early mark-making phases are not sharply delineated stages, but rather, periods indicating roughly when infants and toddlers acquire new behavior. The first two phases involve exploration without any representation, during which infants and toddlers become fascinated with and delighted by what *they* can make happen. The third phase includes some representational behavior, although children do not yet approach paper intending to create anything specific. Still, they sometimes attribute meaning to their marks after making them.

Figure 7.2. While her mother supervises, Chara sits at the kitchen table using a pen and notebook, which she requested after noticing her mother use them.

Phase 1: Whatever Happens, Happens

Between about 10 to 12 and 18 to 20 months, children's facial expressions suggest astonishment, as if surprised by and in awe of the traces *their* fingers leave. They often make many marks in these explorations and look closely at them. Children love mark making and frequently request the paper, pens, and pencils they spot in others' hands. Adults find it difficult to write within sight of an infant because they want the materials!

Several examples of early markings by Livi (12 months), Adam (14 months), and Chara (14 months) are shown. Livi marked on a piece of lined paper she requested from her mother's pad (Figure 7.3). Adam used ballpoint pen, pencil, and red crayon (Figure 7.4). Chara used several markers of different colors while sitting in her high chair (Figure 7.5).

Figure 7.3. Markings by Livi.

Figure 7.4. Markings by Adam.

Figure 7.5. Markings by Chara.

Phase 2: Controlling and Contrasting Marks

Within a few months of starting to explore marking, children begin to repeat a specific kind of mark, sometimes in ways that contrast it with another kind in the same drawing. This behavior is seen as early as 16 to 17 months, and usually no later than 20 to 24 months, in children who have marked frequently from about 1 year old.

At 16 months, Chara created a patch of dots (Figure 7.6), which she separated from the other scribble on her paper. Much later, at 28 months, she often scribbled with abandon on one part of her paper and created controlled *C*-like marks on other parts that were separate from the scribbles (Figure 7.7).

Grayden began controlling marks on a whiteboard easel at about 22 months. Sometimes, he even approached the surface with specific forms in mind. He labeled the marks in one session as spirals (Figure 7.8).

Interestingly, Grayden's father, an artist, sometimes drew for and with Grayden, showing him specific forms and naming them. Chara's mother, an early childhood educator, wrote words and named letters for Chara. These two children picked up specific forms from their parents. Thus, Grayden created and named line forms, while Chara created and named *C*s.

Some of Adam's line contrast markings appear in Figure 7.9. It shows vertical and horizontal lines made with single strokes. This deliberate marking occurred a few months after drawings that included both circular and straighter back-and-forth lines on the same paper. The exploration shown even suggests that he conducted a little study to compare two kinds of mark.

Figure 7.6. Chara's marks (16 months).

Figure 7.7. Chara's marks (28 months).

Figure 7.8. Grayden's spirals.

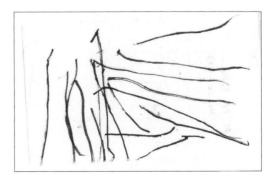

Figure 7.9. Adam's contrasting lines (22 months).

Figure 7.10. Adam's *G*s (20 months).

Figure 7.11. Lucy's mark-making exploration with markers.

Figure 7.12. Sydney's *S* (24 months).

At 20 months, Adam deliberately repeated a specific kind of mark after first creating it accidentally amid several small circular marks (Figure 7.10). He knew the shape and name of *G* from asking for the names of magnetic letters on the refrigerator door and raised letters on the rim of his dish. When he spotted the *G*-like designs, he said, "A *G*!" as if surprised. Then, he made two more, announcing, "'Nother *G*, 'nother one."

At 26 months, Lucy explored colors and contrasting strokes using her older brother's markers (Figure 7.11). Starting in the top-left corner and moving from left to right down the page, she filled the paper with multiple "down ups" and clusters of dots. Occasionally announcing color names as she removed marker caps, she varied the pressure of her grip to create thick, bold lines and thin, wispy lines. Although some strokes overlapped, those on the right side of the page were separate, linear, and word-like in length. Her exploration spanned the gamut of curiosity and autonomy: using her brother's markers; removing marker caps; naming colors; making marks of differing design, pressure, and color; controlling the position of marks on the page; filling the paper; and smiling in satisfaction upon completion. Lucy had seen her 5-year-old brother write and draw and was exposed to her parents' creation of lists and notes for a variety of functions. She seemed delighted by the process and the product of her discovery.

While drawing at 24 months, Sydney started with large, red, free-flowing circular scribbles, to which she added smaller shapes with a blue marker (some closed and reversed curves). Then, she made an *S* in the left middle of her paper—her first one ever (Figure 7.12).

Children's control over their marks increases as they continue exploring with mark-making tools. But adults see already the beginnings of both control and intention when children repeat a form they made accidentally the first time (Adam's *G*s) or deliberately make several specific marks (Grayden's spirals). In these instances, the child adapts their movement to create a specific form. Without a doubt, infants and toddlers are remarkable observers and learners!

Phase 3: Attributing Meaning to Marks

Beginning between 20 and 24 months, toddlers sometimes attribute meaning to marks that start out random and then by chance coalesce into forms that resemble familiar objects. This behavior occurs infrequently for a few months, and then increases.

While drawing at 22 months, Adam announced, "A man . . . mouth and eyes!" (Figure 7.13). His surprised tone of voice and wide eyes indicated that he did not intend to draw something in particular. In fact, he had just completed another drawing to which he did not attribute meaning, even though it contained similar marks and shapes. Apparently, the marks in the previous drawing did not remind Adam of anything, while the arrangement of the marks in this one did.

Adam also sometimes attributed meaning to paintings (Figure 7.14), but not until several months after he had done this with drawings. Perhaps paint invites children to make large spots of color and fewer defined shapes and designs, especially when the brush used is fairly wide. No research about this was found, but we authors wonder whether (1) drawing with finer-tipped mark-making tools (e.g., crayons, pens, pencils) elicits more attributions of meaning from children than does painting and (2) adults more often ask a child to tell them about their work when they draw compared to when they paint.

Around 22 months, Molly's neighbor painted a picture for her birthday using an entire palette of watercolors (Figure 7.15). After covering the paper with designs, he decided to make a dog with a purple body and pink legs in the bottom right corner. The idea for the dog preceded the marks. This planned attribution of meaning might have been inspired by his exploration of materials when making the design or prior experience with and support for art and writing at home.

Sometimes older toddlers add a bit of detail to a drawing that has reminded them of something, perhaps to increase the similarity between their

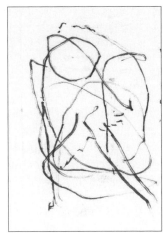

Figure 7.13. Adam's drawing with attribution of meaning.

Figure 7.14. Adam's snakes.

Figure 7.15. Young neighbor's watercolor painting with a dog in the bottom-right corner.

scribbles and the object the scribbles have suddenly brought to their mind. For example, 31-month-old Livi added rocks to the right side and the base of her mountain after having seen in her scribbles the likeness of a volcano (Figure 7.16).

After creating some straight and curved lines, seemingly without any deliberate intention, 27-month-old Sydney looked at her paper and said, "This is an *X* and this is a rainbow" (Figure 7.17). Then, on a second piece of paper, she deliberately recreated the same kinds of lines. When finished, she told her mom, "This is an *X* and this is a rainbow again" (Figure 7.18). After seeing some meaningful objects in one of her scribble drawings, Sydney seemed to realize that she didn't need to wait for forms to coalesce inadvertently on each occasion of scribbling but instead could intend to make them from the start.

Interestingly, a book about colors that Sydney's parents had recently read to her included a picture of a rainbow. Her parents had also named *X* and other letters as Sydney played with magnet letters on the refrigerator door and in other contexts.

At about this age, children also start using one object to represent another in pretend play, even when the object they select bears little resemblance to the one the child wants to represent. Prior to 2 years old, children do not make such substitutions, instead using small replicas of the actual object or other objects with similar features. (See Box 7.1 for information about pretend play development and its connection to writing.)

The onset of this mental flexibility—and perhaps also a new insight that drawings, unlike photos, need not be realistic—allows the child to see more in the organization of marks than was possible just a few months earlier. There are also social influences, as educators and family members show interest in children's drawings and paintings and make comments and ask questions (e.g., "Tell me about your drawing" or "I am curious what you were thinking about here").

Some approaches to inquiring are less assuming (e.g., "Tell me about it") than others (e.g., "What did you make?"). While it may be tempting to ask a child "What are you making?," the authors advise against it. This question might make children feel as if they *must* be making something, which could squelch motivation to explore, or as if their drawing isn't a sufficient representation of their idea if an adult has to ask.

Figure 7.16. Livi's volcano with rocks added.

Figure 7.17. Sydney's original drawing, in which she notices an *X* and a rainbow.

Figure 7.18. Sydney's recreation of the lines.

Box 7.1. Milestones in Children's Pretend Play Behavior

Children begin to pretend at about 12 months old, but pretending at this young age is very simple. Over the next two to three years, pretending changes dramatically. Pretend play requires **object substitution,** or the attribution of meaning to one object used to stand for another (e.g., using a stick as a fishing pole, a block as a cup). This is a symbolic (i.e., representational) activity, akin to a child giving meaning to marks on paper.

When pretending becomes sociodramatic (i.e., pretending that you are someone and coordinating your role with other players' roles), it requires thinking about others' thinking (e.g., what they know, how they feel, what their goals are). These are the same kinds of considerations required when comprehending or creating a story.

The milestones for pretending provided here indicate the major shifts in pretend play over the course of the infant, toddler, and preschool years:

> **Prior to 10 months:** No pretending (Fenson et al. 1976). Explores objects separately, not functionally (e.g., bangs pot lid on floor, mouths its edge, and hits it with a hand, but does not put it on top of the cooking pot).

> **From 10 to 12 months:** Uses objects meaningfully (e.g., puts lids on pots, cups on saucers, and spoons in bowls), but does not pretend (e.g., does not pretend to take a bite of food from the spoon or stir in the bowl as if mixing food) (Bretherton 1984; Fenson et al. 1976).

> **From 12 to 13 months:** Simple pretending of their own ordinary actions (e.g., to sleep when not sleeping, to drink from an empty cup). Does not include others in pretend; materials must be real or replicas (McCune-Nicolich 1981).

> **From 13 to 15 months:** Begins to direct play actions toward others (e.g., pretends to feed a parent or doll, pretends that a doll is asleep) (Fein 1984; Fenson & Ramsay 1980).

> **From 20 to 24 months:** Combines several distinct behaviors into a connected series (e.g., feeds the doll, pushes doll in stroller, puts doll to bed). Uses objects that are not replicas if they have similar features. Begins to use actions that they have not yet performed in real life but have observed others perform (e.g., pretends to cook in a pot or reads to a doll). Begins to animate dolls (e.g., makes them talk, puts spoon in their hand) (Fenson 1984; Fenson & Ramsay 1980).

> **From 26 to 30 months:** Begins to use objects that do not closely resemble the object pretended (e.g., a block as a cup, even though it lacks an essential feature—a cavity) (Fein 1975).

> **At 30 months:** Pretends to be someone else. Indicates they are "in role" by tone of voice or announces the role they have adopted (e.g., "I am Elmo's Mommy") (Dunn 1998). Manages the play of two characters—self and a doll (e.g., the toddler is the Daddy and the doll is a baby; the child puts both "in role") (Goncu 1998). Uses more and more language that is typical of the roles played (e.g., to a doll baby, "It's good. Eat" and "Go to sleep now") and tells others what they are playing (e.g., "I am the Mommy. I'm going shopping") (Fenson 1984).

> **From 30 to 48 months:** Learns to coordinate own role play with roles of other players (Bretherton 1984; Goncu 1998).

> **At 48 months:** Resists using objects with specific known functions as substitutes for other objects but increases flexibility in using nonspecific objects to represent objects in play (Ungerer et al. 1981).

Another approach is to share an interpretation, such as "Oh, this big splash of blue here in the middle of your painting makes me think of the pond where we visit the ducks." In this case, the adult indicates that marks *can* convey meaning and that people are likely to interpret a child's drawings, while not suggesting that the adult's interpretation is what the child intended or that the child should always portray something specific.

It is frequently appropriate and helpful to children for educators and family members to talk with them as they draw and paint. Consider the rich information adults can provide, as illustrated by these examples:

> "I think you made a new color right here. (*Points to it.*) You mixed the red and blue paint together. That spot looks purple to me."

> "Oh, paint isn't food, we don't eat it. Does the paint remind you of mushy food you have on your high chair tray sometimes?"

> "When you put your hand down like this after you put some finger paint on it, it makes a print of your hand. (*Demonstrates with own hand on a blank space on the paper.*)"

> "The paint splatters in our faces when you slap it hard like that. We don't want paint in our eyes. Maybe you can slap it softly, like this. (*Demonstrates.*)"

Notice that these are not demanding comments—a child would not feel compelled to respond. Thus, they do not disrupt the child's own activity. Moreover, the comments about the use of the materials provide reasons for changing behavior, rather than ordering a child to stop doing something (e.g., "No! Stop that!"). Children are much more likely to change their behavior if adults help them understand the effects of their behaviors on others and objects (i.e., induction) (Baumrind 1989).

Creating Accessible Mark-Making Experiences for Infants and Toddlers

Children can create markings at home or in an early learning setting when the environment is organized for these experiences. This section describes a variety of effective strategies to foster infants' and toddlers' early markings by providing particular materials and organizing them in certain ways.

Opportunities in High Chairs

An infant's first opportunities to mark with their fingers will likely occur on the high chair tray as they enjoy a meal. As Hirsh-Pasek and Golinkoff (2007) note, "the high chair becomes a canvas and baby foods the paints. [. . .] It's all about the feel—truly high touch instead of high tech" (8). These language researchers also give this advice: "Don't rush to clean up that mess; there's potential in those mashed potatoes" (Hirsh-Pasek & Golinkoff 2007, 8).

We authors agree but also understand that educators cannot always replicate the leisurely pace of an infant eating and playing in a high chair at home. After all, in an early learning setting, care and attention must be given to more than one child at a time. Potential benefits of the infant's exploration of soft foods might still be realized in early learning settings by having one educator attend to a table with seating suitable for a few infants.

Infants between 12 and 14 months often enjoy finger paint or markers. A bit of finger paint can be placed directly on the high chair tray or table in front of each child's place for the child to explore. If desired, a print of the child's marks in it can be made by placing easel paper over the marks and pressing so the marks transfer. Families might enjoy seeing these, although infants just enjoy the process of squishing the finger paint and smearing it all around. That said, sometimes they are quite deliberate in making marks with their fingers and looking at what they have done.

When paper is offered for an infant to smear paint on directly, use masking tape to secure it to the tray or table. Always offer markers without their caps. They are difficult for children to remove or replace; more importantly, once removed they are choking hazards.

Opportunities at Easels

By 2 years old, children can easily stand at a toddler-size easel to paint. Place a small amount of paint in two or three open cups, providing a different color in each. You might put a paintbrush in each cup or provide just one for use across all; toddlers usually use the first paintbrush they pick up to dip into other cups, even when each cup has its own paintbrush. Toddlers don't care when colors become mixed. Special chubby paintbrushes are not necessary, as toddlers can grasp a thinner one just fine, if not better. It is a good idea, however, to choose paintbrushes with shorter handles because these are easier for a toddler to manipulate.

Educators should expect that toddlers will touch both the bristles of the paintbrush and the wet paint they apply to the paper to feel the paint. This is all part of their exploration. Some toddlers might stick a finger that has paint on it in their mouth to take a taste, especially if they have been given opportunities to explore and make marks with food as described earlier. Keep damp paper towels handy to wipe fingers clean as you say calmly, "We shouldn't eat paint. It's not food. Paint goes on the paper."

Children can also finger paint at an easel. Provide finger paint paper (i.e., glossy or laminated paper) to allow for it to be wiped clean and reused. Place the finger paint in shallow cups in the easel tray. Children just dip their fingers into the paint, and away they go! When finished, a child can wash their hands at a sink before a teacher helps them remove their painting smock.

Opportunities at Water Tables and Other Places to Finger Paint

Toddlers can also explore finger paint in clear plastic tubs designed for water play. In this context, gel paint works best because it dissolves more easily when the tub is washed. Place a small amount of two or three colors in the tub for children to smear around its bottom and sides.

The stands available for water table tubs can also be used to create a good place for children to finger paint. A stand's nonporous cover allows painting to take place directly on it. Alternately, large plastic trays can be used as painting surfaces. Be sure that the color of the finger paints placed on the cover or tray contrasts with the cover or tray's color so that the finger paint is easily visible. These options provide more social and emotional and language opportunities than an easel surface as children paint across from or next to each other. They also offer stability for children who need physical support to stand. The large surface of the stand's cover fosters gross motor movement (arm and core), while the trays are portable and can be used in the laps of children using wheelchairs.

Opportunities at Activity Tables

In a toddler room, it is not safe to place pencils, markers, and crayons out on shelves in a writing and drawing center because toddlers are likely to walk around with these items in their hands. If they should fall, the item could injure them. Instead, place the materials at a table each time the activity is offered to toddlers and make sure an adult stays at the table continuously to supervise.

It is also far better to place a few mark-making tools in a small flat tray (e.g., a shoebox lid) at each toddler's place on the table than to put them in sets organized in cans or plastic containers. Toddlers have trouble pulling one marker or crayon out of a cup or can without tipping the whole thing over. They might also resort to dumping them all out on the table rather than selecting just one. Furthermore, toddlers need only two or three markers, crayons, or colored pencils, not a full set.

Pencils, both standard graphite and colored, should be fairly short and have dull tips. Use handheld sharpeners to create a short tip, then dull it by running it back and forth across a piece of paper. Thick-diameter (chubby) crayons do not break as easily as thin crayons under the pressure applied by toddlers. Plastic crayon holders are also available to prevent breakage. Both thick and thin markers should be placed out on a flat tray, again without their caps. Materials such as adaptive paint brushes with egg-shaped handles or wide bases facilitate an easier grip for children with disabilities. Tempera paint blocks allow children with fine motor challenges to swish broadly across the paint with a brush.

Paper will stay put as a young toddler draws on it if it is anchored at its top and bottom with masking tape. Older toddlers might use one hand to stabilize the paper while drawing with the other, but it's fine if they see no need to do so. Slanted writing surfaces and paper secured to the table can facilitate stability during mark making. Lowering easels to accommodate use while seated and providing footrests for children seated at tables provide support to those who need opportunities for core strength and balance.

When a toddler is finished mark making, a teacher can give the toddler a chance to write their name, likely a scribble version. The teacher can then offer to write the toddler's name, using and naming alphabet letters and commenting that this is how grownups write it, as the toddler watches. This approach supports the toddler's efforts and provides instruction. Developmentally appropriate screen-based technologies can also provide excellent exposure to mark-making experiences (see Box 7.2).

Box 7.2. Technology and Mark Making

Kathleen A. Paciga

It is critical that children learn how to use digital tools to create, communicate, and participate in a world linked and governed by internet-connected devices—in other words, they need to develop digital literacy. Just as print literacy emerges as children develop their understandings about marks, tools for mark making, and the forms and functions of print, children can begin to shape their digital literacy by learning about the tools, forms, and functions of various technology (e.g., phones, tablets, computers, cameras, gaming consoles). The foundations of digital literacy begin in the early years when conversations about the intended audiences and purposes for the marks accompany mark making (Rogow 2022; Turner et al. 2017). It is also important for the physical environment to allow for playful exploration (Maureen, van der Meij, & de Jong 2020; Neumann, Finger, & Neumann 2017).

Digital Mark Making

There are many advantages to using digital devices for mark-making experiences: (1) the use of a writing tool (e.g., fingers) that neither breaks (like crayons or chalk) nor dries out (like markers or paint); (2) choking hazards are nearly eliminated, as there are no caps or broken pieces; (3) it requires little cleanup; (4) the ease of sharing children's work with families, friends, and the community (when permissions allow); and (5) the possibilities to explore a wider range of multimodal compositions, such as voice, video, and image capturing. Of course, there are several drawbacks as well. Children do not experience the sensory learning provided by making marks with various substances. Furthermore, using a finger as a writing tool rather than one that needs to be grasped (e.g., a paintbrush, a pencil) does not provide the same opportunities to practice their fine motor skills, such as a pincer grip. For these reasons and more, digital mark-making experiences should be provided as a supplement to traditional print mark making.

Digital mark making can sometimes replicate the traditional print mark-making experiences children engage in with paper, crayons, pencils, markers, paints, hole punches, stamps, and more. Most devices

Figure 7.19. Purple and red circles drawn with crayon tools (19 months).

Figure 7.20. A nighttime sky, created with stamp and spray paint tools (3 years, 5 months).

Figure 7.21. Children reading, created with photo, stencil, pen, and paint fill tools (5 years, 1 month).

Box 7.2. Technology and Mark Making (continued)

can access a range of apps that include tools and functions that mimic virtual versions of these materials. For example, a child can draw on screen with the tip of their finger or a stylus just as they might with finger paint on an easel or a marker on paper. Experiences like these can be appropriate when supported by adults in home and early learning settings, especially when traditional mark-making tools may not be accessible or practical (Shuler 2009).

Three examples of digital marks made by children using various devices and digital mark-making software are featured in Figures 7.19, 7.20, and 7.21.

Digital mark making can also significantly differ from print mark making in appearance, function, time, process, and effort. With digital technology, a simple click of a button captures what we see in the world on screen. Another few clicks and the image is altered with filters, overlays, and markups. A few more and the image is sent out to an audience with an accompanying verbal message that might also be converted into a written message. Learning how to accomplish the goals for multimodal compositions requires both simple one-step actions (e.g., creating marks, undoing marks, redoing marks) and more complex, multistep actions (e.g., adding sound, photos, or videos; creating a new document; sending a drawing via email).

Figure 7.22 captures an interaction between Charlie (age 7 years, 2 months) and his younger sister Rosie (age 3 years, 3 months) at the public library. Charlie helped Rosie learn how to import a photo into a word processing app and then allowed Rosie to type some random strings of letters below the photo. They also recorded her voice as she described what was in the photo. Later, they played back the recording, slowing down the speed of Rosie's voice and giggling as they called their mother over to look and listen. Their mother took the opportunity to engage them in media literacy inquiry by questioning what was represented, exploring the reasons why they created the composition, and reflecting on what they learned along the way.

Figure 7.22. Charlie helps Rosie learn how to perform multistep actions on a digital device.

In this example, the marks made were comprised of typed strings of letters, photos, and (altered) voice recordings—a relatively new form of marks young children might explore (e.g., Rowe & Miller 2016).

Shared Experiences That Expand and Extend Digital Mark Making

As noted in Chapter 2, many child health authorities around the world have issued guidelines on screen time for children (AAP Council on Communications and Media et al. 2016; Australian Government Department of Health and Aged Care 2021; Canadian Paediatric Society, Digital Health Task Force 2019; RCPCH 2019; WHO 2019), concluding that there is limited evidence to suggest screen time could benefit the youngest children. "For children younger than 2 years, evidence for benefits of media is still limited, adult interaction with the child during media use is crucial, and there continues to be evidence of harm from excessive digital media use" (AAP Council on Communications and Media et al. 2016, 3). Exploration of digital tools can positively contribute to children's literacy development, especially when older children or adults join in the play and scaffold the child's experiences (Jing et al. 2023; Marsh et al. 2021). Figures 7.19 through 7.21 are examples of developmentally appropriate digital mark-making experiences shared with an adult in ways similar to the print mark-making experiences described throughout this chapter.

Technology also allows adults to share and discuss the marks a child makes with a wide audience. Sharing is appropriate for home, community, and early learning contexts when the child has provided verbal assent and the family has consented. In one such example, a parent discussed emailing a screenshot of digital marks created by Annie (age 19 months) to her grandma (see Figure 7.19). Annie's mother talked to Annie about what she was doing with the message and involved Annie: "Would you like to send this drawing to Grandma? Okay, so let's take a picture of your drawing. Help me press this button and I'll press the one over here at the same time. Then we can press this button with the box and the arrow. That means 'send it.'" Annie's mother went on to compose the message to her grandma. To do so, she typed, inviting Annie to press some of the letters for words that were important to her (e.g., one or more letters in her own name, the *L* in *love*) and the number 4 to tell her grandma how many circles appear in the drawing. The message read, *Dear Grandma, Hope you like the 4 circles I drew for you. Love, Annie.* Grandma replied, *Annie, what BEAUTIFUL purple and red circles! Thank you for sharing. Love, Grandma.*

Message Content in the Making: A Look Inside the Minds of Infants and Toddlers

Infants and toddlers are busy learning a lot about the physical and social worlds. For example, they acquire knowledge about how objects in the physical world behave, the differences between animate and inanimate objects, and the feelings and intentions of people. They also learn to communicate with others and to pretend. Soon after the early period of mark making, children begin to pull more and more from this foundation as they draw and write and use language more and more to tell others all about those markings.

Although the discussion here cannot do justice to all that children learn during the first two or three years of life, we authors have tried to give the reader some sense of how busy infants and toddlers are, not only in acting on the world physically, but also in observing and thinking about what goes on around them. Evidence of all their knowledge is not seen in their early markings or verbal expressions noted here; however, it is evident later in the content of pictures that preschoolers and older children draw and paint, as well as in what they tell adults and what they write about in stories or informational pieces. This knowledge acquisition is discussed here to fill out the picture of the learning during the infant and toddler years that contributes to aspects of writing other than mark making.

Knowledge About the Behavior of Physical Objects

During the first year of life, infants learn some rules that govern the behavior of objects in the physical world. For example, by 7 months old, infants expect a box to fall off a table if pushed very far beyond the table's edge. In laboratory experiments, researchers can prevent boxes in this position from falling by using a hidden prop. Infants look for a very long time at such impossible events because they know objects do not ordinarily behave in this way (Baillargeon, Needham, & DeVos 1992). Infants this age also show surprise (i.e., look longer) when a ball rolls up rather than down an inclined board (Kim & Spelke 1992) and when an object moving through the air stops and remains suspended without anything appearing to support it (Spelke, Phillips, & Woodward 1995).

Within the first year, infants also learn about cause and effect in the physical world. For example, they learn how objects behave when other objects knock into them. Because infants are not yet talking, researchers must infer what infants know and think from how long they look (i.e., longer when surprised or puzzled). Here's what infants figure out:

> **At 6 months,** they act surprised (i.e., look longer) when any object does not move when another object collides with it.

> **At 8 months,** they know that objects move longer and farther when the colliding object is larger rather than smaller one (Baillargeon 1995; Kotovsky & Baillargeon 1994, 1998, 2000).

> **At 9 months,** they no longer show surprise when some tall, narrow objects don't move when hit. For example, infants learn from exploring while crawling that table and chair legs and the poles between a railing and stairs are attached and don't budge when pushed, pulled, or bumped into (Wang, Kaufman, & Baillargeon 2003).

> **At 10 months,** they no longer show surprise when an unattached object doesn't move when hit. Experiences like pulling books off shelves, trying to push heavy baskets of magazines, and manipulating various pots and pans teach infants that some items are hard to move—are heavy—while others are easy to move—are lighter (Wang, Kaufman, & Baillargeon 2003).

Given the knowledge they are acquiring, it is no wonder that toddlers painting at an easel return paintbrushes to a cup or tray rather than release them midair or show no surprise when a hole appears in their paper after they have rubbed a paint-filled brush over and over it, while no hole is worn in the solid easel frame behind it. It is also no wonder that, when representing object relations and their actions, preschoolers know enough to make comments, such as, "The ball knocked into that wall and then landed over here. (*Points to the wall and where the ball was deflected in painting.*) It didn't hit a window like my brother's ball did one time."

Categories of Things

By 11 months, infants also know some specific behaviors and functions associated with many categories of things. For example, they are more likely to give a toy person a ride in a vehicle of any kind than they are to give a ride to a toy person on an animal. Conversely, they are likely to put any kind of animal to bed after seeing someone model this behavior, but they are highly unlikely to put vehicles to bed (Mandler & McDonough 1998; McDonough & Mandler 1998).

Between 7 and 9 months old, infants can distinguish among the actions they see actors on screen perform, such as walking, jumping, or bending. They recognize each action's unique features, even when each action is performed somewhat differently by different people (Pulverman et al. 2006). When drawing and painting later, preschoolers and older children depict people in ways that portray these different actions using this early understanding. Furthermore, they use the correct term (*walk, bend, jump*) for each action as they describe it if they have heard adults link each specific term to its respective action.

Infants also begin very early to distinguish between animate and inanimate objects. For example, by 2 months old, they more frequently vocalize to and smile at a live person than to a doll (Legerstee 1992; Legerstee, Corter, & Kienapple 1990). By 6 months, they begin to realize that people behave differently toward animate and inanimate things (Legerstee 1991) and that these two categories of things also behave differently. For example, 7-month-olds look longer at a ball or a chair that appears to move spontaneously than at a person who moves because they know that inanimate objects are *not* supposed to do this (Poulin-Dubois & Shultz 1990; Spelke, Phillips, & Woodward 1995). Similarly, 16-month-olds show no surprise when a dog or a person climbs stairs or jumps over a block in a movie, but they are surprised (i.e., look longer) when a movie shows a car or a bus jumping over a wall (Poulin-Dubois & Forbes 2006).

Older infants also attribute intentions to humans (Myowa-Yamakoshi et al. 2011). For example, in one study, 18-month-olds saw either a human model or a mechanical model perform the very same action of placing beads beside a cup. When it was their turn to handle the beads, toddlers who watched the human model's placement of beads put the beads in the cup, while toddlers who observed the mechanical model's placement of beads put the beads on the table, just as they had observed (Meltzoff 1995). The researchers concluded that the first group of toddlers assumed, based on the knowledge acquired from observing humans, that the human models intended to put the beads in the cup but failed.

Knowing the typical behavior of things allows children to create something funny by subverting expected behavior in a drawing or a painting. This knowledge about animate versus inanimate things also allows preschoolers and older children to appreciate fiction without becoming terribly misinformed about the real world. Inspired by his love of the television show, *Veggie Tales*, 3-year-old Alex drew a picture of radishes (Figure 7.23). (In this picture, he also included letters in his name.) This showed his dual appreciation—delight in the talking veggies and knowledge about the real ones.

Figure 7.23. Alex's radishes (pink marks) and letters in his name (blue marks) (3 years, 9 months).

Building Blocks of Communication: Emotional Expression and Identification, Emotional Understanding, and Empathy

Writing is the expression of ideas and information using symbolic representation. This section overviews how very young children develop basic communicative skills that become the basis for creating messages they capture with emergent writing during the preschool years and with conventional writing later on.

Newborns cry when hungry or uncomfortable and prefer looking at faces over objects (Meltzoff & Kuhl 2016). Adults interpret an infant's gaze toward their face as regard for them and respond (Kaye & Fogel 1980). Between 1 and 2 months, infants begin to smile socially at people who smile at and talk to them, and they begin to gaze more at people's eyes (Brazelton et al. 1975; Stern et al. 1975). By 3 months, infants use smile and gaze to regulate their interactions with family members and educators. Specifically, they break gaze to stop an interaction and maintain gaze and coo more to keep one going. A list of milestones for social interaction and language from 3 to 36 months is provided in Table 7.1.

Emotional expression and identification. Infants and toddlers are also learning about emotions and social behavior. Infants express emotions from the minute they are born, and adults can soon tell when an infant is happy, sad, angry, or surprised. Infants smile a lot by 2 or 3 months when people talk and smile at them, but not when viewing a sad face (Termine & Izard 1988). By 4 months, infants laugh (Sroufe & Wunsch 1972). By 6 months, they show anger and sadness to unresponsive mothers (Weinberg & Tronick 1996) and look at family members or educators to understand an unfamiliar person or event (Walle, Reschke, & Knothe 2017). Between 18 and 24 months, toddlers add more complicated, self-conscious emotions to their repertoires (e.g., guilt, embarrassment, and shame) (Lewis et al. 1989). Pride is expressed a bit later, at around 28 months (Lewis, Alessandri, & Sullivan 1992).

In addition to experiencing and expressing emotions, infants gradually learn to distinguish facial expressions that signal different emotions in others. By 7 or 8 months, infants have learned to distinguish expressions for happiness, sadness, fear, anger, and surprise (Barrera & Maurer 1981; Bornstein et al. 2011; Di Lorenzo et al. 2019; LaBarbera et al. 1976).

Between 18 and 30 months, toddlers build a vocabulary for naming and talking about many emotions and affective behaviors. These words include *happy, sad, funny, mad, yucky, cry, laugh, surprised, scared,* and many more (Bretherton & Beeghly 1982; Dunn, Bretherton, & Munn 1987).

Emotional understanding. Although 7- or 8-month-olds use visual information to distinguish among different facial expressions, they do not yet understand the meanings of the emotions they see people express. By 10 months, however, infants engage in ***social referencing***— looking back and forth between a familiar adult and something in their immediate environment that is of concern to the infant, such as a stranger or an unfamiliar toy (Sorce et al. 1985; Vaish & Sriano 2004). For example, if an infant's parent smiles at a stranger, the infant is more likely to approach the stranger than if the infant's parent scowls or looks worried when a stranger is present. Although infants this age use emotion information they infer from facial expressions to guide their *own* behavior, they are not able to use the facial expressions they observe alone to

Table 7.1. Typical Milestones in Social Interaction and Verbal Communication

Age	Milestones
3 months	• Begin to coordinate their smiles, vocalizations, gazes, and other responses with adults (Bloom 1977; Condon 1979) • Begin to imitate and repeat pitch, loudness, and duration of mother's vocalization to communicate and connect (Gratier & Devouche 2011)
6 months	• Begin to follow others' head and eye movements, but look only in the general direction not at the specific target and are distracted by intermediary objects (Butterworth & Jarrett 1991)
7 months	• Respond more consistently to the pauses that mothers leave for them and more often use vocalizations rather than other behaviors (e.g., yawns, smiles, burps) when taking their turn (Snow 1977) • Often verbalize to greet a familiar person who looks at them (Kaye & Fogel 1980)
9 to 11 months	• Locate the target of another's gaze, if pointing is combined with it, when objects are in visual field (Corkum & Moore 1995) • Understand intentions of others to communicate (Stephens & Matthews 2014)
12 months	• Follow point and gaze more reliably to targets not close to the visual field (Flom et al. 2004) • Are skilled in the alternating pattern of interaction typical of conversation in their culture (Broerse & Elias 1994) • Understand quite a few words and begin to speak a few
18 to 20 months	• Combine words to form rudimentary sentences • Expressive vocabulary begins to increase fairly rapidly
24 to 36 months	• Syntactic and grammatical skills increase steadily • Use gaze fairly skillfully to signal listening to a conversational partner (i.e., look at the speaker in sustained way); look away as they begin taking a turn before looking back at the listener to make sure they are listening (Rutter & Durkin 1987) • Respond quite consistently when spoken to and initiate verbal interactions • Learn to talk about the causes of feelings and other mental states in relation to themselves and others • Use mental state talk in pretend play (Bretherton & Beeghly 1982; Dunn, Bretherton, & Munn 1987)

predict the future behavior of others until they are about 18 months old (Repacholi & Gopnik 1997).

The development of empathy. In laboratory studies, infants between 1 and 9 months cry when they hear the recorded cry of another infant (Geangu et al. 2010). However, in natural settings with their mothers and other infants, 6-month-olds rarely cry when a peer cries. Instead, they might try to touch the infant, only transitioning from showing concern to becoming distressed themselves when another child's crying continues for a long time (Hay, Nash, & Pederson 1981).

Although infants between 6 and 12 months respond with affect and concern to others' distress and prefer people who help rather than hinder others' actions (Hamlin, Wynn, & Bloom 2007), they do not yet try to provide comfort to the distressed person (e.g., pat them on the back, offer words of comfort) or seek help (e.g., call to an adult). By 16 months, these prosocial behaviors are quite common, unless the other person's distress continues for a long time or is very intense. In these situations, the toddler becomes distressed quickly and is unable to act for the benefit of the other person. There are, however, individual differences, with some babies more likely than others to become distressed quickly when observing distress in others (Roth-Hanania, Davidov, & Waxler 2011; Ungerer et al. 1990).

Studies about emotional understanding also indicate that, by 18 months, toddlers begin to realize that different people can have different feelings about the same thing. Such understanding, which continues to develop for years, also positions the young child to understand the characters in stories and the conflicts that might occur among them. The topics of other people's feelings and differences in feeling among people also begin to appear in young children's writing and drawing.

Concluding Thoughts

Infants' first early marks take form on the paper by accident, not by design. But before long, toddlers begin to exert some control by repeating marks whose accidental appearance catches their attention. This behavior marks the transition from the first to the second phase of early mark making. A bit later, something new begins. As Gardner (1980) describes it, "the child is establishing a vocabulary of lines and forms—the basic building blocks of a graphic language—which, like the sounds of language, eventually combine into meaningful, referential units" (11). The dawning of the idea that marks can represent meaning is the transition from the second to the third phase of early mark making described in this chapter.

In early learning settings, educators can display photographs of children engaged in drawing or painting, along with the markings they have created, on a bulletin board where families can see them. These might inspire some families to provide similar experiences at home, if they do not already do so. For a variety of reasons, though, sometimes mark-making experiences cannot be provided at home. These families will be especially grateful to teachers who make an effort to provide their children with these experiences.

Infants and toddlers are very busy learners who acquire the understanding that humans have goals and intentions and that conditions sometimes hinder their ability to achieve them. This knowledge positions older toddlers and young preschoolers to both understand and generate stories in which humans and animals behave differently than inanimate objects. By preschool, children subvert these typical ways of behaving in the real world to create some humor in their everyday life and fictional stories.

This chapter also discussed young children's understandings of facial expressions. It is no wonder that toddlers sometimes show great interest in the facial expressions of children and adults they see in books or that they can label characters' feelings when adults read to them. Feelings also sometimes show up in young preschoolers' first representational drawings and paintings.

Some of the strong correlations between early book-reading experiences and later success in reading might come from the fact that books for toddlers involve some of the knowledge and understandings that they are just beginning to acquire (see Chapter 2). When adults share books and talk with toddlers about a book's content, children's knowledge is strengthened, and children also learn more language that is needed to talk about it. Even in this early period, it is evident how reading books to children and offering opportunities for children to tell all about what they draw and write are mutually supportive.

CHAPTER 8

WRITING DURING THE PRESCHOOL YEARS

Chara, 34 months old, creates two short vertical lines in her finger painting. When finished, she looks up and says, "Two legs." After she makes a horizontal line above the legs, she glances up again and announces, "A mouth." Next, she makes a small curved line that resembles an arch. "It's sad," she explains. Before breaking gaze, she adds, "I need a head." Chara turns back to her finger painting and draws a circle around the two mouths.

"Why did you make the face sad?" Chara's teacher asks. Chara looks up and replies, "I want it sad." She smears paint over the lines, making them disappear. Next, she looks up, smiles, and looks back down as she says, "I need more paint." After the finger paint is replenished, Chara continues to explore by squishing it in her hands, rubbing her paint-filled palms up and down her arms, and spreading paint all over her paper.

At almost 3 years old, Chara knew the names and relative locations of basic human body parts and understood the facial expressions that matched many feelings. Additionally, her language was adequate for engaging in a conversation, and she knew how people in her culture use gaze to monitor a conversational partner's listening and the beginning and ending of turns.

Given Chara's hefty store of knowledge about all sorts of things and her long history of mark making (almost two years of experience by 34 months), this soon-to-be preschooler was not only poised to draw something that was in her mind, but also equipped to tell all about it.

In this chapter, the discussion of both mark making and representational skill begun in Chapter 7 continues. This chapter discusses how preschool children combine picture making (i.e., drawing or painting) and writing marks to capture their meanings. It also considers preschoolers' uses of writing and drawing, the complexity and content of their drawings, and their interest in these activities. The chapter is organized around four phases that match the following ages:

> Phase 1: 2½ to 3 years old

> Phase 2: 3 to 4 years old

> Phase 3: 4 to 5 years old

> Phase 4: 5 years to about 5 years, 9 months old (including children who turn 5 during the school year)

It is important to note that the age range for each phase is an approximation. As noted in Chapter 7, providing mark-making experiences for infants and toddlers is not as common as reading to very young children. Consequently, the age at which various writing and drawing behaviors appear is likely to vary more widely than the age at which language and vocabulary skills develop. In other words, children with more mark-making experiences may reach later phases sooner than their peers with fewer mark-making experiences.

For each phase of writing and drawing, the chapter provides a general picture of what children do and links it to learning on three fronts: physical mark making (i.e., writing letters and drawing pictures), word creation, and meaning making. Comments about conditions that support both skill acquisition and interest are offered throughout.

Phase 1: Writing Begins to Look Like Writing and "Says" Something

In Chapter 7, Chara and Sydney included letter-like forms in scribble drawings, and Grayden made spiral marks. Although Chara and Sydney knew that *C* and *S* were in their respective names, neither child said, "That says . . . " or "Oh, that's me!" Likewise, after making spirals, Grayden did not say, "Those are pinwheels." Letters and spirals were simple depictions, identified by name. At best, the letters were associated with someone (e.g., "*C* is for Chara," "*T* is for Tricia").

This mark-making behavior resembles an early form of pretend play in which children relate objects functionally but are not "in role." Role playing, such as taking on the role of mommy cooking or daddy feeding a baby, appears around 28 to 30 months. (For more on pretend play behavior, see Box 7.1 in Chapter 7.) A somewhat similar transformation toward the symbolic use of letters and other designs appears in drawing and writing behavior around 30 months. Although children still sometimes depict various lines and alphabet letters, as well as people and other items (Figure 8.1), they also now use lines or individual marks *as writing*—the marks "say" something. Sometimes, children now also set out to draw something specific, rather than attribute meanings to paintings and drawings only after exploratory mark making brought something specific to mind. Finally, preschoolers separate drawing marks from their writing marks fairly consistently and organize writing marks linearly.

Getting into the Role of Writer

At 32 months, Chara wrote a grocery list using wavy lines. As she wrote, she named food items aloud (e.g., "eggs, milk, beets"), mimicking her mother's list-making behavior. Her mother also wrote words on Chara's paper when she requested it. (See Figures 5.1 and 5.3 in Chapter 5.) Starting at about 34 months, Chara sometimes wrote alphabet letters—approximations, not conventional forms—without intending to convey any meaning. In other words, she was not making a list or writing a note to someone. Instead, she was writing as if practicing. Most letters she wrote did not resemble their conventional forms very closely. In Figure 8.2, she wrote three *C*s as she was saying, "*C, C, C, C.*" Then, she said "*H, I, J, K*" as she made additional marks.

Adam used wavy lines to write his father's name on an envelope for a Father's Day card that he made in response to his mother's suggestion (Figure 8.3). He wrote his name as a return address by making a wavy line across the top of the envelope. A few days later, he placed himself in the role of writer to make "a letter to Daddy," using similar wavy lines.

Separating Writing and Drawing and Organizing Writing into Lines

In the grocery list, card envelope, and letter examples, Chara and Adam used only writing— wavy lines or individual marks organized linearly. However, in much of their mark making at this time, they used both pictures (or decorations) and writing, which they separated.

Figure 8.1. Adam's picture of the letter *A* and people at 34 months.

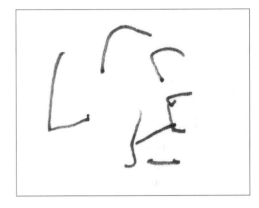

Figure 8.2. Chara's letter practice.

Figure 8.3. Adam's Father's Day card envelope.

Figure 8.4. Chara's card with her name signed at the bottom (34 months).

Figure 8.5. Adam separates writing from pictures.

For example, Chara added letter-like marks (apparently her name) to a card she created for a friend (Figure 8.4) without writing on top of paper decorations she made on it. Her mother had written messages recently in some valentines they made together, which modeled separating writing from decorations.

Adam also separated writing and picture marks. Adam explained that his scribble words (lower right) said "Dear Mommy, I love you. Dear Daddy, I love you too" (Figure 8.5). The authors have seen this awareness across many children, including their acknowledgment of the distinctions between writing and pictures. For example, one 5-year-old explained, "This is my picture, and my name, and lots of words." Another commented "my name" while pointing to wavy lines at the bottom edge of their paper and "my picture" when gesturing toward a scribble mass.

Although many children distinguish between writing and picture marks by about 3 years old, some do not. For example, Tyler (3 years, 5 months) wrote his name on paper in the block area using a mass of scribble that an adult could easily have thought was a picture. He had limited marking experience prior to preschool, but once enrolled, Tyler spent considerable time in the block area with children who routinely made signs for their buildings. He also watched his teacher write in some whole group situations.

With access to writing tools and adult models to observe in preschool, Tyler figured out that marks intended as writing are organized differently than picture marks. Several months later (at 3 years, 8 months), he began using individual marks, all lined up, for his name. A few months after that, his marks somewhat resembled the letters in his name.

Attributing Meaning to Pictures

Although preschoolers continue to paint and draw freely without attributing meaning to their marks, they are more inclined to attribute meaning to their marks than they were as toddlers. By now, they realize that people use marks primarily to represent meaning. For example, after painting with watercolors one day, an adult asked Chara to tell them about her paintings. Chara said that one was "The sun and all the world" (Figure 8.6) and the other was "A trail with cool, soft, squelchy mud" (Figure 8.7).

Chara borrowed the words for Figure 8.7 from a favorite book, *Rain,* by Manya Stojic. When the rain stops in the book, the rhino says that he can no longer feel the rain, but he can "lie in the cool, soft, squelchy mud." Chara liked these words and sometimes repeated them during readings of this book. Interestingly, her mother had also recently modeled using text from a book in a message that she wrote on a gift tag for some baked goods. Chara's idea of using book wording to label her painting marks might have been inspired by her mother's example.

Chara could have attributed any number of meanings to her watercolor paintings because they did not strongly resemble any specific thing. But just as with dramatic play, younger preschoolers are willing to use one object to stand for another, even when the object does not closely look like what it represents. Only a hint of resemblance in the picture (i.e., a few brown spots) is reason enough for Chara to give it meaning (i.e., "cool, soft, squelchy mud"). This willingness to see something in almost anything declines in the 4-year-old.

Sometimes, children now also set out intentionally to draw a picture, rather than attribute meaning only to marks already made as before. This new behavior indicates increased cognitive growth, including the beginning of the ability to plan. An example with a single item depicted is shown in Figure 8.8.

Figure 8.6. Chara's "sun" painting.

Figure 8.7. Chara's "trail" painting.

Figure 8.8. Adam's person (35 months).

Summing Up Phase 1

By about age 3, children get into the role of writer and often create that writing using wavy lines or individual letter-like squiggles that are all lined up. Many children this age begin to separate writing from picture marks. They also sometimes try to write their names, although their marks don't always resemble actual letters. Children are increasingly likely to attribute meaning to pictures that start out as explorations. They also begin to draw pictures intentionally. Sometimes, information and scenes from familiar books inspire the meanings children attribute to their drawings and paintings.

When assessing a child's understanding, such as their knowledge about the organization of picture marks versus writing marks, multiple samples of marking should be drawn from a range of contexts. The child's intention for each sample should also be considered because these influence their behavior. For example, if a preschool teacher were assessing Adam's understanding, it would be appropriate to consider the samples shown in Figures 8.1 and 8.5, among others.

Finally, a child's history of experience must also be taken into account when drawing conclusions following an assessment. Even at this age, writing and drawing skills vary widely among children because their experiences have differed. For example, Tyler had virtually no mark-making experience before entering preschool. Not surprisingly, his writing level differed from Adam's and Chara's, but with access, acceptance, and support, Tyler's writing developed just fine. If you are interested in a more in-depth assessment of young children's writing, consult Chapter 6 in *Writing in Preschool* (Schickedanz & Casbergue 2009).

Phase 2: Names, Mock Words, and Detailed Pictures

When children are between 3 and 4 years old, they become quite interested in trying to write their names and other words, and they include more details in their drawings and paintings. Children also have more to say when adults talk with them about their writing and drawing.

Children Write Their Names

The evolution of Adam's name writing is shown in Figures 8.9 through 8.13. In the first sample (Figure 8.9), one mark resembled *A,* but the others did not resemble any letters in his name. By 33 months, Adam had added an *M* of sorts, using a little circle inside "goal posts" to carve out its inside (Figure 8.10). By 41 months, Adam's *A*s and *M*s were very recognizable, and his *D* was a circle whose left side Adam "flattened" by adding lines (Figure 8.11). Adam knew how the conventional forms of these letters looked, and he managed to create better and better versions through experimentation. At this point, he could not figure out any other way to make *D* straight on its left side. By 43 months, Adam had solved this problem (Figures 8.12 and 8.13), probably from information he obtained from his mother's demonstrations. She would say, "Here's another way to make *D* with a straight side," and then modeled using two separate strokes, starting with a straight vertical line on the left and then adding a curved line to its right side.

Figure 8.9. Adam's name writing at 32 months.

Figure 8.10. Adam's name writing at 33 months.

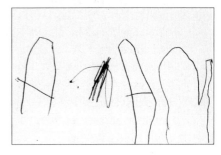

Figure 8.11. Adam's name writing at 41 months.

Figure 8.12. Adam's name writing at 43 months, first version.

Figure 8.13. Adam's name writing at 43 months, second version.

Because children typically see letters that have already been formed, they do not realize that more than one stroke is made to compose most letters. They also sometimes envision more strokes than are actually used in a letter (e.g., two short horizontal lines to form the top of *T,* not one continuous line). The letter clue game described in Box 5.3 in Chapter 5 helps preschoolers understand that letters are composed of multiple segments.

Some children are content for a while to use mostly placeholders for the letters in their names. For example, when signing a picture at preschool, 3-year-old Audrey wrote six circles as she recited the names of each letter in her name aloud in order. *R* and *Y* are difficult letters to form, which encourages placeholder use. Additionally, when Audrey entered preschool, she was familiar with Chinese characters, not English letters. Within a few months, however, the English letters she formed became quite recognizable.

Figure 8.14. Adam's writing of the word *Daddy*.

Figure 8.15. Zola writes *I love you* and signs her name.

Figure 8.16. Adam's writing of *tiger* at 44 months, which he copied from his mother's writing on the chalkboard.

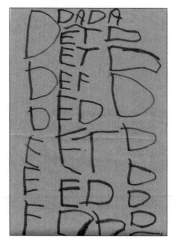

Figure 8.17. Adam's list of mock words.

Interest in Words

Children often become interested in words other than their names. These include names of siblings, preschool friends, and parents and grandparents (e.g., *mommy, nana, papa, daddy*). Children copy these words or write the letters needed for a name as an adult dictates them. At 39 months, Adam wrote *daddy* on a birthday card envelope as his mother dictated each letter (Figure 8.14).

While chatting with her mother in Mandarin and English, Zola (45 months) wrote a note to her mother in English that said *I love you* and signed her name above the message (Figure 8.15). The letters were recognizable and mostly conventional. With name-writing knowledge from preschool in mind, she likely applied letter and sound knowledge to the spelling of her message. She might have seen hearts associated with messages of love and decided to color in the last mark accordingly.

When they are a bit older, children are sometimes interested in spelling the names of familiar things. For example, when at school with his mother one day, Adam wanted to see a classroom. He noticed the chalkboard and asked his mother to write words that he dictated. She wrote *cat, tiger, dragon, picture,* and other words, which he copied onto pieces of paper (Figure 8.16). A month later, at home, Adam requested the word game again. Just as before, he dictated the words, and then copied them after his mother had written them down.

Sometimes, 3-year-olds also create mock words, which are based on visual information acquired from observing words in the environment. But visual information alone does not provide information about how letters are selected. (See Table 8.1 later in this chapter for a discussion of the various strategies preschoolers use to create words.)

At 43 months, Adam started with a known word (*dada*) and then, using these and a few other letters (*E, F, T*), created several mock words (Figure 8.17).

Children often make grocery lists when in the house area to support their dramatic play. Teachers can put paper there as a prop for this purpose as well as others, such as creating lists of instructions for babysitters who were "called" to take care of the doll babies. Lily used letter strings to create a list of people she wanted to attend her birthday party (Figure 8.18).

Pictures Become More Detailed

Children's pictures become more detailed and often tell a story, rather than simply depict a single object. For example, at 37 months, Livi drew several people and said, "This is our family at the circus" (Figure 8.19). At 42 months, Adam drew "a cave with frosting decorations and a mommy, daddy, brother, and sister inside" (Figure 8.20).

Sometimes, children still draw single items or people, but these typically include more details than pictures they drew when younger (Figure 8.21).

Every drawing provides an opportunity to talk with a child if that child is interested. In the process, language development is nurtured, knowledge is expanded, and narrative and expository skills are honed. These conversations have consequences for children's later composing skills (Peterson, Jesso, & McCabe 1999). Talking with children about their drawings is discussed further in Box 8.1.

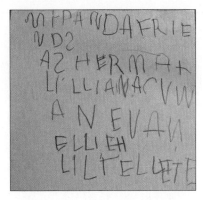

Figure 8.18. Lily's list of invitees to her birthday party (4 years, 8 months).

Figure 8.19. Livi's picture of her family at the circus, where they recently visited.

Figure 8.20. Adam's picture of a family in a cave.

Figure 8.21. Adam's "man with a beard."

Box 8.1. Talking with Children About Their Drawings

When sharing books with young children, talking together about the book is as important as reading it. Although there is no specific research about the effect of talking with young children about their drawings, what is known from studies of parental talking with young children about their immediate past experiences (e.g., Peterson, Jesso, & McCabe 1999) and from studies of the effects of teacher-child talk in a variety of preschool contexts (e.g., Dickinson & Porche 2011; Rowe & Snow 2020) can apply.

In general, studies point to several features of talk that support children's language development:

> Teachers extend conversation—keep it going—by contributing information and asking questions.

> Teachers use sophisticated vocabulary (i.e., higher-level words) rather than more common words.

> Teachers correct inaccuracies of fact in children's statements. For example, they might say, "Oh, that's called a *whisk* not a *broom*. Brooms have bristles, and we sweep with them. This whisk has wire loops, and we mix things up with it."

A picture, such as Livi's of her family at the circus (Figure 8.19), which was drawn at home, could be used to help Livi tell personal narratives. Consider the richness of this potential conversation Livi's mom and dad might have with her:

Mom: Oh, yes, we did go to the circus last week. How did we get there?

Livi: We drove a long time.

Mom: Yes, we had to drive all the way into Boston, and that's quite a long distance.

Dad: After we parked the car, we had to ride the train to the circus, didn't we?

Livi: And the sky went away.

Dad: Yes, we rode underground on the trolley, and we couldn't see the trees or buildings or the sky for a while.

Mom: What animal at the circus did you like the best?

Livi: I like the elephant, and the people ride on him!

Mom: Oh, yes, the elephants were carrying people in seats on their backs, weren't they? Were there any other animals you liked a lot?

Summing Up Phase 2

Between 3 and 4 years old, children become more aware of letters, especially those in their names, and they write them in ways that resemble more closely each letter's conventional form. There is variation in skill across children due to differences in fine motor skill and differences among children in their familiarity with specific letter forms.

Children also become interested in writing words at this time, and they create letter strings that look like words. Of course, children have little, if any, understanding at this point of how letters are *actually* selected to make words.

Children's pictures become more detailed and provide wonderful starting points for conversations with adults.

Phase 3: Writing and Drawing Come into Full Bloom

During this phase, which spans 4 to 5 years old, children put writing to even more uses, create letters that are closer and closer to conventional form, and begin to understand why specific letters are selected to spell each word. Drawings also become more complex because children have more cognitive power and a wider range of experience from which to draw content.

The samples in this section are from a diverse group of children, some monolingual, some multilingual, and some with developmental challenges. This section discusses several children by showing multiple samples of their writing and drawing that were created in different contexts across a few months. For others, only a sample or two are provided.

Using Writing for a Variety of Purposes

Tracey (4½ years old) wanted to gift her mother with a watercolor painting, and she determined she needed a gift tag (Figure 8.22). She knew how to write her name and the word *love*. (She had requested it many times.) Like many 4-year-olds, however, Tracey did not plan the use of the limited space on the small piece of paper she selected for making her gift tag. After finishing *T, R, A,* and *C* and realizing that she would likely run out of space, she made a very skinny *E*. Even with this adaptation, she still lacked enough space for the top of *Y*. To solve this problem, she placed the *Y*'s top on the line above, after the *E* in *love,* and then drew its long lower part down to join the other letters in her name.

Figure 8.22. Tracey's gift tag.

One day, after building a library in the block area, Angelina wanted to make a sign to label it. The teacher she asked for help in spelling *library* segmented the sounds in the word, one by one, and dictated the letters used to represent each one. When Angelina reached the paper's edge after writing *R,* the teacher noticed and advised, "Go over to the other side and put *A* under *L*."

Figure 8.23. Angelina's library sign.

But Angelina insisted that *A* belonged under *R*, explaining, "They have to go together" (i.e., letters that follow in a word should be placed close together physically). She had not yet learned to sweep to the left and then move to the right when placing print on paper or some other surface, or when reading it (Figure 8.23).

Tracey and Angelina wrote for many other purposes as well, and so did Gabriela. Her writing during preschool is featured in Figures 8.24 through 8.27. For example, she wrote her nickname, Gabi, and decorated it and added funny letters and an overabundance of the lowercase *i*, which she turned into flowers (Figure 8.24). Once she wrote a name (Brownie) for a new classroom gerbil. A teacher segmented the sounds in this word, and Gabi selected letters to represent these sounds and wrote the words. After realizing that she didn't have a letter to represent /n/ in *Brownie*, Gabi squeezed one in, writing *M* rather than *N* (Figure 8.25). Gabi also wrote a sign for block play that said *Danger, Alligators* (DNG LGAT) and another saying *No Pets* (NO PATS) (Figures 8.26 and 8.27). In response to her request for spelling help, a teacher segmented the sounds in the words, and Gabi selected letters to represent them.

Figure 8.24. Decorated form of *Gabi* (4 years, 5 months).

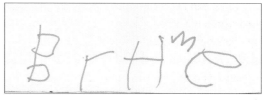

Figure 8.25. *Brownie,* a suggested gerbil name (4 years, 6 months).

Figure 8.26. *Danger, Alligators* block area sign (4 years, 8 months).

Figure 8.27. *No Pets* block area sign (4 years, 8 months).

Purposes for writing also include sharing understandings from stories or curricular content, and examples may reflect a broad spectrum of young writers' skills. Figure 8.28 is a journal message by 5-year-old Lucy in which she tries to pinpoint the crux of Rainbow Fish's struggle in *The Rainbow Fish,* by Marcus Pfister. Using a variety of uppercase and lowercase letters in phonologically based spellings, she wrote *He did not want to give up a fin* (He Dit not Wut to GiVua fn). She knew the spellings of a few common words (*he, not, to*) and adhered carefully to her own pronunciations of the words to spell the rest. (Lucy was also learning vocabulary specific to the story, such as a *scale* versus a *fin*.) When writing about more open-ended possibilities for a character in a different story a few weeks later, Lucy opted for lengthy letter strings (Figure 8.29), perhaps because encoding all of her ideas seemed daunting.

Within a unit about community helpers, 5-year-old Noah used mostly conventionally spelled words to share an understanding about firefighters while still working out the finer details of form, writing uppercase and lowercase *F* (Figure 8.30).

One day at preschool, Adam copied the name of a favorite song, "Head, Shoulders, Knees, and Toes," from a list of songs he saw on a large piece of chart paper (Figure 8.31). At home, during an episode of solitary pretend play, he left a sign on the sofa warning creatures to stay away (Figure 8.32).

In the next set of examples, children wrote letters to the authors or family members to share a variety of special messages. After their teacher shared a book Judy (one of the authors) had sent and suggested that the children write thank-you letters to her, a child drew a picture and wrote mock words (Figure 8.33).

Figure 8.28. Lucy's message about Rainbow Fish's dilemma.

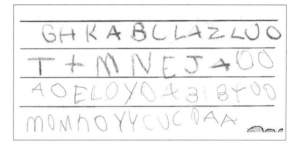

Figure 8.29. Lucy's letter strings about an idea for a character in a story.

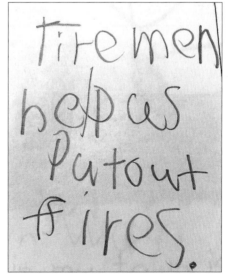

Figure 8.30. Noah's note about community helpers.

Figure 8.31. Adam's favorite song in preschool (4 years, 8 months).

Figure 8.32. Adam's note to tell creatures to stay away (4 years, 6 months). Mock words are used, but *Roo*—name of preschool pet gerbil—is included as a base.

Figure 8.33. Thank-you letter to Judy from a 4-year-old.

Figure 8.34. Message in condolence card and corresponding drawing.

Figure 8.35. A 5-year-old's letter in Korean.

When Molly's (one of the authors) mother passed away, two young neighbors, ages 6 and 3, wrote a condolence card and drew a picture, respectively (Figure 8.34). A 5-year-old learning Korean and English wrote his grandparents a letter with the message *Grandma, I love you. Grandpa, I love you,* and then signed his name (Figure 8.35).

The children ranged in age from 3 years old to a bit over 6 years old. No matter the level of skill, adults accepted all of the children's marks.

Making Words

Young 4-year-olds often use mock words to fill pages of a book, write multiword messages, or create artifacts for pretend play. In all situations, children know they can convey their message when telling interested teachers or peers what the writing they have created says.

For older preschoolers, mock words often coexist with words they make using other strategies. For example, 4-year-old Ella used mock words to create a turn-taking signup list for a pretend sandbox in the block area because she said it could accommodate only two children at a time (Figure 8.36). All but one of the names she created for her list (*Coco*) were mock words (the pretend children's names). Interestingly, though, Ella's competence at the time far exceeded the mock word approach. For example, just a few months after making this list, she made a maze game with blocks and a poster to advertise it. She generated spellings for the ad by segmenting sounds in words and matching these to letter names (*Please come to the . . .*). After making the poster, she also wrote a note to invite the teacher (*Please come*) (Figure 8.37).

At about the same time, Ella made a book by stapling half-size pieces of paper together. Her book was about fairies. Ella invented spellings on the first page (*One day the fairies went out and they saw a toad*) and used some invented spellings on the second page (Figure 8.38). For the third page, she resorted to writing mock words. Beginning on the fourth page and continuing through page 24, she used scribble writing. Most likely, she changed her approach because generating spellings for words, and even writing specific letters for mock words, was too much work for the long book that she had in mind.

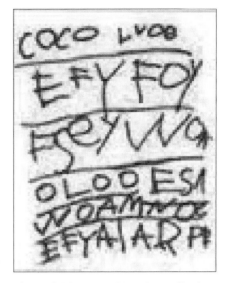

Figure 8.36. Turn-taking signup list for the sandbox (4 years, 5 months).

Figure 8.37. Note inviting the teacher to see the maze game (4 years, 10 months).

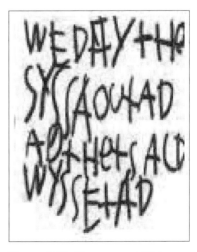

Figure 8.38. First page of Ella's book, "The Fairies."

Figure 8.39. Adam's words copied from mother's paper after he dictated them (3 years, 9 months).

Figure 8.40. Adam's words copied from mother's paper after he dictated them, with *cat* spelled with a *K* instead of a *C* (3 years, 9 months).

As is true with most learning, children are proficient at any time with some word-creation strategies, while their grasp of others is tentative. Since tentative strategies take considerably more effort than familiar ones (Siegler & Alibali 2005), children use these when writing only a little or for just the first page when writing a lot. Children give up scribble writing when they can form letters quickly enough to make this strategy as practical as scribble writing (see Table 8.1).

Sometimes, younger children also generate spellings (Read 1975). For example, Adam asked his mother to write down some words he dictated to her so that he could then copy them. After she had spelled *cat*, Adam copied it (Figure 8.39). He then rewrote *cat* on a different piece of paper (Figure 8.40) without looking at his copied version. This time, he used *K*, not *C*, as the first letter.

Perhaps his mother's segmentation of first sounds in this word and others before writing them for Adam to copy had an effect (e.g., "Okay, *cat*—/k/at. We use *C* to write the first sound in *cat*"). Adam linked the /k/ sound to the first sound in the letter *K*'s name and wondered why his mother had used *C* (i.e., /k/ is not the sound we hear when naming the letter *C*). Maybe he decided to rewrite the word, thinking, "This time, I'm going to write it right!"

Following this episode, Adam did not generate any phonemic-based spellings for about a year. Instead, he used syllable-based spellings, asked for spellings, and sometimes created mock words. Often, when he asked for spellings, his preschool teacher segmented the sounds in the words he wanted and matched a letter to them, or she asked Adam to select a letter that he thought would go with the sounds. (See Box 8.2.)

At 56 months, when adding *peanuts* and *cheese crackers* to a grocery list (Figure 8.41), Adam first wrote *P* and *E* when spelling *peanuts*, and then asked, "What's next?" His mother said *A* and then segmented /n/ before saying the letter *N*'s name. Adam determined on his own that the letters *T* and *S* were needed to finish writing *peanuts* (PEANTS).

Before starting to write *cheese*, he asked how to write /ch/. His mother said that *C* and *H* are used together. He wrote *C* and lowercase *h,* and then represented the next sound he heard in *cheese* with one letter *E*. Then he added *S*. After writing *C, R,* and *A* for *crackers*, he asked whether he should use *C* or *K* next. His mother said that he could use either one. (Today, she would tell him instead that both letters are used together in this word to write the sound. At the time, she didn't want him to become overly concerned about which letters to use.) He said, "I'll use both." After writing *C* and *K*, he added *R* and *S* to finish *cheese crackers* (ChES CRACKRS).

Older 4-year-olds Tina, Lania, and Kate generated spellings when they needed just a word or two and sometimes when writing more, if they had time. While playing with a doll in the dramatic play area, Tina pretended that her child, Flower, had drawn a picture and needed to write her name on it. When Tina asked for help in spelling *Flower*, the teacher said the word slowly, enunciating each sound. Tina wrote FLR to represent the sounds she heard.

At about the same time, Tina and several classmates interviewed the person who ran a food cart in the lobby of their preschool to find out what foods she sold. The children wrote down in little notebooks what the lady at the cart told them. Their teacher repeated each word slowly, enunciating sounds. Tina selected letters to write each sound in each food word to write *hot dogs* (HOIDG), *fruit* (FROT), *muffins* (MFNS), *soup* (SOOO), *salad* (SLD), and *juice* (JOC). A few months later, Tina drew a snake and wrote BOA. She segmented the word's first sound (/b/) and mapped it to the letter *B*. She mapped the word's second sound to *O*. The last sound in *boa* has no letter-name match, but Tina knew to represent it with *A* because the last sound in her name was the same.

Lania wrote KASAL SAV (*castle save*) by herself to label a block building (Figure 8.42). She was very attuned to sounds in words, perhaps because she had knowledge of more than one language—Lania was trilingual. When she wrote this piece, she was finishing her second year in an English immersion preschool.

Figure 8.41. Adam's grocery list with *peanuts* and *cheese crackers.*

Figure 8.42. *Castle Save* by Lania (4 years, 10 months).

Table 8.1. Preschoolers' Word Creation Hypotheses

Children's hypotheses	Children's reasoning and strategies	Moving their understanding forward
Words are physically related to what they represent	• Words capture aspects of the physical appearance of objects they represent. • Words usually have more marks if they are for larger objects and fewer if for smaller ones (Ferreiro & Teberosky 1982; Papandropoulos & Sinclair 1974). For example, a child might use three squiggles for *grasshopper* and seven for *cow*.	• Provide situations that contradict the idea, such as using children's names. The child thus observes that taller children do not always have names with many letters and shorter children do not always have names with few letters. • Read and underline labels under pictures in books. As a child observes, they obtain key information.
Each word is a stable and arbitrary sequence of letters	• Any sequence of letters is a word. • Each word has its own letters (i.e., children don't know that 26 letters spell all English words). Young children sometimes say, "Hey, that's my name!" when seeing any word beginning with their name's first letter.	• Comment to help children learn that the same letters appear in many different words. For example, "Yes, Juanita, your name starts with *J*, but so does José's. Your name does not have an *S* in the middle. See the *N* and *T*?"
Letter strings are based on some visual rules	• Every letter string (i.e., mock word) is considered by a child to be a real word if it follows certain rules: (a) it has a variety of letters, not multiples of just one (Lavine 1977); (b) it is not too long or too short (i.e., has between four and seven characters); and (c) it has a unique order of letters when the same letters are reused in different "words" (i.e., just as *eat* and *tea* are two different words even though they have the same letters, the mock words *adma, ddaa,* and *dmma* are also assumed by the child to be different words) (Clay 1975; Lavine 1977).	• Sound out children's mock words if they ask what they say. This demonstrates that letters represent sounds in spoken words and that not every collection of letters is a real word. • Children will then ask for spellings more and create mock words less, except when pretending to write.

Children's hypotheses	Children's reasoning and strategies	Moving their understanding forward
Large units of sound are linked to letters	• At first only larger speech units (i.e., syllables) are detected. • Letters are used to represent entire syllables. For example, in Figure 8.10 Adam wrote *AO* for his name, using *O* for *D*. When asked to "tell about these two letters," he pointed first to the *A* and said, "/a/," and then to *O* and said, "/dam/."	• As children continue to see their names and other words in the environment spelled out, this hypothesis will fade. Children gradually realize syllabic spelling doesn't look right. • Helping children to gain more phonological awareness skill also aids them in giving up this approach (see Chapter 5).
Word spellings are phoneme-based	• As letter names are learned, children match sounds in spoken words to letters whose names contain the sounds. • Children are able first to segment the first sounds in spoken words. They gradually can segment more sounds in spoken words. • If children cannot link a letter name to a word's isolated first sound, they ask adults how to spell the sound, just as Adam did with *cheese* (see Figure 8.41). • Children gradually learn to segment ending and middle sounds in spoken words, but preschoolers usually need a lot of help.	• Sounding out words for children to spell helps them develop phoneme-level awareness (Ball & Blachman 1991). • Tell children the letter(s) used to write the sounds you have segmented in spoken words. • Later, isolate sounds for children and encourage them to select the letters that are used to write the sounds. • Prompt children to segment sounds in spoken words as they gain skill. Help with sounds in the middle and at the end of words as needed.

Young children use a variety of strategies to create words, basing each one on an idea about how the writing system works. Because these ideas build on one another, the pattern of hypotheses seen in one child usually closely resembles the pattern seen in other children. That said, there are variations because children's experiences vary. When adults understand children's hypotheses, they can interact in ways that move children's understanding forward. Children who enter first grade with a great deal of knowledge about word making usually have benefited from countless hours of informative adult interactions (Durkin 1966; Read 1975).

Box 8.2. How Do Children Create Spellings?

When children create phoneme-based spellings (e.g., KAT for *cat,* SALE for *Sally),* adults often wonder how they do it. Preschoolers' invented spellings are actually rule-based decisions, rather similar to some rule-based oral language decisions that they make. For example, although very young children use the correct verbs they have heard adults say (e.g., "I went," "I ran"), some months later, they begin to say "I goed" and "I runned" (Fenson et al. 1994). These errors emerge after the child notices that the past tense for most verbs uses the morpheme *ed* and then applies this general rule to irregular verbs. This behavior— **overregularization**—diminishes gradually as children continue to hear adults use the irregular past tense verbs (e.g., ran, taught, went) and learn to use them.

What "Rules" Are Children Using to Create Spellings?

This section discusses the basis for young children's thoughtful, though incorrect, spelling decisions.

Code Only What You Hear

This is a good general rule for spelling in an alphabetic writing system because alphabet letters (i.e., graphemes) code phonemes in spoken words. However, the problem in English is that many words' spellings include letters that do not represent a specific sound that is heard in the word (e.g., cak**e**, **k**not, e**a**t). When children are unaware of this fact, they spell these words by representing only the sounds they hear in the words: KAK, NT and ET, respectively.

Use the Letter Whose Name Contains the Sound

When spelling words, young children also match sounds in letter names to sounds they detect in spoken words or hear when adults isolate sounds as they assist with spelling. For example, Adam used this approach when spelling the first and last sounds of *cat* (KAT). Many sounds are indeed spelled with letters whose names contain them (e.g., *B* /b/; *D* /d/; *M* /m/; *T* /t/). Some letter names have sounds they commonly code *at the beginning of their name* (e.g., *B, D, J, K, P, T, V, Z),* while other letter names have sounds they commonly code *at the end of their names* (e.g., *F, L, M, N, R, S, X).*

Letter-name matching works well not only for many consonant phonemes, but also for tense vowel phonemes (e.g., **e**at, **E**than). The problem, of course, is that lax vowel phonemes are also spelled with the same letters (e.g., s**e**t, t**e**ll, **e**very), even though these letters' names do not contain these sounds. To spell lax vowel sounds, young children often search for the letter name whose phonetic features match most closely the vowel sound they hear in the lax vowel they want to spell. For example, they spell the middle vowel phoneme in *pen* and *mess* with the letter *A* (i.e., *pan* for *pen; mass* for *mess).* If our readers say the names of *A* and *E* and pay attention to the lax vowel phoneme in *pen* or *mess* when they say these words, they can feel a closer resemblance to the speech features in *A* than in *E* (Read 1975).

Some sounds are not contained in any letter's name. For example, consider W ("duh-bl-u"), *H* ("aich"), *Q* ("k-yoo"), and *Y* ("wi-e"). Children sometimes use these letters incorrectly to spell a word because the sounds in the letters' names are misleading. For example, they might spell *dog* as **W**G, *wind* as **Y**D, *chicken* as **H**KN, and *queen* as **K**WEN.

English spelling is also complicated because some letters can represent more than one sound (e.g., *C* in *city* and *candy; G* in *giraffe* and *goat; Y* in *yes* and *mommy)* and different letters can represent the same sound. For example, both *C* and *K* are used to write /k/

(e.g., *candy* and *kitten*); both *Ph* and *F* are used to write /f/ (e.g., *phone* and *funny);* and both *Ch* and *Sh* are used to write /sh/ (e.g., *Charlene* and *Sharon*). And consider this: in the word *cricket*, the very same sound at its beginning and in its middle is spelled in two different ways.

Sounds Vary in Different Contexts

Children make additional spelling errors because the same letter actually represents sounds that vary somewhat in different word contexts. For example, when /t/ is followed by /r/ (e.g., /t/ in *truck, train, try*), it has the feature of **affrication** (i.e., slow release of air when saying the sound). When /t/ is not followed by /r/, as in *time, talk,* and *tomato*, there is no affrication. Thus, a young child must learn not to spell *truck* as CHK (i.e., *Ch* represents affrication, such as in the first sound heard in *cherry* or *chicken*). The child learns to ignore the affrication speech feature and focus on the additional speech features in /t/ in words when /t/ is followed by /r/.

Helping Young Children Move Toward Conventional Spellings

Exposing children to text in storybook titles and on classroom signs, labels, and charts helps children move gradually toward conventional spelling. Writing in a group situation, such as when taking dictation for a list of what children learned from their study of some topic, can also help. In these situations, children learn the most when teachers segment words they write down on their chart paper into some of their constituent sounds and select the letters that represent these sounds, commenting about spellings when they are somewhat unusual as needed.

For example, suppose a child dictates, "I learned that spiders have eight legs." A teacher could say, "Okay, I'll add *spiders* to our list. *Spiders*—/s/piders; we use *S* to write /s/, the first sound we hear when we say *spiders*." Continuing, the teacher says *spiders* again and isolates the next phoneme (i.e., s . . . /p/ . . . iders). "I hear /p/ next in *spiders*. We use the letter *P* to write /p/." For the next to the last phoneme, the teacher would say, "Spid . . . /er/ . . . s. I hear /r/ next, but I'll write a letter *E* before I write the *R* because I know *E* comes before *R* in this word, even though we don't hear a sound for it when we say the word." After isolating the last sound, the teacher could say, "The last sound in *spiders* is /z/. We use *S* to write that sound, even though you might think we use *Z* because we hear /z/."

When children create their own spellings, teachers answer their questions in ways that show respect for their good thinking. For example, if a child asks "Is that how you spell *cat*?" after writing KT, a teacher could say, "I can read it because *cat* begins with a /k/ sound, and we use the letter *K* to write /k/ in many words. But we write the first sound in *cat* with a *C* not a *K*. It's kind of tricky." If a child asks why, answer honestly: "I don't know. Somebody decided *cat* should be spelled this way, and that's how grown-ups write it. Grown-ups also put an *A* in the middle, and you can add that letter, if you'd like." If the child says, "I'm going to leave it this way," the teacher might say, "That's okay. Maybe next time you will want to try writing *cat* with the letters *C-A-T*."

While it's important to avoid squelching children's interest in and attention to the phonemes in words by insisting on corrections of their early spellings, teachers also don't want children to see only their own invented spellings. Looking at these invented spellings repeatedly affects children's later spelling, so it is important for children to see conventional spellings frequently throughout this period. A teacher should also explain any violations of children's current spelling assumptions in situations where they are guiding the spelling of words in a group situation.

Alphabet Letter Formation

Skill in letter formation changes quite a lot between 4 and 5 years old. It also varies considerably from child to child for a variety of reasons, including variations in children's experiences and interests. Additionally, some alphabet letters are more difficult than others for any preschooler to write. These include *B, K, R,* and *Y,* as seen in Figures 8.22, 8.23, and 8.43. Preschoolers also have difficulty making letters uniform in size and getting their proportions right. The letter *E* is interesting because children seem to realize that there is no confusion between *E* and any other letter, no matter how many short horizontal lines drawn to the right they squeeze onto the vertical line. The *E* in *Tracey* (Figure 8.22) demonstrates this knowledge and may have resulted from efforts to "fix" the placement of initially misplaced horizontal lines. Although the *E* in *Robert* (Figure 8.43) departs in a different way from a conventional *E* (i.e., its horizontal lines are bunched high up on the vertical line), there are three lines, not two, which indicate that this is *E* not *F.*

Preschoolers also work hard at the orientation of letters so that curves, lines, and intersections are positioned accurately to reflect the letter intended. Consider how these factors distinguish between *C* and *U, K* and *X,* and *V* and *Y.* To make one letter distinct from another requires knowing where to start and stop each stroke, planning the lengths of lines, and anticipating where lines and curves touch. For example, the orientation of Lucy's *C*s and *U*s became more conventional over time, perhaps as a result of experience, tutelage, and her own scrutiny of the letters (Figures 8.44 through 8.47). The intersection and positioning of lines in uppercase *Y* differ from those of lowercase *y,* which may have influenced the variations seen between, for example, Figures 8.45 (which features an uppercase *Y*) and 8.46 (which features a lowercase *y*). Dots in lowercase letters are often initially attached to the letter as children learn to organize space (Figure 8.48). (For more on letter formation in preschool, see Box 8.3.)

Figure 8.43. Example of *B, E,* and *R* in *Robert.*

Figure 8.44. The orientations of *C* and *U* are similar in Lucy's name (4 years, 3 months).

Figure 8.45. The orientations of *C* and *U* are conventional in Lucy's name (5 years, 2 months).

Figure 8.46. The intersection and orientation of lines for *Y* are developing in Lucy's name (5 years, 8 months)

Figure 8.47. The intersections and orientations of all letters in Lucy's name are conventional (5 years, 10 months).

Figure 8.48. Lucy writes *Fuji,* the name of her favorite type of apple (5 years, 2 months).

Box 8.3. Helping Young Children Learn to Form Letters

Although the preschool years are not the time for formal lessons in handwriting, teachers can assist children in ways that will help them develop some skill.

A Good Visual Image

Children gain information about the form of each letter from opportunities to see and contrast letters with one another. Matching alphabet letters using various materials (see Chapter 5) and playing with alphabet puzzles help children to learn the shape of each letter. Some matching materials should use highly confusable letters in a set (e.g., *B* and *R*, *C* and *G*, *E* and *F*, *N* and *K*, *O* and *Q*). Alphabet puzzles that have a space for each letter shape, not a letter stamped on jigsaw puzzle pieces, are better from an instruction point of view.

Line Segments

Looking at and comparing letters provide information about each letter's overall design, but these processes are not informative about each letter's line segments. Many young children use just one continuous line to make everything except the middle horizontal line of *E* because this is how *E* looks to them. However, *E* is actually comprised of four lines: one long vertical line forming its left side and three horizontal lines positioned out to the right from the vertical line.

When children watch as letters are written, they get information about the lines used to form them. The teacher can provide demonstrations by playing the letter clue game (see Box 5.3 in Chapter 5) about once a week after the first month or two of school. Focusing on just one or two letters in each game session takes no more than five to six minutes.

The Sequence and Direction of the Lines That Form Letters

The sequence and direction of drawing the lines to form a letter cannot be discerned from looking at already-formed letters, nor can they be grasped easily from worksheets with arrows and numbers marking lines in a model letter. The best learning about letter formation comes from watching demonstrations an adult provides. The letter clue game helps, and teachers can also demonstrate letter formation in authentic tasks, such as when the class composes a thank-you letter or creates an experience chart following a field trip.

Describe the formation of letters very explicitly as you write them. Later in the year, you can ask, "Okay, what kind of line should I make first for *B*? Yes, a long vertical line! Should I draw it up like this or down like this? (*Moves finger in the air to demonstrate each direction.*)"

Teachers can also provide demonstrations individually to children at the writing center, at the easel, or anywhere else that children write and ask for help. While younger preschoolers are usually happy to make a design that resembles the intended letter just a little bit, older 4-year-olds sometimes want their letters to look more conventional. They might say, "Hey, I can't make a *K* right! You do it!" Show the child how they can write the letter or model writing it yourself, judging which approach to use in each situation.

Box 8.3. Helping Young Children Learn to Form Letters (continued)

When demonstrating, use a separate piece of paper rather than the child's. You can make the letter once, line by line, and describe the actions. For example, for the letter *R*, a teacher might say, "To make *R,* we start with a long vertical line like this. Then, we go back to the top of the line and make a curved line that goes out like this and then comes back to the middle of the vertical line. Then, we make a short diagonal line that goes down and out." After writing the letter once as the child watches, start over, this time making one line at a time and inviting the child to write that line on their own paper after watching you. The child's writing will not be perfect, but demonstrations give children an idea of how to proceed in getting letters to look more as they might wish.

Materials to Avoid

Dot-to-dot letters and letter stencils are not helpful. Children cannot learn strokes or the direction and order in which to make them from their guidance. In fact, children connect the dots in any way they wish, and they can randomly choose to move their writing tool in any direction within the openings of a stencil. Worksheets with a model letter and a blank row for children to practice writing a letter multiple times are also of little use, and they also run the risk of turning writing into a tedious chore.

Large wall charts are not handy as guides to writing letters where children want to write. Small, individual letter guides are better resources, not only for a writing center but also for taking to the block center for labeling structures, the art center for incorporating writing into their paintings, outdoors for creating chalk drawings, and any other area where a child might be inspired to write. If the teacher uses individual letter guides as a reference when demonstrating for a child at the easel or the writing table, they will learn how to use the reference by watching.

Some children are very skilled in forming letters, including their lowercase forms, by the time they are around 5 years old, as Figures 8.49 and 8.50 illustrate.

In all preschoolers, fine motor skills are still developing, and this affects children's writing. (See Box 8.4.) Children with fine motor issues sometimes have considerable difficulty forming letters, but if teachers accept and respect their efforts, they draw and write just as much as other children.

One child with fairly significant motor delays drew a very interesting picture of her dog lying down, and then wrote the dog's name (mock word) (Figures 8.51 and 8.52). Near the end of the year, she made a thank-you note with a lot of pink paint for the school director whose garden the children had visited to plant flowers. She wrote *for Judy* on her painting (Figure 8.53).

Some children need special assistance and explicit help, and this child received an abundance of both. Moreover, difficulties with the physical aspects of writing should not provide a barrier to children in generating ideas and in explaining these verbally when their physical marks for drawing or writing alone cannot convey their full meanings.

Most importantly, children need the freedom to draw and write as they wish when they explore, play, and learn in every area of the early learning setting. Engagement in meaningful writing experiences not only keeps children interested and motivated to write but also provides many opportunities for them to learn about writing.

Figure 8.49. Example of high-level letter formation skill on a party invitation by a child (4 years, 8 months).

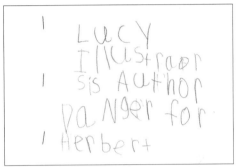

Figure 8.50. Example of high-level letter formation skill on the cover of a book by a child (5 years, 5 months).

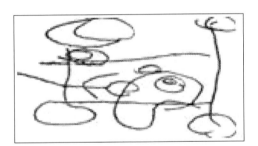

Figure 8.51. Drawing of dog lying down (4 years, 7 months).

Figure 8.52. Dog's name (mock word) (4 years, 7 months).

Figure 8.53. Thank-you note to Judy (4 years, 11 months).

Box 8.4. Fine Motor Development

Fine motor development refers to the increasing ability over a number of years to use the fingers of both hands. Children use a number of early grasps as their fine motor skills—the use of their fingers to manipulate objects—are maturing (Carlson & Cunningham 1990). All of these grasps result in larger writing and a lack of precision in creating and connecting lines to form letters.

Children first use a fist grasp to hold writing and drawing tools, using the muscle in the upper arm to move the whole arm and hand (i.e., the pivot is at the shoulder). Various overhand and stiff finger grips usually follow before children arrive at a mature grip, which uses the index finger, middle finger, and thumb. With a mature grip, the side of the hand rests on the tabletop, taking the weight off the writing or drawing tool's point and allowing its flexible movement by the fingers. Until children have mature fine motor skills, their lines look a bit wobbly and overruns dominate where lines intersect. Nevertheless, it is almost always possible to interpret correctly which letters a child intended.

Children vary greatly in fine motor development, which is affected strongly by maturation. Some have a rather mature finger grip at 3 years old; others do not have a mature group until they are 5 or 6. Children with significant fine motor delays and other motor issues will have different trajectories of fine motor development.

Some children with fine motor issues need assistance from an occupational therapist. Often, such specialists also provide helpful suggestions for early childhood educators. For example, they might recommend providing vertical surfaces (e.g., an easel) or covering an entire table with a large piece of paper. These modifications allow a child with fine motor issues to use larger muscles in the upper arm to move writing or drawing tools, and they provide larger surfaces for writing, which accommodates the larger marks a child will make when guiding a writing tool with their entire arm.

While there are other modifications that might be appropriate for an individual child, children with fine motor issues can still experiment with making letters and will also learn something about their line segments and the order in which they are drawn. Luckily, young children do not need much fine motor skill to enjoy writing and drawing, as long as adults are accepting of the marks they make.

More Complex Pictures

Pictures that children draw or paint increasingly tell whole stories or have stories under the surface, if adults ask the child about them. For example, one child who lives in southern California, where it rarely rains, drew a picture of a walk in the rain with his grandparents when they visited from Korea. He explained the picture by saying, "On a rainy day my family takes a walk" (Figure 8.54). Another child, who drew a scene depicting an apple-picking adventure at an orchard, said when explaining the picture, "Mom, I love you" (Figure 8.55).

Families and teachers of older preschoolers can use technology to support children's content knowledge acquisition, provide new ways for children to tell and write both story and informational texts, and nurture children's word creation knowledge. Examples of appropriate applications are discussed in Box 8.5.

Figure 8.54. Family holding umbrellas on a walk in the rain (5 years).

Figure 8.55. Scene from an orchard picking apples with mom (4 years, 5 months).

Summing Up Phase 3

Using writing and drawing to communicate and for enjoyment become commonplace for some children during the period between 4 and 5 years old. It is just something they do—*if* adults are accepting, sensitive, and helpful in response to their efforts and provide many opportunities. Skill increases by leaps and bounds during this year, especially when children have the benefit of educators who respond genuinely to their ideas and thinking and help them in ways that support literacy skills learning (e.g., segmenting sounds in words, linking letters to isolated sounds, noticing the specific features of letters).

With all that is at stake for a child's learning and their recognition that adult attention is genuine, families and teachers should be careful not to slip into responding to children's writing and drawing with quick pat praise (e.g., "Good job," "Fantastic!"). This kind of language is devoid of content, and its frequent use limits the diversity of the language that children hear from adults. Less diversity in language used with children limits the vocabulary and content to which children are exposed through conversation, which in turn is related negatively to children's language development (Pan et al. 2005). An additional consequence of pat praise is that children begin to think that they are inherently good at something and that effort and practice do not matter. Research indicates that an effort mindset serves children's academic achievement better in the long run than the mindset of "I am smart" (Dweck 2017).

Box 8.5. Preschoolers, Message Composition, and Technology

Kathleen A. Paciga

Box 7.2 in Chapter 7 provided information about developmentally appropriate digital marking tools for toddlers. During the preschool years, children can expand their content knowledge by using technology and digital media to gain exposure to books, videos, games, and simulations connected to the curriculum or children's interests. Children can then demonstrate what they learn using the myriad interactive applications (apps) for computers, tablets, or smartphones. The examples explored here expand on the content in Box 8.1 (children talking about their pictures) and Box 8.2 (word creation strategies and spelling).

Apps That Build Content Knowledge and Support Message Creation

Virtual experiences help children develop knowledge about the qualities and behaviors of people and things. Well-designed interactive apps, such as those recognized by the Association for Library Service to Children (a division of the American Library Association), build on children's content knowledge and have characters that replicate human and/or animal needs or emotions. Of course, the child's interactions should be accompanied by language-rich conversations with adults as passive interactions with screen media are less effective in building children's vocabulary and knowledge than joint media engagement (Korat, Atishkin, & Segal-Drori 2022).

Toca Boca's award-winning apps provide playful opportunities that complement and extend traditional dramatic play explorations. For example, in Toca Doctor, children take care of a virtual person by removing splinters, cleaning and bandaging a wound, or fixing a broken leg.

Digital books and short-form video content available through online libraries, such as Epic or Unite for Literacy, also expand language. In these libraries, children have access to books addressing a range of topics—animals, sports, seasons, celebrations, family, friends, and more. The concepts that pique children's interest when choosing what to read will often be integrated into their play and composition (e.g., Dyson 2020; Wohlwend 2015).

Even though children need mostly real experiences with animals and people, like traditional books, virtual experiences can extend a child's real experiences or provide opportunities not available to a child in real life (e.g., a child with allergies might not have a pet, but they can care for a virtual pet). And just as with traditional books, interactions with adults are critical to the child's learning.

Composing Messages Digitally

Many authors and artists use digital tools that help them create works in ways that were previously unimaginable. The use of multimedia components in digital texts has evolved as the capacity for elements such as hyperlinks, photos, data visualizations, text and graphic overlays on photos, audio narration, videos, and content generated by artificial intelligence have become possibilities for anyone with access to digital devices. The following are some options for preschool children to explore composing:

> Puppet Pals supports storytelling. The Director's Pass (an in-app purchase) allows use of a child's own photos as character puppets or settings. For example, teachers or children can snap pictures of the events and people involved in a field trip and then import them into Puppet Pals. Children then utilize the pictures as components of story—characters, settings, and/or events. Children narrate the stories as they wish.

> With Toontastic 3D, a child selects or draws a setting, inserts characters (from their own drawings or the menu of premade choices), and then dictates a story about those characters. The app records the child's dictation as well as their movement and coordination of the characters on the screen. The child can then play back the recording to watch their story unfold.

Technology Supports Word Knowledge and Emergent Spelling

Practicing composing and reading messages provides children with opportunities to grow their knowledge about words, images, and other multimedia. Learning about how these work through technology motivates children, and it has proven to be an effective way to grow a range of early literacy skills, including letter awareness, print awareness, phonological awareness, phonics, vocabulary, and emergent spelling (e.g., Strouse, Newland, & Mourlam 2019). (See Box 5.7 in Chapter 5 for apps that focus on letter knowledge.)

There is a need for teacher-guided instruction on literacy skills in early learning settings, and some time must be devoted daily to this. But preschoolers also need to use writing in play and for authentic purposes, such as writing letters, notes, signs, and lists. Skilled teachers can work literacy instruction in as they help children meet their goals. (See Box 8.6.)

Phase 4: More and More of Everything

In the period that spans 5 years to 5 years, 9 months old, children's writing and drawing change somewhat remarkably, especially in children with a long history of writing and drawing experience. Although children who have not had experiences with mark making in infancy and toddlerhood can catch up during preschool if adequate opportunities and support are provided, children who enter kindergarten without a multitude of writing and drawing experiences usually struggle to catch up.

As this book has explored, the knowledge children gain from early writing and drawing experiences include code-related skills, such as phonological awareness and letter-sound associations, and oral language skills acquired from talking with adults about their drawings and paintings. During this period of more and more of everything, children write about more topics, including knowledge they gain from personal experiences or informational books. Children write for more purposes, such as to share, to entertain, or to inform, and their writing reflects text features of their genre (e.g., lists and labels for expository purposes, sentences to share events in narratives).

Box 8.6. Enhancing Story Creation Skills in Dramatic Play Through Teacher Involvement

Dramatic play involves mental composing, which is an important aspect of writing, even though dramatic play scenarios are not written down. Children's dramatic play provides wonderful opportunities for teachers to support children's ability to create stories and hone their literacy-related skills, as the example provided here illustrates:

> After two children build a boat in the block area, one child says, "Get in! There are sharks in the water!" Their teacher, who is listening, comments, "Oh, my. Maybe you should make a sign to warn people who might be swimming. Signs are often posted at beaches when it isn't safe to go into the water and swim. Signs say something like, 'Swim at your own risk. Shark-infested waters.'"
>
> The children jump out of the boat and get writing materials and tape from the supplies. One child writes BVOVOHR. He also draws two pictures, and then writes another string of letters beneath them (TOPBIV). Next, he tears off a piece of tape and begins taping the sign to the boat while his friend holds it in position.
>
> At this point, the teacher asks in a worried tone, "What if you go out to sea and people don't see the sign? They won't know they should take precautions." The children stop for a moment to think before taking their sign to the block area and taping it to one end of the block shelves. "That's a good idea," says the teacher. "Now, it's where everyone can see it."

When something like this play episode transpires, the teacher might also comment to children's families at the end of the day (e.g., "Oh, be sure to ask Devone about the boat he built today and the sign he made about sharks"). The teacher might also place some books about sharks in the book area and encourage the children to take a look. If the children engage with the books and learn more about sharks, the teacher might ask if they might like to write a book about what they know.

Teachers have other opportunities to support multiple aspects of writing in dramatic play. Here's a list of some dramatic play contexts, the writing materials that children might use with each one, and the play opportunities that teachers might support.

Vignette adapted from J.A. Schickedanz, "Setting the Stage for Literacy Events in the Classroom." *Child Care Information Exchange* 123, Sept./Oct. (1999): 54.

Doctor's Office Play

> Child-created signs (e.g., Doctor Is In/Out; No Smoking; Please Silence Cell Phones)

> Message pad, appointment log (mock computer with keyboard), and pencil for receptionist

> Clipboard with photocopied blank health charts for the doctor to fill out for each patient

> Index cards (cut into quarters) for appointment cards for the office receptionist to fill in

> Pad of blank prescription forms for the doctor to fill in

Grocery Store Play

> Message pad and pencils for making grocery shopping lists

> Child-created labels for store departments (e.g., Dairy, Produce, Bakery) and self-serve food items on a hot food or salad bar

> Brown paper bags on which children have written the store name

> Child-created signs with store hours

Restaurant Play

> Magnetic letters and board on which children can write and post names of specials

> Placemats made by children from paper with the restaurant's name on it (laminated)

> Notepads and pencils for wait staff to use for taking orders

> Child-created signs (e.g., Open and Closed, one with business hours)

> Child-created labels (e.g., Takeout Orders Placed Online)

Post Office Play

> Child-created signs (e.g., one with business hours)

> Stationery and envelopes

> Child-created play money

> Cardboard boxes with Post Office written on them by children for mailing letters

> Adhesive labels to be cut and used for child-created postage stamps

Transportation Play

> Child-created paper tickets

> Poster with arrival and departure times for buses and trains

> Child-created play money and credit cards

> Child-created route maps for trains, buses, or subways

> Child-created signs for taxi and rideshare pickup locations

Examples of children who drew and wrote very little before reaching kindergarten are not provided here. Instead, the samples that follow illustrate what children *can* do by this age if they have had many experiences, starting either as a young 2-year-old or by 3 years old in an excellent preschool.

In the first two samples, Lucy dictated the text and drew pictures for her true story, "Danger for Herbert," recounting the capers that ensued when her aunt and uncle brought Herbert, a friend's guinea pig, to visit at Thanksgiving. Figure 8.56 shows the dramatic scene when the family cat discovered Herbert's cage in the middle of the night. On an earlier page, Lucy drew images for a list of supplies and equipment needed to care for a guinea pig (Figure 8.57).

Figure 8.56. The family cat climbs onto Herbert's cage in the middle of the night while everyone sleeps (5 years, 5 months).

Figure 8.57. Lucy's drawing of supplies and equipment to care for Herbert (5 years, 5 months).

Five-year-old Lily wrote and illustrated an autobiographical story about her love of gymnastics. Illustrations complemented the text by revealing important details, including the blue tumbling mat, team colors in the leotards, and gymnasts' hair pulled back into buns (Figure 8.58).

At nearly 6 years old, Noah drew and labeled the body parts of an insect (Figure 8.59). He created this drawing during a writing activity that took place after his teacher shared information about insects and the names of the various parts of their bodies.

A child who was a little past 5 years old was excited about an upcoming trip to see her grandmother in South Korea. During the period when her family was planning their trip, the child wrote a note, all by herself, to her grandmother, saying, *Hi, Grandma. We will be leaving America* (Hi, GAMA. WE WILL BE LEVING AMARAC). The family spoke primarily Korean at home, and the child learned English from an English immersion preschool, which she attended for two years (see Box 8.7).

Even children who are in kindergarten when they are between 5 years and 5 years, 9 months old can benefit from additional writing experiences at home and in after-school programs. For example, Adam drew the pictures of a castle and of a man on a horse with a dog in November and January, respectively, of his kindergarten year (Figures 8.60 and 8.61). During this time, he also attended an afternoon family child care program. Time was short in his morning-only kindergarten, and many of the writing activities involved drawing and writing about an assigned topic or focus.

Kindergarten typically involves more specific writing assignments than does preschool, and it gives more attention to both handwriting and code-related skills. Opportunities to draw and write at home or in an after-school program help children maintain a high level of motivation while kindergarten provides the support that helps children develop additional literacy skills.

Figure 8.58. "I am good at competing in gymnastics."

Figure 8.59. Noah's diagram of an insect's body parts (5 years, 11 months).

Figure 8.60. Adam's castle with knights, drawn at home (5 years, 4 months).

Figure 8.61. Adam's man on a horse, drawn in the early learning setting (5 years, 6 months).

Box 8.7. Invented Spelling Skill in Preschoolers Who Are Multilingual Learners

In discussing individual writing samples, this chapter noted that some children were bilingual or trilingual. Although the authors did not conduct systematic studies over the years, it has seemed to us that children learning more than one language often developed higher levels of phonological awareness compared to their monolingual peers. Specifically, they often developed skill in creating phonemic-based spellings, independently (e.g., KASAL SAV for *castle save*). We often wondered why.

As indicated throughout this chapter, many samples were collected in early learning settings where English was the language of instruction and children created most of the invented samples near the end of their second year of preschool. Additionally, in all of the early learning settings from which samples were drawn, teachers scaffolded the spelling of words when children requested help (i.e., segmented the words into their phonemes, linked these sounds to letters that represent them). They also "talked out loud" in the same way about spellings when writing words in a group situation, such as when children dictated something about a recent field trip or the content for a thank-you note to a classroom volunteer or other guest.

The early learning settings also included high levels of language interaction, not only between adults and children but also among the children in a variety of play settings, and provided a curriculum rich in content and oral language, including vocabulary. As noted in Box 3.5 in Chapter 3, children learn vocabulary better when they are provided information about the words, compared to learning only simple labels for objects and actions without any associated information.

Finally, as discussed in Chapter 5, size of vocabulary is related to phonological awareness skill. One hypothesis about the nature of this relationship suggests that a larger vocabulary prompts reorganization of stored words, based on global sound characteristics, to more segmental features (i.e., smaller units of sound).

All of these features of the social setting, and of the early learning setting's curriculum and instruction, would likely increase an older preschooler's skill in creating phonemic-based spellings on their own, but they do not explain why a multilingual child in such settings might develop greater skill than their monolingual peers. Research on the effects of bilingualism on the brain provides some clues.

Recent research on monolingual speakers and bilingual speakers indicates an advantage for bilingual speakers in phonological learning related to improved auditory skills (Spinu, Hwang, & Vasilita 2023). Learning multiple languages changes the brain's auditory system and seems associated with the ability to pay more attention to sounds (Sharifinik, Ahadi, & Rahimi 2021). Researchers have found that learning a second language actually changes the brain's auditory system. Instead of multilingual children becoming confused by the two (or three) languages they are learning, the researchers concluded that plasticity in the brain allows them to develop more efficient and flexible auditory systems, which leads to greater auditory attention.

After reading this research, the authors also recalled that many of the multilingual children watched the teacher's mouth as the words requested were spoken and segmented into their phonemes and as the letters needed to write the sounds were named. Monolingual children, on the other hand, did not tend to watch the teacher's mouth, probably because they could simply listen to a word and remember it and understand more easily exactly what letter the teacher had named. Multilingual children, on the other hand, sometimes checked about the letter's name (e.g., *M* when a teacher had said *N*) to get clarification.

Monolingual children's greater familiarity with English vocabulary led to less attention to the teacher's instructional help, and perhaps elicited less instructional help. In the long run, looking at the teacher's mouth and listening more attentively to letters named to make sure they knew what had been said might have led to more phonological awareness skill in the multilingual children. Teachers might have been more explicit, and perhaps also repeated information more often, when assisting multilingual children with spellings because they thought more explicitness was necessary. Alternately, teachers simply might have responded with more information when children seemed more attentive—that is, when they looked more often at the teacher and watched the teacher's mouth.

These thoughts are offered as reflections about the authors' experience because data were not collected systematically. The research raises curiosity about whether there might be a phonological awareness benefit for children whose first language is English if they too had opportunities during the preschool years to learn another language, such as would occur in a multilingual program.

Concluding Thoughts

During the preschool years, the alphabet letters that children write become better and better approximations to their conventional forms. Children also develop some understanding of how letters are used to create words, and this understanding is informed by their development of phonological awareness (see Chapter 5). When a fairly good grasp of phonological awareness is coupled with the insight that letters function to represent sounds in spoken words (i.e., they have acquired the alphabetic principle), some older preschoolers start to invent spellings.

Preschoolers' drawings and paintings also begin to resemble the objects and actions that children intend to depict, and their content becomes more and more complex. Because children cannot yet "tell all" with pictures or with writing, it is extremely important for adults to prompt children to relate the meanings and messages they want to convey more fully by using their oral language.

As with all aspects of development, children vary greatly in their writing and drawing behavior. Some 3-year-olds enter preschool with about two years of marking and message-making experience, while others enter with virtually none. Preschool teachers should *expect* wide variations in children's mark-making behavior and interest, while not *accepting* low levels of skill as "a given" (i.e., as inborn differences in capacity). If early childhood educators nurture and support writing and message creation in all children, no matter the status of their interest and skill when they start, all children will have a chance to learn and thrive in these areas.

LIST OF CHILDREN'S LITERATURE CITED

Chapter 1

Chickens Aren't the Only Ones. 1999. R. Heller. New York: Penguin Random House.

Gilberto and the Wind. 1963. M.H. Ets. New York: Viking Children's Books.

Mama Built a Little Nest. 2014. J. Ward. Illus. S. Jenkins. San Diego: Beach Lane Books.

One Dark Night. 2001. H. Hutchins. Illus. S.K. Hartung. New York: Viking Children's Books.

The Snowy Day. 1962. E.J. Keats. New York: Viking Children's Books.

Water Is Water. 2015. M. Paul. Illus. J. Chin. New York: Roaring Brook Press.

Whistle for Willie. 1964. E.J. Keats. New York: Viking Children's Books.

Chapter 2

8 Little Planets. 2018. C. Ferrie. Illus. L. Doyle. Naperville, IL: Sourcebooks Explore.

10 Things I Love About You! 2022. D. McLean. Illus. G. Habib. Wilton, CT: Tiger Tales.

Animal Parade. 2019. Illus. J. Ho. Baltimore: duopress labs.

Animals Move. 2022. J. Whittingham. Toronto, ON: Pajama Press.

Babies Love Animals. 2022. S. König. New York: Philomel.

Baby EyeLike series. New York: PlayBac.

Baby Faces. 2022. J. Harbison. Morton Grove, IL: Little Grasshopper Books.

Bedtime for Duckling. 2022. A. Hepworth. Illus. A. Doherty. Wilton, CT: Tiger Tales.

Black on White. 1993. T. Hoban. New York: Greenwillow Books.

Bilingual Bright Baby series. R. Priddy. New York: Priddy Books.

Boats. 1998. B. Barton. New York: HarperFestival.

Brown Bear, Brown Bear, What Do You See? 1992. B. Martin Jr. Illus. E. Carle. New York: Holt, Rinehart, & Wilson.

California, Baby! 2023. C. Szalay. Self-published.

Color Me: Who's in the Water? 2018. S. Sajnani. London: Happy Yak.

Curious George series. M. Rey. Illus. H.A. Rey. New York: Clarion.

Dinosaur Dance! 2016. S. Boynton. New York: Boynton Bookworks.

Don't Tickle the Monkey! 2023. S. Taplin. Illus. A.M. Larranaga. London: Usborne.

Dr. Seuss's ABC: An Amazing Alphabet Book. 1991. Dr. Seuss. New York: Random House.

Ducks Away! 2016. M. Fox. Illus. J. Horacek. San Diego: Beach Lane Books.

Everywhere Babies. 2001. S. Meyers. Illus. M. Frazee. New York: Clarion.

Feast for 10. 1993. C. Falwell. New York: Clarion.

Freight Train. 1978. D. Crews. New York: Greenwillow Books.

Getting Dressed. 2020. P. Oud. New York: Clavis.

Give Me a Snickle! 2022. A. Sevigny. Victoria, BC: Orca.

Go Sleep in Your Own Bed! 2017. C. Fleming. Illus. L. Nichols. New York: Schwartz & Wade.

The Going to Bed Book. 1982. S. Boynton. New York: Boynton Bookworks.

Goodnight, Goodnight, Construction Site. 2011. S.D. Rinker. Illus. T. Lichtenheld. San Francisco: Chronicle Books.

Goodnight Moon. 1947. M.W. Brown. Illus. C. Hurd. New York: Harper & Row.

Hanukkah Nights. 2022. A. Hoffman. Minneapolis, MN: Kar-Ben Publishing.

Happy in Our Skin. 2018. F. Manushkin. Illus. L. Tobia. Somerville, MA: Candlewick.

Hey, Water! 2019. A. Portis. New York: Neal Porter.

Hidden Hippo. 2009. J. Gannij. Illus. C. Beaton. Concord, MA: Barefoot Books.

Hugs and Kisses. 2022. R.G. Intrater. New York: Cartwheel Books.

Hush! A Thai Lullaby. 1996. M. Ho. Illus. H. Meade. London: Orchard Books.

I Thought I Saw a Crocodile! 2020. Illus. L. Nichols. London: Templar.

In My Barn. 2012. S. Gillingham. Illus. L. Siminovich. San Francisco: Chronicle Books.

In the Air. 2022. N. Durley. New York: Abrams.

In the Wild. 2022. Illus. S. Muthomi. Melville, NY: Little Hippo Books.

Kindness. 2024. P. Rossa. Illus. K. Klein. Rolling Meadows: Cottage Door Press.

Leo Gets a Checkup. 2018. A. McQuinn. Illus. R. Hearson. Watertown, MA: Charlesbridge.

Let's Find the Tiger. 2019. Illus. A. Willmore. Wilton, CT: Tiger Tales.

Little Blue Truck. 2008. A. Schertle. Illus. J. McElmurry. San Diego: Harcourt.

Little Feet Love. 2009. A. Nex. Ashland, OH: Piggy Toes Press.

Little Nature Explorers series. A. Hendricks. Illus. G. Scott. Mankato, MN: Amicus.

Llama Llama Misses Mama. 2009. A. Dewdney. New York: Viking Children's Books.

LunarTale: A New Year's Adventure. 2023. S. Hong. New York: Abrams.

The Mitten. 1989. J. Brett. New York: Putnam Juvenile.

Moo, Baa, La La La! 1982. S. Boynton. New York: Boynton Bookworks.

Mr. Brown Can Moo! Can You? 1970. Dr. Seuss. New York: Random House.

My Big Truck Book. 2011. R. Priddy. New York: Priddy Books.

My Neighborhood. 2018. M. Frost. New York: Workman.

Nighty Night, Little Green Monster. 2013. E. Emberly. New York: LB Kids.

Nursery Times series. Frome, England: Jo and Nic's Crinkly Cloth Books.

Olivia . . . and the Missing Toy. 2003. I. Falconer. New York: Atheneum Books for Young Readers.

On Mother's Lap. 1972. A.H. Scott. Illus. G. Coalson. New York: Clarion.

Owl Babies. 1992. M. Waddell. Illus. P. Benson. Somerville, MA: Candlewick.

¡Pío Peep! 2003. Eds. A.F. Ada & F.I. Campoy. Trans. A. Schertle. Illus. V. Escrivá. Nashville: HarperCollins Español.

Planes. 1998. B. Barton. New York: HarperFestival.

See, Touch, Feel series. R. Priddy. New York: Priddy Books.

The Snowy Day. 1962. E.J. Keats. New York: Viking Children's Books.

Stir Crack Whisk Bake: A Little Book About Little Cakes. 2019. America's Test Kitchen Kids & M. Frost. Naperville, IL: Sourcebooks Explore.

Sumo Counting. 2021. S. Ishida. Seattle: Little Bigfoot.

Sunny Days. 2022. D. Kerbel. Illus. M. Sato. Toronto, ON: Pajama Press.

Tails. 2003. M. Van Fleet. Boston: Houghton Mifflin Harcourt.

Tails series. Shenzhen, China: beiens.

Te amo, bebé/Love You, Baby. 2020. A. Pixton. Illus. S. Lomp. New York: Workman.

Ten Little Fingers and Ten Little Toes. 2008. M. Fox. Illus. H. Oxenbury. New York: Clarion.

That's Not My Teddy . . . 1999. Fiona Watt. Illus. R. Wells. London: Usborne.

Things That Go. 2023. S. Wing. Illus. M. Hogan. Rolling Meadows: Cottage Door Press.

Time for a Trip. 2018. P. Gershator. Illus. David Walker. New York: Union Square Kids.

Touch and Feel/Tacto y textura series. London: DK.

The Touch Book. 2021. N. Edwards. Illus. T. Elliott. Wilton, CT: Tiger Tales.

Trains. 1998. B. Barton. New York: HarperFestival.

Truckery Rhymes. 2009. J. Scieszka. Illus. D. Shannon, L. Long, & D. Gordon. New York: Simon & Schuster Books for Young Readers.

Tub Time Books series. Montreal, QC: Land of B.

Tummy Time! 2022. Tunbridge Wells, England: Mama Makes Books.

The Wheels on the Bus. 2020. Illus. Y. Huang. London: Nosy Crow.

Where's Spot? 1980. E. Hill. New York: Penguin Young Readers Group.

Whose Knees Are These? 2019. J. Asim. Illus. L. Pham. New York: LB Kids.

Chapter 3

Alphabet Under Construction. 2002. D. Fleming. New York: Henry Holt.

Amos and Boris. 1971. W. Steig. New York: Farrar, Straus, and Giroux.

Bathe the Cat. 2022. A.B. McGinty. Illus. D. Roberts. San Francisco: Chronicle Books.

Bee-Bim Bop! 2005. L.S. Park. Illus. H.B. Lee. New York: Clarion.

Can an Aardvark Bark? 2017. M. Stewart. Illus. S. Jenkins. San Diego: Beach Lane Books.

Caps for Sale. 1947. E. Slobodkina. New York: HarperCollins.

Corduroy. 1968. D. Freeman. New York: Viking Children's Books.

Dog's Colorful Day. 2001. E. Dodd. London: Puffin Books.

Dreams. 1974. E.J. Keats. London: Puffin Books.

Duck in the Truck. 1999. J. Alborough. New York: HarperCollins.

Farmer Duck. 1992. M. Waddell. Illus. H. Oxenbury. Somerville, MA: Candlewick.

Fish Is Fish. 1974. L. Lionni. Decorah, IA: Dragonfly Books.

Gilberto and the Wind. 1963. M.H. Ets. New York: Viking Children's Books.

A Hat for Minerva Louise. 1994. J.M. Stoeke. London: Puffin Books.

Henny Penny. 1968. P. Galdone. New York: Clarion.

Inch by Inch. 1995. L. Lionni. New York: HarperCollins.

Knuffle Bunny. 2004. M. Willems. New York: Hyperion.

Last Stop on Market Street. 2015. M. de la Peña. Illus. C. Robinson. New York: Putnam Young Readers.

The Little Red Hen (Makes a Pizza). 1999. P. Sturges. Illus. A. Walrod. London: Puffin Books.

Max's Dragon Shirt. 2000. R. Wells. London: Puffin Books.

Mouse Paint. 1989. E.S. Walsh. San Diego: Harcourt.

Peter's Chair. 1967. E.J. Keats. London: Puffin Books.

Possum and the Peeper. 1998. A. Hunter. Boston: Houghton Mifflin.

Possum's Harvest Moon. 1996. A. Hunter. Boston: Houghton Mifflin.

The Puddle Pail. 1997. E. Kleven. London: Puffin Books.

Rabbits and Raindrops. 1997. J. Arnosky. London: Puffin Books.

Raccoon on His Own. 2001. J. Arnosky. London: Puffin Books.

Some Smug Slug. 1996. P.D. Edwards. Illus. H. Cole. New York: HarperTrophy.

Stellaluna. 1993. J. Cannon. San Diego: Harcourt.

The Street Beneath My Feet. 2017. C. Guillain. Illus. Y. Zommer. London: words & pictures.

Swimmy. 1973. L. Lionni. Decorah, IA: Dragonfly Books.

Vámonos a Tegucigalpa/Let's Go to Tegucigalpa. 2021. P. Rodriguez & A. Stein. Illus. A. Godinez. Los Angeles: Lil' Libros.

Whistle for Willie. 1964. E.J. Keats. New York: Viking Children's Books.

Windows. 2017. J. Denos. Illus. E.B. Goodale. Somerville, MA: Candlewick.

Chapter 4

A Is for Africa. 1993. I. Onyefulu. London: Puffin Books.

About . . . series. C. Sill. Illus. J. Sill. Atlanta: Peachtree.

The Airport: The Inside Story. 2023. J. Walton. Illus. H. Abbo. London: Neon Squid.

The All-Together Quilt. 2020. L. Rockwell. New York: Knopf Books for Young Readers.

Animal Architects. 2021. A. Cherrix. Illus. C. Sasaki. San Diego: Beach Lane Books.

Bear Has a Story to Tell. 2012. P.C. Stead. Illus. E.E. Stead. New York: Roaring Brook Press.

A Beetle Is Shy. 2016. D.H. Aston. Illus. S. Long. San Francisco: Chronicle Books.

The Boat Alphabet Book. 1998. J. Pallotta. Illus. D. Biedrzycki. Watertown, MA: Charlesbridge.

Butterfly. 2007. M. Ling. London: DK.

Can an Aardvark Bark? 2017. M. Stewart. Illus. S. Jenkins. San Diego: Beach Lane Books.

Carry Me! Animal Babies on the Move. 2008. S. Stockdale. Atlanta: Peachtree.

Crayfish. 2002. L.M. Schaefer. Portsmouth, NH: Heinemann Library.

Eating the Alphabet. 1989. L. Ehlert. San Diego: Harcourt Brace.

An Egg Is Quiet. 2006. D.H. Aston. Illus. S. Long. San Francisco: Chronicle Books.

Elmore. 2018. H. Hobbie. New York: Random House.

Farfallina and Marcel. 2002. H. Keller. New York: Greenwillow Books.

Feathers: Not Just for Flying. 2014. M. Stewart. Illus. S.S. Brannen. Watertown, MA: Charlesbridge.

Food Trucks! 2014. M. Todd. New York: Clarion.

The Frog Alphabet Book. 1990. J. Pallotta. Illus. R. Masiello. Watertown, MA: Charlesbridge.

From Wheat to Bread. 2013. S. Taus-Bolstad. Minneapolis, MN: Lerner.

Hiders Seekers Finders Keepers: How Animals Adapt in Winter. 2022. J. Kulekjian. Illus. S. Perera. Toronto, ON: Kids Can Press.

Honeybee: The Busy Life of Apis Mellifera. 2020. C. Fleming. Illus. E. Rohmann. New York: Neal Porter.

A House for Hermit Crab. 1987. E. Carle. Natick, MA: Picture Book Studio.

Just Ducks! 2012. N. Davies. Illus. S. Rubbino. Somerville, MA: Candlewick.

The Magic of Sleep: A Fascinating Guide to the World of Slumber. 2021. V. Woodgate. London: DK.

Magnetic and Nonmagnetic. 2008. A. Royston. Portsmouth, NH: Heinemann Library.

Make Way for Ducklings. 1941. R. McCloskey. New York: Viking Children's Books.

More. 2012. I.C. Springman. Illus. B. Lies. Boston: Houghton Mifflin.

On the Wing. 2014. D. Elliott. Illus. B. Stadtlander. Somerville, MA: Candlewick.

Over and Under the Snow. 2011. K. Messner. Illus. C.S. Neal. San Francisco: Chronicle Books.

Over and Under the Waves. 2022. K. Messner. Illus. C.S. Neal. San Francisco: Chronicle Books.

P Is for Pakistan. 2007. S. Razzak. Photog. P. Das. London: Frances Lincoln Children's Books.

Porcupines. 2021. A. McDonald. Minnetonka, MN: Bellwether Media.

Raccoon on His Own. 2001. J. Arnosky. London: Puffin Books.

Ready, Set, Run! The Amazing New York City Marathon. 2023. L. Kimmelman. Illus. J. Hartland. New York: Random House Studio.

A Rock Is Lively. 2015. D.H. Aston. Illus. S. Long. San Francisco: Chronicle Books.

A Seed Grows. 2022. A. Portis. New York: Neal Porter.

Snooze-O-Rama: The Strange Ways That Animals Sleep. 2021. M. Birmingham. Illus. K. Reed. Toronto, ON: Owlkids.

Stellaluna. 1993. J. Cannon. San Diego: Harcourt.

Unbeatable Beaks. 1999. S.R. Swinburne. Illus. J. Paley. New York: Henry Holt.

Whale Fall: Exploring an Ocean-Floor Ecosystem. 2023. M. Stewart. Illus. R. Dunlavey. New York: Random House Studio.

Wildlife Anatomy: The Curious Lives and Features of Wild Animals Around the World. 2023. J. Rothman. With L. Hiley. North Adams, MA: Storey Publishing.

The Yucky Reptile Alphabet Book. 1989. J. Pallotta. Illus. R. Masiello. Watertown, MA: Charlesbridge.

Chapter 5

Bee-Bim Bop! 2005. L.S. Park. Illus. H.B. Lee. New York: Clarion.

Beep Beep/Piip piip. 2019. P. Horacek. Somerville, MA: Candlewick.

Mamá Goose. 2005. A.F. Ada & F.I. Campoy. Illus. M. Suárez. New York: Little, Brown Books for Young Readers.

Roadwork. 2008. S. Sutton. Illus. B. Lovelock. Somerville, MA: Candlewick.

Salsa Lullaby. 2019. J. Arena. Illus. E. Meza. New York: Knopf Books for Young Readers.

Wombat. 2023. P. Bunting. Watertown, MA: Charlesbridge.

Chapter 8

Rain. 2000. M. Stojic. New York: Crown Books for Young Readers.

The Rainbow Fish. 1992. M. Pfister. Trans. J.A. James. New York: NorthSouth Books.

REFERENCES

AAP (American Academy of Pediatrics) Council on Communications and Media, D. Hill, N. Ameenuddin, Y.R. Chassiakos, C. Cross, J. Hutchinson, A. Levine, R. Boyd, R. Mendelson, M. Moreno, & W.S. Swanson. 2016. "Media and Young Minds." *Pediatrics* 138 (5): e20162591.

Adams, M.J. 1990. *Beginning to Read: Thinking and Learning About Print.* Cambridge, MA: MIT Press.

Anthony, J.L., C.J. Lonigan, K. Driscoll, B.M. Phillips, & S.R. Burgess. 2003. "Preschool Phonological Sensitivity: A Quasi-Parallel Progression of Word Structure Units and Cognitive Operations." *Reading Research Quarterly* 38 (4): 470–87.

Australian Government Department of Health and Aged Care. 2021. "Physical Activity and Exercise Guidelines for Infants, Toddlers, and Preschoolers (Birth to 5 Years)." Last modified May 6. www.health.gov.au/topics/physical-activity-and-exercise/physical-activity-and-exercise-guidelines-for-all-australians/for-infants-toddlers-and-preschoolers-birth-to-5-years.

Baghban, M. 1984. *Our Daughter Learns to Read and Write: A Case Study from Birth to Three.* Newark, DE: International Reading Association.

Baillargeon, R. 1995. "A Model of Physical Reasoning in Infancy." In *Advances in Psychological Science*, Vol. 9, eds. C. Rovee-Collier & L.P. Lipsitt, 305–71. Norwood, NJ: Ablex.

Baillargeon, R., A. Needham, & J. DeVos. 1992. "The Development of Young Infants' Intuitions About Support." *Early Development and Parenting* 1 (2): 69–78.

Ball, E.W., & B.A. Blachman. 1991. "Does Phoneme Awareness Training in Kindergarten Make a Difference in Early Word Recognition and Developmental Spelling?" *Reading Research Quarterly* 26 (1): 49–66.

Barrera, M.E., & D. Maurer. 1981. "The Perception of Facial Expressions by the Three-Month-Old." *Child Development* 52 (1): 203–06.

Bartlett, F. 1958. *Thinking: An Experimental and Social Study.* London: Allen & Unwin.

Bates, E., & J.C. Goodman. 1997. "On the Inseparability of Grammar and the Lexicon: Evidence from Acquisition, Aphasia and Real-Time Processing." *Language and Cognitive Processes* 12 (5–6): 507–84.

Baumrind, D. 1989. "Rearing Competent Children." In *Child Development Today and Tomorrow,* ed. W. Damon, 349–78. San Francisco: Jossey-Bass.

Beck, I.L., & M.G. McKeown. 2001. "Text Talk: Capturing the Benefits of Read-Aloud Experiences for Young Children." *The Reading Teacher* 55 (1): 10–20.

Beck, I., M. McKeown, & L. Kucan. 2002. *Bringing Words to Life: Robust Vocabulary Instruction.* New York: Guilford.

Bell, M.A., & C.D. Wolfe. 2004. "Emotion and Cognition: An Intricately Bound Developmental Process." *Child Development* 75 (2): 366–70.

Beneke, S.J., M.M. Ostrosky, & L.G. Katz. 2008. "Calendar Time for Young Children: Good Intentions Gone Awry." *Young Children* 63 (3): 12–16.

Benson, M.S. 1997. "Psychological Causation and Goal-Based Episodes: Low-Income Children's Emerging Narrative Skills." *Early Childhood Research Quarterly* 12 (4): 439–57.

Bergelson, E., & R. Aslin. 2017. "Semantic Specificity in One-Year-Olds' Word Comprehension." *Language Learning and Development* 13 (4): 481–501.

Bergelson, E., & D. Swingley. 2012. "At 6–9 Months, Human Infants Know the Meanings of Many Common Nouns." *Proceedings of the National Academy of Sciences* 109 (9): 3253–58.

Berhenke, A., A.L. Miller, E. Brown, R. Seifer, & S. Dickstein. 2011. "Observed Emotional and Behavioral Indicators of Motivation Predict School Readiness in Head Start Graduates." *Early Childhood Research Quarterly* 26 (4): 430–41.

Best, R.M., R.G. Floyd, & D.S. McNamara. 2008. "Differential Competencies Contributing to Children's Comprehension of Narratives and Expository Texts." *Reading Psychology* 29 (2): 137–64.

Bialystok, E. 2015. "Bilingualism and the Development of Executive Function: The Role of Attention." *Child Development Perspectives* 9 (2): 117–21.

Biemiller, A., & C. Boote. 2006. "An Effective Method for Building Meaning Vocabulary in Primary Grades." *Journal of Educational Psychology* 98 (1): 44–57.

Bintz, W.P., & L.M. Ciecierski. 2017. "Hybrid Text: An Engaging Genre to Teach Content Area Material Across the Curriculum." *The Reading Teacher* 71 (1): 61–69.

Birckmayer, J., A. Kennedy, & A. Stonehouse. 2008. *From Lullabies to Literature: Stories in the Lives of Infants and Toddlers*. Washington, DC: NAEYC; Castle Hill, Australia: Pademelon Press.

Bishop, R.S. 1990. "Mirrors, Windows, and Sliding Glass Doors." *Perspectives* 6 (3): ix–xi.

Bloom, K. 1977. "Patterning of Infant Vocal Behavior." *Journal of Experimental Child Psychology* 23 (3): 367–77.

Booth, A.E. 2009. "Causal Supports for Early Word Learning." *Child Development* 80 (4): 1234–50.

Bornstein, M.H., M.E. Arterberry, C. Mash, & N. Manian. 2011. "Discrimination of Facial Expressions by 5-Month-Old Infants of Nondepressed and Clinically Depressed Mothers." *Infant Behavior & Development* 34 (1): 100–06.

Bourgeois, K.S., A.W. Khawar, S.A. Neal, & J.J. Lockman. 2005. "Infant Manual Exploration of Objects, Surfaces, and Their Interrelations." *Infancy* 8 (3): 233–52.

Brazelton, T.B., E. Tronick, L. Adamson, H. Als, & S. Weise. 1975. "Early Mother-Infant Reciprocity." In *Parent-Infant Interaction* (Ciba Foundation Symposium. No. 33). Amsterdam: Elsevier.

Bretherton, I. 1984. "Representing the Social World in Symbolic Play." In *Symbolic Play: The Development of Social Understanding*, ed. I. Bretherton, 3–41. New York: Academic Press.

Bretherton, I., & M. Beeghly. 1982. "Talking About Internal States: The Acquisition of an Explicit Theory of Mind." *Developmental Psychology* 18 (6): 906–21.

Broerse, J., & G. Elias. 1994. "Changes in the Content and Timing of Mothers' Talk to Infants." *British Journal of Developmental Psychology* 12 (1): 131–45.

Brooks, R., & A.N. Meltzoff. 2015. "Connecting the Dots from Infancy to Childhood: A Longitudinal Study Connecting Gaze Following, Language, and Explicit Theory of Mind." *Journal of Experimental Child Psychology* 130: 67–78.

Brown, R. 1973. *A First Language: The Early Stages*. Cambridge, MA: Harvard University Press.

Bus, A., M.H. van IJzendoorn, & A.D. Pellegrini. 1995. "Joint Book Reading Makes for Success in Learning to Read: A Meta-Analysis on Intergenerational Transmission of Literacy." *Review of Educational Research* 65 (1): 1–21.

Bushnell, E.W., & J.P. Boudreau. 1993. "Motor Development and the Mind: The Potential Role of Motor Abilities as a Determinant of Aspects of Perceptual Development." *Child Development* 64 (4): 1005–21.

Butterworth, G.E., & N. Jarrett. 1991. "What Minds Have in Common in Space: Spatial Mechanisms Serving Joint Visual Attention in Infancy." *British Journal of Developmental Psychology* 9 (1): 55–72.

Byers-Heinlein, K., & C. Lew-Williams. 2013. "Bilingualism in the Early Years: What the Science Says." *LEARNing Landscapes* 7 (1): 95–112.

Cahill, P. 2023. "How Many Characters Are There in Chinese?" *Chinese Language Institute,* December 9. https://studycli.org/chinese-characters/number-of-characters-in-chinese.

Campos, J., C. Frankel, & L. Camras. 2004. "On the Nature of Emotional Regulation." *Child Development* 75 (2): 377–94.

Canadian Paediatric Society, Digital Health Task Force. 2019. "Digital Media: Promoting Healthy Screen Use in School-Aged Children and Adolescents." *Paediatrics & Child Health* 24 (6): 402–08.

Carey, S. 1978. "The Child as Word Learner." In *Linguistic Theory and Psychological Reality*, eds. M. Halle, J. Bresnan, & G.A. Miller, 359–73. Cambridge, MA: MIT Press.

Carey, S. 1985. *Conceptual Change in Childhood*. Cambridge, MA: MIT Press.

Carlson, K., & J.L. Cunningham. 1990. "Effects of Pencil Diameter on the Grapho-Motor Skills of Preschoolers." *Early Childhood Research Quarterly* 5 (2): 279–93.

Cartmill, E.A., B.F. Armstrong, L.R. Gleitman, S. Goldin-Meadow, T.N. Medina, & J.C. Trueswell. 2013. "Quality of Early Parent Input Predicts Child Vocabulary 3 Years Later." *Proceedings of the National Academy of Sciences of the United States of America* 110 (28): 11278–83.

Chall, J.S., & V.A. Jacobs. 2003. "Poor Children's Fourth-Grade Slump." *American Educator* 27 (1): 14–15, 44.

Chambre, S., L.C. Ehri, & M. Nest. 2020. "Phonological Decoding Enhances Orthographic Facilitation of Vocabulary Learning in First Graders." *Reading and Writing* 33 (5): 1133–62.

Christ, T., & X.C. Wang. 2012. "Supporting Preschoolers' Vocabulary Learning: Using a Decision-Making Model to Select Appropriate Words and Methods." *Young Children* 67 (2): 74–80.

Christ, T., X.C. Wang, M.M. Chiu, & E. Strekalova-Hughes. 2019. "How App Books' Affordances Are Related to Young Children's Reading Behaviors and Outcomes." *AERA Open* 5 (2). doi:10.1177/2332858419859843.

Cioffi, G. 1984. "Observing Composing Behaviors of Primary-Age Children: The Interaction of Oral and Written Language." In *New Directions in Composition Research*, eds. R. Beach & L.S. Bridwell, 171–90. New York: Guilford.

Clay, M.M. 1975. *What Did I Write?* Auckland, New Zealand: Heinemann.

Cohen, L.B., & B.A. Younger. 1984. "Infant Perception of Angular Relations." *Infant Behavior & Development* 7 (1): 37–47.

Cole, P.M., S.E. Martin, & T.A. Dennis. 2004. "Emotion Regulation as a Scientific Construct: Methodological Challenges and Directions for Child Development Research. *Child Development* 74 (2): 317–33.

Collins, M.F. 2010. "ELL Preschoolers' English Vocabulary Acquisition from Storybook Reading." *Early Childhood Research Quarterly* 25 (1): 84–97.

Collins, M.F. 2016. "Supporting Inferential Thinking in Preschoolers: Effects of Discussion on Children's Story Comprehension." *Early Education and Development* 27 (7): 932–56.

Collins, M.F. 2023. "Beyond Questions: A Fellowship of Opportunities for Fostering Preschoolers' Story Comprehension." *The Reading Teacher* 76 (4): 400–11.

Colonnesi, C., G.J.J.M. Stams, I. Koster, & M.J. Noom. 2010. "The Relation Between Pointing and Language Development: A Meta-Analysis." *Developmental Review* 30 (4): 352–66.

Common Sense Media. 2011. *Zero to Eight: Children's Media Use in America—A Common Sense Media Research Study.* Report. San Francisco: Common Sense Media. www.commonsensemedia.org/sites/default/files/research/report/zerotoeightfinal2011.pdf.

Condon, S. 1979. "Neonatal Entrainment and Enculturation." In *Before Speech: The Beginning of Interpersonal Communication*, ed. M. Bullowa, 131–48. Cambridge, MA: Cambridge University Press.

Connolly, K., & M. Dalgleish. 1989. "The Emergence of Tool-Using Skill in Infancy." *Developmental Psychology* 25 (6): 894–912.

Conradi-Smith, K., & E.H. Hiebert. 2022. "What Does Research Say About the Texts We Use in Elementary School?" *Phi Delta Kappan* 103 (8): 8–13.

Copeland, K.A., S. Sherman, C.A. Kendeigh, H.J. Kalkwarf, & B.E. Saelens. 2012. "Societal Values and Policies May Curtail Preschool Children's Physical Activity in Child Care Centers." *Pediatrics* 129 (2): 265–74.

Copple, C., ed. 2012. *Growing Minds: Building Strong Cognitive Foundations in Early Childhood*. Washington, DC: NAEYC.

Corbetta, D., & W. Snapp-Childs. 2009. "Seeing and Touching: The Role of Sensory-Motor Experience on the Development of Infant Reaching." *Infant Behavior and Development* 32 (1): 44–58.

Corkum, V., & C. Moore. 1995. "Development of Joint Visual Attention in Infants." In *Joint Attention: Its Origins and Role in Development*, eds. C. Moore & P. Dunham, 61–83. Hillsdale, NJ: Erlbaum.

Correia, M.P. 2011. "Fiction vs. Informational Texts: Which Will Kindergartners Choose?" *Young Children* 66 (6): 100–04.

Council of Chief State School Officers. 2012. "Framework for English Language Proficiency Development Standards Corresponding to the Common Core State Standards and the Next Generation Science Standards." Washington, DC: Council of Chief State School Officers.

Coyne, M., D.B. McCoach, S. Loftus, R. Zipoli, & S. Kapp. 2009. "Direct Vocabulary Instruction in Kindergarten: Teaching for Breadth vs. Depth." *Elementary School Journal* 110 (1): 1–18.

Crosson, A.C., & N.K. Lesaux. 2010. "Revisiting Assumptions About the Relationship of Fluent Reading to Comprehension: Spanish Speakers' Text-Reading Fluency in English." *Reading and Writing* 23 (5): 475–94.

Cunningham, A., & J. Zibulsky. 2011. "Tell Me a Story: Examining the Benefits of Shared Reading." In *Handbook of Early Literacy Research*, Vol. 3, eds. S.B. Neuman & D.K. Dickinson, 396–411. New York: Guilford.

Curcic, D. 2023. "Children's Book Sales Statistics." *WordsRated,* January 30. https://wordsrated.com/children-book-sales.

Dahl, K., & P. Freppon. 1995. "A Comparison of Inner-City Children's Interpretations of Reading and Writing Instruction in the Early Grades in Skills-Based and Whole Language Classrooms." *Reading Research Quarterly* 31 (1): 50–74.

De Jong, M.T., & A.G. Bus. 2002. "Quality of Book-Reading Matters for Emergent Readers: An Experiment with the Same Book in a Regular or Electronic Format." *Journal of Educational Psychology* 94 (1): 145–55.

De Jong, M.T., & A.G. Bus. 2004. "The Efficacy of Electronic Books in Fostering Kindergarten Children's Emergent Story Understanding." *Reading Research Quarterly* 39 (4): 378–93.

Di Lorenzo, R., A. Blasi, C. Junge, C. van den Boomen, R. van Rooijen, & C. Kemner. 2019. "Brain Responses to Faces and Facial Expression in 5-Month-Olds: An fNIRS Study." *Frontiers in Psychology* 10: 1240. doi:10.3389/fpsyg.2019.01240.

Dickinson, D.K., R.M. Golinkoff, & K. Hirsh-Pasek. 2010. "Speaking Out for Language: Why Language Is Central to Reading Development." *Educational Researcher* 39 (4): 305–15.

Dickinson, D.K., A. McCabe, N. Clark-Chiarelli, & A. Wolf. 2004. "Cross-Language Transfer of Phonological Awareness in Low-Income Spanish and English Bilingual Children." *Applied Psycholinguistics* 25 (3): 323–47.

Dickinson, D.K., K. Nesbitt, M. Collins, E. Hadley, K. Newman, B. Rivera, H. Ilgaz, A. Nicolopoulou, R. Golinkoff, & K. Hirsh-Pasek. 2019. "Teaching for Breadth and Depth of Vocabulary Knowledge: Learning from Explicit and Implicit Instruction and the Storybook Text." *Early Childhood Research Quarterly* 47 (2): 341–56.

Dickinson, D.K., & M.V. Porche. 2011. "Relation Between Language Experiences in Preschool Classrooms and Children's Kindergarten and Fourth-Grade Language and Reading Abilities." *Child Development* 82 (3): 870–86.

Dickinson, D.K., & M.W. Smith. 1994. "Long-Term Effects of Preschool Teachers' Book Readings on Low-Income Children's Vocabulary and Story Comprehension." *Reading Research Quarterly* 29 (2): 105–22.

Duke, N. 2000. "3.6 Minutes per Day: The Scarcity of Informational Texts in First Grade." *Reading Research Quarterly* 35 (2): 202–24.

Duke, N.K., & V.S. Bennett-Armistead. With A. Huxley, M. Johnson, D. McLurkin, E. Roberts, C. Rosen, & E. Vogel. 2003. *Reading and Writing Informational Text in the Primary Grades: Research-Based Practices.* New York: Scholastic.

Duke, N.K., & J. Carlisle. 2011. "The Development of Comprehension." In *Handbook of Reading Research,* Vol. IV, eds. M.L. Kamil, P.D. Pearson, E.B. Moje, & P.P. Afflerbach, 199–228. New York: Routledge.

Duke, N.K., A.-L. Halvorsen, & J.A. Knight. 2012. "Building Knowledge Through Informational Text." In *Knowledge Development in Early Childhood: Sources of Learning and Classroom Implications,* eds. A.M. Pinkham, T. Kaefer, & S.B. Neuman, 205–19. New York: Guilford.

Duke, N.K., & J. Kays. 1998. "'Can I Say Once Upon a Time?': Kindergarten Children Developing Knowledge of Information Book Language." *Early Childhood Research Quarterly* 13 (2): 295–318.

Duke, N.K., K.L. Roberts, R.R. Norman, N.M. Martin, J.A. Knight, P.M. Morsink, & S.L. Calkins. 2010. "What We've Been Learning About Children's Visual Literacy and What It Might Mean for Assessment and Instruction." Paper presented at the annual meeting of the International Reading Association, in Chicago, IL.

Duke, N.K., A.E. Ward, & P.D. Pearson. 2021. "The Science of Reading Comprehension Instruction." *Reading Teacher* 74 (6): 663–72.

Dunn, J. 1998. "Young Children's Understanding of Other People: Evidence from Observation Within the Family." In *Cultural Worlds of Early Childhood,* eds. M. Woodhead, D. Faulkner, & K. Littleton, 101–16. New York: The Open University.

Dunn, J., I. Bretherton, & P. Munn. 1987. "Conversations About Feeling States Between Mothers and Their Young Children." *Developmental Psychology* 23 (1): 132–39.

Durkin, D. 1966. *Children Who Read Early: Two Longitudinal Studies.* New York: Teachers College Press.

Dweck, C.S. 2017. "From Needs to Goals and Representations: Foundations for a Unified Theory of Motivation, Personality, and Development." *Psychological Review* 124 (6): 689–719.

Dyson, A.H. 2000. "Writing and the Sea of Voices: Oral Language in, Around, and About Writing." In *Perspectives on Writing: Research, Theory, and Practice,* eds. R. Indrisano & James Squire, 45–65. Newark, DE: International Reading Association.

Dyson, A.H. 2020. "'We're Playing Sisters, on Paper!': Children Composing on Graphic Playgrounds." *Literacy* 54 (2): 3–12.

Ehri, L.C. 2022. "What Teachers Need to Know and Do to Teach Letter-Sounds, Phonemic Awareness, Word Reading, and Phonics." *Reading Teacher* 76 (1): 53–61.

Ehri, L.C., & J. Sweet. 1991. "Fingerpoint-Reading of Memorized Text: What Enables Beginners to Process the Print?" *Reading Research Quarterly* 26 (4): 443–62.

Evaluation and Training Institute. 2016. *UPSTART Program Evaluation: Year 6 Program Results*. Cohort 6 Technical Report. Culver City, CA: Evaluation and Training Institute. www.waterford.org-uploads.s3.amazonaws.com/wp-content/uploads/2015/12/14175207/ETI-UPSTART-Cohort-6-Evaluation-Report-1.pdf.

Fang, Z. 2008. "Going Beyond the Fab Five: Helping Students Cope with the Unique Linguistic Challenges of Expository Reading in Intermediate Grades." *Journal of Adolescent & Adult Literacy* 51 (6): 476–87.

Fantz, R.L. 1963. "Pattern Vision in Newborn Infants." *Science* 140 (3564): 296–97.

Fein, G.G. 1975. "A Transformational Analysis of Pretending." *Developmental Psychology* 11 (3): 291–96.

Fein, G.G. 1984. "The Self-Building Potential of Make-Believe Play, or 'I Got a Fish, All by Myself.'" In *Child's Play: Developmental and Applied*, eds. T.D. Yawkey & A.D. Pellegrini, 125–42. Hillsdale, NJ: Lawrence Erlbaum.

Fenson, L. 1984. "Developmental Trends for Action and Speech in Pretend Play." In *Symbolic Play: The Development of Social Understanding*, ed. I. Bretherton, 249–70. New York: Academic Press.

Fenson, L., P.S. Dale, J.S. Reznick, E. Bates, D.J. Thal, & S.J. Pethick. 1994. "Variability in Early Communicative Development." *Monographs of the Society for Research in Child Development* 59 (5): Serial No. 242.

Fenson, L., J. Kagan, R. Kearsley, & P. Zelazo. 1976. "The Developmental Progression of Manipulative Play in the First Two Years." *Child Development* 47 (1): 232–36.

Fenson, L., & D.S. Ramsay. 1980. "Decentration and Integration of the Child's Play in the Second Year." *Child Development* 51 (1): 171–78.

Ferreiro, E. 1986. "The Interplay Between Information and Assimilation in Beginning Literacy." In *Emergent Literacy: Writing and Reading*, eds. W.H. Teale & E. Sulzby, 15–49. Norwood, NJ: Ablex.

Ferreiro, E., & A. Teberosky. 1982. *Literacy Before Schooling*. Trans. K.G. Castro. Portsmouth, NH: Heinemann.

Fisch, S.M., J.S. Shulman, A. Akerman, & G.A. Levin. 2002. "Reading Between the Pixels: Parent-Child Interaction While Reading Online Storybooks." *Early Education and Development* 12 (4): 435–51.

Fletcher, K.L., & W.H. Finch. 2015. "The Role of Book Familiarity and Book Type on Mothers' Reading Strategies and Toddlers' Responsiveness." *Journal of Early Childhood Literacy* 15 (1): 73–96.

Fletcher, K.L., & E. Reese. 2005. "Picture Book Reading with Young Children: A Conceptual Framework." *Developmental Review* 25 (1): 64–103.

Flom, R., G.O. Deak, C.G. Phill, & A.D. Pick. 2004. "Nine-Month-Olds' Shared Visual Attention as a Function of Gesture and Object Location." *Infant Behavior & Research* 27 (1): 181–94.

Flynn, R.M., & R.A. Richert. 2015. "Parents Support Preschoolers' Use of a Novel Interactive Device." *Infant and Child Development* 24 (6): 624–42.

Frank, M.C., E. Vul, & S.P. Johnson. 2009. "Development of Infants' Attention to Faces During the First Year." *Cognition* 110 (2): 160–70.

Franks, A.M., C. Seaman, E.K. Franks, W. Rollyson, & T. Davies. 2022. "Parental Reading to Infants Improves Language Score: A Rural Family Medicine Intervention." *Journal of the American Board of Family Medicine* 35 (6): 1156–62.

Gardner, H. 1980. *Artful Scribbles: The Significance of Children's Drawings*. New York: Basic Books.

Geangu, E., O. Benga, D. Stahl, & T. Striano. 2010. "Contagious Crying Beyond the First Days of Life." *Infant Behavior and Development* 33 (3): 279–88.

Gelman, R., & K. Brenneman. 2004. "Science Learning Pathways for Young Children." *Early Childhood Research Quarterly* 19 (1): 150–58.

Gelman, S.A., & J.D. Coley. 1990. "The Importance of Knowing a Dodo Is a Bird: Categories and Inferences in 2-Year-Old Children." *Developmental Psychology* 26 (5): 796–804.

Genishi, C., & A.H. Dyson. 2009. *Children, Language, and Literacy: Diverse Learners in Diverse Times*. New York: Teachers College Press; Washington, DC: NAEYC.

Gerde, H.K., & G.E. Bingham. 2023. "Using the Science of Early Literacy to Design Professional Development for Writing." In *Handbook on the Science of Early Literacy*, eds. S.Q. Cabell, S.B. Neuman, & N.P. Terry, 236–52. New York: Guilford.

Gersten, R., K. Haymond, R. Newman-Gonchar, J. Dimino, & M. Jayanthi. 2020. "Meta-Analysis of the Impact of Reading Interventions for Students in the Primary Grades." *Journal of Research on Educational Effectiveness* 13 (2): 401–27.

Gesell, A., & F.L. Ilg. 1937. *Feeding Behavior of Infants*. Philadelphia: Lippincott.

Gibson, E.J. 1975. "Theory-Based Research on Reading and Its Implications for Instruction." In *Toward a Literate Society*, eds. J.B. Carroll & J.S. Chall, 288–321. New York: McGraw-Hill.

Gilkerson, J., J.A. Richards, S.F. Warren, D.K. Oller, R. Russo, & B. Vohr. 2018. "Language Experience in the Second Year of Life and Language Outcomes in Late Childhood." *Pediatrics* 142 (4): e20174276. doi:10.1542/peds.2017-4276.

Gogate, L., & G. Hollich. 2016. "Early Verb-Action and Noun-Object Mapping Across Sensory Modalities: A Neuro-Developmental View." *Developmental Neuropsychology* 41 (5–8): 293–307.

Gola, A.A.H. 2012. "Mental Verb Input for Promoting Children's Theory of Mind: A Training Study." *Cognitive Development* 27 (1): 64–76.

Golinkoff, R.M., D.D. Can, M. Soderstrom, & K. Hirsh-Pasek. 2015. "(Baby)Talk to Me: The Social Context of Infant-Directed Speech and Its Effects on Early Language Acquisition." *Current Directions in Psychological Science* 24 (5): 339–44.

Goncu, A. 1998. "Development of Intersubjectivity in Social Play." In *Cultural Worlds of Early Childhood*, eds. M. Woodhead, D. Faulkner, & K. Littleton, 117–32. New York: The Open University.

Gratier, M., & E. Devouche. 2011. "Imitation and Repetition of Prosodic Contour in Vocal Interaction at 3 Months." *Developmental Psychology* 47 (1): 67–76.

Graves, D. 1981. "A Case Study Observing the Development of Primary Children's Composing, Spelling, and Motor Behavior During the Writing Process." Final report. (NIE Grant No. G-78-0174; ED 218–653.) Durham, NH: University of New Hampshire.

Grolig, L. 2020. "Shared Storybook Reading and Oral Language Development: A Bioecological Perspective." *Frontiers in Psychology* 11: 1818. doi:10.3389 /fpsyg.2020.01818.

Guernsey, L., & M.H. Levine. 2015. *Tap, Click, Read: Growing Readers in a World of Screens.* San Francisco: Jossey-Bass.

Hamlin, J.K., K. Wynn, & P. Bloom. 2007. "Social Evaluations by Preverbal Infants." *Nature* 450 (7169): 557–60.

Hammer, C.S., E. Hoff, Y. Uchikoshi, C. Gillanders, D. Castro, & L.E. Sandilos. 2014. "The Language and Literacy Development of Young Dual Language Learners: A Critical Review." *Early Childhood Research Quarterly* 29 (4): 715–33.

Hammer, C.S., S. Scarpino, & M.D. Davison. 2011. "Beginning with Language: Spanish-English Bilingual Preschoolers' Early Literacy Development." In *Handbook of Early Literacy Research*, Vol. 3, eds. S.B. Neuman & D.K. Dickinson, 118–35. New York: Guilford.

Hay, D.F., F. Nash, & J. Pederson. 1981. "Responses of Six-Month-Olds to the Distress of Their Peers." *Child Development* 52 (3): 1071–75.

Hayes, J.R. 2000. "A New Framework for Understanding Cognition and Affect in Writing." In *Perspectives on Writing: Research, Theory, and Practice*, eds. R. Indrisano & J.R. Squire, 6–41. Newark, DE: International Reading Association.

Hepburn, E., B. Egan, & N. Flynn. 2010. "Vocabulary Acquisition in Young Children: The Role of the Story." *Journal of Early Childhood Literacy* 10 (2): 159–82.

Hirsh-Pasek, K., & R.M. Golinkoff. 2007. *Celebrate the Scribble: Appreciating Children's Art.* Easton, PA: Crayola Beginnings Press.

Hoff, E., C. Core, S. Place, R. Rumiche, M. Señor, & M. Parra. 2012. "Dual Language Exposure and Early Bilingual Development." *Journal of Child Language* 39 (1): 1–27.

Hoffman, J.L., & K.A. Paciga. 2014. "Click, Swipe, and Read: Sharing E-Books with Toddlers and Preschoolers." *Early Childhood Education Journal* 42 (6): 379–88.

Holland, J.W. 2008. "Reading Aloud with Infants: The Controversy, the Myth, and a Case Study." *Early Childhood Education Journal* 35 (4): 383–85.

Hollich, G.J., K. Hirsh-Pasek, R. Golinkoff, R.J. Brand, E. Brown, H.L. Chung, E. Hennon, C. Rocroi, & L. Bloom. 2000. "Breaking the Language Barrier: An Emergentist Coalition Model for the Origins of Word Learning." *Monographs of the Society for Research in Child Development* 65 (3): 1–135.

Hood, M., E. Conlon, & G. Andrews. 2008. "Preschool Home Literacy Practices and Children's Literacy Development: A Longitudinal Analysis." *Journal of Educational Psychology* 100 (2): 252–71.

Horner, S.L. 2004. "Observational Learning During Shared Book Reading: The Effects on Preschoolers' Attention to Print and Letter Knowledge." *Reading Psychology* 25 (3): 167–88.

Horst, J.S., K.L. Parsons, & N.M. Bryan. 2011. "Get the Story Straight: Contextual Repetition Promotes Word Learning from Storybooks." *Frontiers in Psychology* 2: 17. doi:10.3389/fpsyg.2011.00017.

International Literacy Association. 2019. "Digital Resources in Early Childhood Literacy Development." Position statement and research brief. Newark, DE: International Literacy Association.

IOM (Institute of Medicine) & NRC (National Research Council). 2015. *Transforming the Workforce for Children Birth Through Age 8: A Unifying Foundation.* Report. Washington, DC: National Academies Press.

Jahdhami, S.A. 2023. "Motherese in Omani Arabic." *British Journal of English Linguistics* 11 (2): 1–31.

Jing, M., T. Ye, H.L. Kirkorian, & M.L. Mares. 2023. "Screen Media Exposure and Young Children's Vocabulary Learning and Development: A Meta-Analysis." *Child Development* 94 (5): 1398–418.

Johnson, D.D. 2000. "Just the Right Word: Vocabulary and Writing." In *Perspectives on Writing: Research, Theory, and Practice*, eds. R. Indrisano & J.R. Squire, 162–86. Newark, DE: International Reading Association.

Johnson, S.P. 2011. "Development of Visual Perception." *Wiley Interdisciplinary Reviews: Cognitive Science* 2 (5): 515–28.

Jones, G., F. Cabiddu, D.K.J. Barrett, A. Castro, & B. Lee. 2023. "How the Characteristics of Words in Child-Directed Speech Differ from Adult-Directed Speech to Influence Children's Productive Vocabularies." *First Language* 43 (3): 253–82.

Justice, L.M., & H.L. Ezell. 2002. "Use of Storybook Reading to Increase Print Awareness in At-Risk Children. *American Journal of Speech-Language Pathology* 11 (1): 17–29.

Justice, L.M., J. Meier, & S. Walpole. 2005. "Learning New Words from Storybooks: An Efficacy Study with At-Risk Kindergartners." *Language, Speech, and Hearing Services in Schools* 36 (1): 17–32.

Justice, L.M., K. Pence, R. Bowles, & A.K. Wiggins. 2006. "An Investigation of Four Hypotheses Concerning the Order by Which 4-Year-Old Children Learn the Alphabet Letters." *Early Childhood Research Quarterly* 21 (3): 374–89.

Justice, L.M., Y. Petscher, C. Schatschgneider, & A. Mashburn. 2011. "Peer Effects in Preschool Classrooms: Classmates' Abilities Are Associated with Children's Language Growth." *Child Development* 82 (6): 1768–77.

Karniol, R. 1989. "The Role of Manual Manipulation Stages in the Infant's Acquisition of Perceived Control over Objects." *Developmental Review* 9 (3): 205–33.

Karrass, J., & J.M. Braungart-Rieker. 2005. "Effects of Shared Parent-Infant Book Reading on Early Language Acquisition." *Journal of Applied Developmental Psychology: An International Lifespan Journal* 26 (2): 133–48.

Kaye, K., & A. Fogel. 1980. "The Temporal Structure of Face-to-Face Communication Between Mothers and Infants." *Developmental Psychology* 16 (5): 454–64.

Kelly, L.B. 2020. "Bilingual Children's Talk About Informational Text: Focus on Ideas, Images, and Print." *Reading Horizons* 59 (2): 20–42.

Kelley, J.G., N.K. Lesaux, M.J. Kieffer, & S.E. Faller. 2010. "Effective Academic Vocabulary Instruction in the Urban Middle School." *The Reading Teacher* 64 (1): 5–14.

Kim, J.E., & J. Anderson. 2008. "Mother-Child Shared Reading with Print and Digital Texts." *Journal of Early Childhood Literacy* 8 (2): 213–45.

Kim, K., & E.S. Spelke. 1992. "Infants' Sensitivity to Effects of Gravity on Visible Object Motion." *Journal of Experimental Psychology: Human Perception and Performance* 18 (3): 385–93.

Kirkorian, H.L., K. Choi, & T.A. Pempek. 2016. "Toddlers' Word Learning from Contingent and Noncontingent Video on Touch Screens." *Child Development* 87 (2): 405–13.

Klop, D., L. Marais, A. Msindwana, & F. de Wet. 2018. "Learning New Words from an Interactive Electronic Storybook Intervention." *South African Journal of Communication Disorders* 65 (1): a601. doi:10.4102/sajcd.v65i1.601.

Korat, O., S. Atishkin, & O. Segal-Drori. 2022 "Vocabulary Enrichment Using an E-Book with and Without Kindergarten Teacher's Support Among LSES Children." *Early Child Development and Care* 192 (9): 1384–401.

Korat, O., O. Kozlov-Peretz, & O. Segal-Drori. 2017. "Repeated E-Book Reading and Its Contribution to Learning New Words Among Kindergartners." *Journal of Education and Training Studies* 5 (7): 60–72.

Korat, O., I. Levin, S. Atishkin, & M. Turgeman. 2014. "E-Book as Facilitator of Vocabulary Acquisition: Support of Adults, Dynamic Dictionary and Static Dictionary." *Reading and Writing* 27 (4): 613–29.

Kotovsky, L., & R. Baillargeon. 1994. "Calibration-Based Reasoning About Collision Events in 11-Month-Old Infants." *Cognition* 51 (2): 107–29.

Kotovsky, L., & R. Baillargeon. 1998. "The Development of Calibration-Based Reasoning About Collision Events in Young Infants." *Cognition* 67 (3): 311–51.

Kotovsky, L., & R. Baillargeon. 2000. "Reasoning About Collision Events Involving Inert Objects in 7.5-Month-Old Young Infants." *Developmental Science* 3 (3): 344–59.

Kuhl, P.K., R.R. Ramírez, A. Bosseler, J.-F.L. Lin, & T. Imada. 2014. "Infants' Brain Responses to Speech Suggest Analysis by Synthesis." *Proceedings of the National Academy of Sciences* 111 (31): 11238–45.

LaBarbera, J.D., C.E. Izard, P. Vietze, & S.A. Parisi. 1976. "Four- and Six-Month-Old Infants' Visual Response to Joy, Anger, and Neutral Expressions." *Child Development* 47 (2): 535–38.

Labbo, L.D. 2009. "'Let's Do the Computer Story Again, Nana': A Case Study of How a 2-Year-Old and His Grandmother Shared Thinking Spaces During Multiple Readings of an Electronic Story." In *Multimedia and Literacy Development: Improving Achievement for Young Learners*, eds. A.G. Bus & S.B. Neuman, 196–210. New York: Routledge.

Labbo, L.D., & M.R. Kuhn. 2000. "Weaving Chains of Affect and Cognition: A Young Child's Understanding of CD-ROM Talking Books." *Journal of Literacy Research* 32 (2): 187–210.

LaBerge, D., & S.J. Samuels. 1974. "Toward a Theory of Automatic Information Processing in Reading." *Cognitive Psychology* 6 (2): 293–323.

Landry, S.E., P.R. Smith, & K.E. Swank. 2006. "Responsive Parenting: Establishing Early Foundations for Social, Communication, and Independent Problem-Solving Skills." *Developmental Psychology* 42: 627–42.

Language and Reading Research Consortium. 2015. "The Dimensionality of Language Skills in Young Children." *Child Development* 86 (6): 1948–65.

Lavine, L. 1977. "Differentiation of Letter-Like Forms in Prereading Children." *Developmental Psychology* 13 (2): 89–94.

Leacox, L., & C.W. Jackson. 2014. "Spanish Vocabulary-Bridging Technology-Enhanced Instruction for Young English Language Learners' Word Learning." *Journal of Early Childhood Literacy* 14 (2): 175–97.

Lee, Y., J. Lee, M. Han, & J.A. Schickedanz. 2011. "Narratives, the Classroom Book Environment, and Teacher Attitudes Toward Literacy Practices in Korea and the United States." *Early Education and Development* 22 (2): 234–55.

Legerstee, M. 1991. "Changes in the Quality of Infant Sounds as a Function of Social and Nonsocial Stimulation." *First Language* 11 (33): 327–43.

Legerstee, M. 1992. "A Review of the Animate-Inanimate Distinction in Infancy: Implications for Models of Social and Cognitive Knowing." *Early Development and Parenting* 1 (1): 59–67.

Legerstee, M., C. Corter, & K. Kienapple. 1990. "Hand, Arm, and Facial Actions of Young Infants to a Social and Nonsocial Stimulus." *Child Development* 61 (3): 774–84.

Lesaux, N.K., & M.J. Kieffer. 2010. "Exploring Sources of Reading Comprehension Difficulties Among Language Minority Learners and Their Classmates in Early Adolescence." *American Educational Research Journal* 47 (3): 596–632.

Leung, C.B. 2008. "Preschoolers' Acquisition of Scientific Vocabulary Through Repeated Read-Aloud Events, Retellings, and Hands-On Science Activities." *Reading Psychology* 29 (2): 165–93.

Lewis, M., S.M. Alessandri, & M.W. Sullivan. 1992. "Differences in Shame and Pride as a Function of Children's Gender and Task Difficulty." *Child Development* 63 (3): 630–38.

Lewis, M., M.W. Sullivan, C. Stanger, & M. Weiss. 1989. "Self Development and Self-Conscious Emotions." *Child Development* 60 (1): 146–56.

Linebarger, D., J.T. Piotrowski, & C.R. Greenwood. 2010. "On-Screen Print: The Role of Captions as a Supplemental Literacy Tool." *Journal of Research in Reading* 33 (2): 148–67.

Lonigan, C.J. 2006. "Conceptualizing Phonological Processing Skills in Preschoolers." In *Handbook of Early Literacy Research*, Vol. 2, eds. D.K. Dickinson & S.B. Neuman, 77–89. New York: Guilford.

López, L.M., & M.M. Páez. 2021. *Teaching Dual Language Learners: What Early Childhood Educators Need to Know*. Baltimore: Brookes.

López-Escribano, C., S. Valverde-Montesino, & V. García-Ortega. 2021. "The Impact of E-Book Reading on Young Children's Emergent Literacy Skills: An Analytical Review." *International Journal of Environmental Research and Public Health* 18 (12): 6510. doi:10.3390/ijerph18126510.

Lundberg, I., J. Frost, & O. Petersen. 1988. "Effects of an Extensive Program for Stimulating Phonological Awareness in Preschool Children." *Reading Research Quarterly* 23 (3): 263–84.

Luo, R., & C.S. Tamis-LeMonda. 2017. "Reciprocity Between Maternal Questions and Child Contributions During Book-Sharing. *Early Childhood Research Quarterly* 38: 71–83.

Mandler, J.M., & L. McDonough. 1998. "Studies in Inductive Inference in Infancy." *Cognitive Psychology* 37 (1): 60–80.

ManyBabies Consortium. 2020. "Quantifying Sources of Variability in Infancy Research Using the Infant-Directed-Speech Preference." *Advances in Methods and Practices in Psychological Science* 3 (1): 24–52.

Marcinowski, E., E. Nelson, J. Campbell, & G. Michel. 2019. "The Development of Object Construction from Infancy Through Toddlerhood." *Infancy* 24 (3): 368–91.

Marsh, J., J. Lahmar, L. Plowman, D. Yamada-Rice, J. Bishop, & F. Scott. 2021. "Under Threes' Play with Tablets." *Journal of Early Childhood Research* 19 (3): 283–97.

Martin, L.E. 1998. "Early Book Reading: How Mothers Deviate from Printed Text for Young Children." *Reading Research and Instruction* 37 (2): 137–60.

Martinez, M., & N. Roser. 1985. "Read It Again: The Value of Repeated Readings During Storytime. *The Reading Teacher* 40 (5): 444–51.

Martinez, M.G., & W.H. Teale. 1989. "Children's Book Selections in a Kindergarten Classroom Library." Unpublished raw data. (Cited in J.S. Fractor, M.C. Woodruff, M.G. Martinez, & W.H. Teale. 1993. "Let's Not Miss Opportunities to Promote Voluntary Reading: Classroom Libraries in the Elementary School." *The Reading Teacher* 46 (6): 476–84.)

Mashburn, A., L.M. Justice, J.T. Downer, & R.C. Pianta. 2009. "Peer Effects on Children's Language Achievement During Pre-Kindergarten." *Child Development* 80 (3): 686–702.

Masonheimer, P.E., P.A. Drum, & L.C. Ehri. 1984. "Does Environmental Print Identification Lead Children into Word Reading?" *Journal of Reading Behavior* 16 (4): 257–71.

Maureen, I.Y., H. van der Meij, & T. de Jong. 2020. "Enhancing Storytelling Activities to Support Early (Digital) Literacy Development in Early Childhood Education." *International Journal of Early Childhood* 52: 55–76.

McArthur, D., L.B. Adamson, & D.F. Deckner. 2005. "As Stories Become Familiar: Mother-Child Conversations During Shared Reading." *Merrill Palmer Quarterly: Journal of Developmental Psychology* 51 (4): 389–411.

McCune-Nicolich, I. 1981. "Toward Symbolic Functioning: Structure of Early Pretend Games and Potential Parallels with Language." *Child Development* 52 (3): 785–97.

McDonough, L., & J.M. Mandler. 1998. "Inductive Generalization in 9- and 11-Month-Olds." *Developmental Science* 1 (2): 227–32.

McGee, L., & D.J. Richgels. 1989. "'K Is Kristen's': Learning the Alphabet from a Child's Perspective." *The Reading Teacher* 39 (2): 216–25.

McGee, L., & J.A. Schickedanz. 2007. "Repeated Interactive Read-Alouds in Preschool and Kindergarten." *The Reading Teacher* 60 (8): 742–51.

Meltzoff, A.N. 1995. "Understanding the Intentions of Others: Re-Enactment of Intended Acts by 18-Month-Old Children." *Developmental Psychology* 31 (5): 838–50.

Meltzoff, A.N., & P. Kuhl. 2016. "Exploring the Infant Social Brain: What's Going on in There?" *ZERO TO THREE* 36 (3): 2–9.

Mermelshtine, R. 2017. "Parent–Child Learning Interactions: A Review of the Literature on Scaffolding." *British Journal of Educational Psychology* 87 (2): 241–54.

Metsala, J.L. 1997. "An Examination of Word Frequency and Neighborhood Density in the Development of Spoken-Word Recognition." *Memory & Cognition* 25 (1): 47–56.

Metsala, J.L. 1999. "Young Children's Phonological Awareness and Nonword Repetition as a Function of Vocabulary Development." *Journal of Educational Psychology* 91 (1): 3–19.

Metsala, J.L., & A.C. Walley. 1998. "Spoken Vocabulary Growth and the Segmental Restructuring of Lexical Representations: Precursors to Phonemic Awareness and Early Reading Ability." In *Word Recognition in Beginning Literacy*, eds. J.L. Metsala & L.C. Ehri, 89–120. Hillsdale, NJ: Erlbaum.

Mills, C.M., J.H. Danovitch, M.G. Grant, & F.B. Elashi. 2012. "Little Pitchers Use Their Big Ears: Preschoolers Solve Problems by Listening to Others Ask Questions." *Child Development* 83 (2): 568–80.

Milteer, K., R. Ginsburg, & D.A. Mulligan. 2012. "The Importance of Play in Promoting Healthy Child Development and Maintaining Strong Parent-Child Bond: Focus on Children in Poverty." *Pediatrics* 129 (1): 204–13.

Mohammed, S., A. Afaya, & A.S. Abukari. 2023. "Reading, Singing, and Storytelling: The Impact of Caregiver-Child Interaction and Child Access to Books and Preschool on Early Childhood Development in Ghana." *Scientific Reports* 13: 13751. doi:10.1038/s41598-023-38439-5.

Montag, J.L., M.N. Jones, & L.B. Smith. 2015. "The Words Children Hear: Picture Books and the Statistics for Language Learning." *Psychological Science* 26 (9): 1489–96.

Morgante, J.D., & R. Keen. 2008. "Vision and Action: The Effect of Visual Feedback on Infants' Exploratory Behaviors." *Infant Behavior and Development* 31 (4): 729–33.

Morris, A.S., J.S. Silk, M.D. Morris, & L. Steinberg. 2011. "The Influence of Mother-Child Emotion Regulation Strategies on Children's Expression of Anger and Sadness." *Developmental Psychology* 47 (1): 213–25.

Morrow, L. 1985. "Reading and Retelling Stories: Strategies for Emergent Readers." *The Reading Teacher* 38 (9): 870–75.

Muhinyi, A., & M.L. Rowe. 2019. "Shared Reading with Preverbal Infants and Later Language Development." *Journal of Applied Developmental Psychology* 64 (July–Sept): 101053.

Myowa-Yamakoshi, M., Y. Kawakita, M. Okanda, & H. Takeshita. 2011. "Visual Experience Influences 12-Month-Old Infants' Perception of Goal-Directed Actions of Others." *Developmental Psychology* 47 (4): 1042–49.

NAEYC. 2019. "Advancing Equity in Early Childhood Education." Position statement. Washington, DC: NAEYC. www.naeyc.org/resources/position-statements/equity.

NAEYC. 2020. "Developmentally Appropriate Practice." Position statement. Washington, DC: NAEYC. www.naeyc.org/resources/position-statements/dap.

NAEYC. 2022. *Developmentally Appropriate Practice in Early Childhood Programs Serving Children from Birth Through Age 8.* 4th ed. Washington, DC: NAEYC.

NAEYC & Fred Rogers Center for Early Learning and Children's Media. 2012. "Technology and Interactive Media as Tools in Early Childhood Programs Serving Children from Birth Through Age 8." Joint position statement. Washington, DC: NAEYC; Latrobe, PA: Fred Rogers Center for Early Learning at Saint Vincent College. www.naeyc.org/files/naeyc/file/positions/PS_technology_WEB2.pdf.

Nagy, W.E., R.C. Anderson, & P.A. Herman. 1987. "Learning Words from Context During Normal Reading." *American Educational Research Journal* 24 (2): 237–70.

Nagy, W., & E.H. Hiebert. 2011. "Toward a Theory of Word Selection." In *Handbook of Reading Research,* Vol. IV, eds. M.L. Kamil, P.D. Pearson, E.B. Moje, & P.P. Afflerbach, 388–404. New York: Routledge.

Nagy, W., & D. Townsend. 2012. "Words as Tools: Learning Academic Vocabulary as Language Acquisition." *Reading Research Quarterly* 47 (1): 91–108.

National Governors Association Center for Best Practices, Council of Chief State School Officers. 2010. "Common Core State Standard (English Language Arts)." Washington, DC: National Governors Association Center for Best Practices, Council of Chief State School Officers. https://corestandards.org/wp-content/uploads/2023/09/ELA_Standards1.pdf.

NCES (National Center for Education Statistics). 2003. *The Nation's Report Card: Writing 2002.* Report NCES 2003-529. Washington, DC: US Government Printing Office. https://nces.ed.gov/nationsreportcard/pdf/main2002/2003529.pdf.

NCES (National Center for Education Statistics). 2008. *The Nation's Report Card: Writing 2007*. Report NCES 2008-468. Washington, DC: US Government Printing Office. https://nces.ed.gov/ nationsreportcard/pdf/ main2007/2008468.pdf.

NCES (National Center for Education Statistics). 2012. *The Nation's Report Card: Writing 2011*. Report (NCES 2012-470). Washington, DC: US Government Printing Office. https://nces.ed.gov/ nationsreportcard/pdf/ main2011/2012470.pdf.

NCES (National Center for Education Statistics). 2022. "NAEP Report Card: Reading." *The Nation's Report Card*, last modified January 12. www.nationsreportcard.gov/ reading/?grade=4.

Nelson, D.G.K., K.A. O'Neil, & Y.M. Asher. 2008. "A Mutually Facilitative Relationship Between Learning Names and Learning Concepts in Preschool Children: The Case of Artifacts." *Journal of Cognition and Development* 9 (2): 171–93.

Neuman, S.B., & D.C. Celano. 2013. *Giving Our Children a Fighting Chance: Poverty, Literacy, and the Development of Informational Capital*. New York: Teachers College Press.

Neuman, S.B., & T. Kaefer. 2018. "Developing Low-Income Children's Vocabulary and Content Knowledge Through a Shared Book Reading Program." *Contemporary Educational Psychology* 52: 15–24.

Neumann, M.M., G. Finger, & D.L. Neumann. 2017. "A Conceptual Framework for Emergent Digital Literacy." *Early Childhood Education Journal* 45 (4): 471–79.

Nevo, E., V. Vaknin-Nusbaum, S. Brande, & L. Gambrell. 2020. "Oral Reading Fluency, Reading Motivation, and Reading Comprehension Among Second Graders." *Reading and Writing* 33 (8): 1945–70.

Newman, R.S., M.L. Rowe, & N.B. Ratner. 2016. "Input and Uptake at 7 Months Predicts Toddler Vocabulary: The Role of Child-Directed Speech and Infant Processing Skills in Language Development." *Journal of Child Language* 43 (5): 1158–73.

NICHD (National Institute of Child Health and Human Development). 2000. *Teaching Children to Read: An Evidence-Based Assessment of the Scientific Research Literature on Reading and Its Implications for Reading Instruction*. Report of the National Reading Panel. Washington, DC: US Government Printing Office. www.nichd.nih.gov/ sites/default/files/publications/ pubs/nrp/Documents/report.pdf.

NICHD (National Institute of Child Health and Human Development). 2008. *Developing Early Literacy: A Scientific Synthesis of Early Literacy Development and Implications for Intervention*. Report of the National Early Literacy Panel. Washington, DC: US Government Printing Office. www.nichd.nih.gov/ sites/default/files/publications/ pubs/documents/NELPReport09.pdf.

NICHD (National Institute of Child Health and Human Development) Early Child Care Research Network. 2005. "Pathways to Reading: The Role of Oral Language in the Transition to Reading." *Developmental Psychology* 41 (2): 428–42.

Ninio, A., & J. Bruner. 1978. "The Achievement and Antecedents of Labelling." *Journal of Child Language* 5 (1): 1–15.

Olaussen, I.O. 2022. "A Playful Orchestration in Narrative Expressions by Toddlers: A Contribution to the Understanding of Early Literacy as Event." *Early Years* 42 (2): 137–50.

Olson, J., & E.F. Masur. 2015. "Mothers' Labeling Responses to Infants' Gestures Predict Vocabulary Outcomes." *Journal of Child Language* 42 (6): 1289–1311.

Ouellette, G.P. 2006. "What's Meaning Got to Do with It: The Role of Vocabulary in Word Reading and Reading Comprehension." *Journal of Educational Psychology* 98 (3): 554–66.

OverDrive Education. 2020. "Schools' Usage of Ebooks and Audiobooks Surges in 2020." *OverDrive* (blog), December 1. https://company.overdrive.com /2020/12/01/schools-usage-of -ebooks-and-audiobooks-surges-in-2020.

Paciga, K.A., & C.M. Cassano. 2023. "Does Knowing the Word Matter for Preschool DLLs? Individualized Vocabulary Words on Phonological Awareness Assessments." Unpublished project dissertation. Ann Arbor, MI: Inter-university Consortium for Political and Social Research. doi:10.3886/E196281V1.

Paciga, K.A., & J.L. Hoffman. 2015. "Realizing the Potential of E-Books in Early Education." In *Encyclopedia of Information Science and Technology*, 3rd ed., Vol. VII, ed. M. Khosrow-Pour, 4787–96. Hershey, PA: IGI Global.

Paciga, K.A., J.L. Hoffman, & W.H. Teale. 2011. "The National Early Literacy Panel and Preschool Literacy Instruction: Green Lights, Caution Lights, and Red Lights." *Young Children* 66 (6): 50–57.

Paciga, K.A., J.G. Lisy, & W.H. Teale. 2013. "Better Start Before Kindergarten: Computer Technology, Interactive media, and the Education of Preschoolers." *Asia-Pacific Journal of Research in Early Childhood Education* 7 (2): 85–104.

Paciga, K.A., J.G. Lisy, W.H. Teale, & J.L. Hoffman. 2022. "Student Engagement in Classroom Read Alouds: Considering Seating and Timing." *Illinois Reading Council Journal* 50 (4): 38–46.

Paciga, K.A., & M. Quest. 2017. "It's Hard to Wait: Effortful Control and Story Understanding in Adult-Supported E-Book Reading Across the Early Years." *Journal of Literacy and Technology* 18 (1): 35–79.

Palmer, C.F. 1989. "The Discriminating Nature of Infants' Exploratory Actions." *Developmental Psychology* 25 (6): 885–93.

Pan, B.A., M.L. Rowe, J.D. Singer, & C.E. Snow. 2005. "Maternal Correlates of Growth in Toddler Vocabulary Production in Low-Income Families." *Child Development* 76 (4): 763–82.

Papandropoulos, I., & H. Sinclair. 1974. "What's a Word? Experimental Study of Children's Ideas on Grammar." *Human Development* 17 (2): 241–58.

Paratore, J.R., C.M. Cassano, & J.A. Schickedanz. 2011. "Supporting Early (and Later) Literacy Development at Home and at School: The Long View." In *Handbook of Reading Research*, Vol. IV, eds. M.L. Kamil, P.D. Pearson, E.B. Moje, & P.P Afflerbach, 106–35. New York: Routledge.

Paris, A.H., & S.G. Paris. 2003. "Assessing Narrative Comprehension in Young Children." *Reading Research Quarterly* 38 (1): 36–76.

Parsons, A.W., S.A. Parsons, J.A. Malloy, L.B. Gambrell, B.A Marinak, D.R. Reutzel, M.D. Applegate, A.J. Applegate, & P.C. Fawson. 2018. "Upper Elementary Students' Motivation to Read Fiction and Nonfiction." *Elementary School Journal* 188 (3): 505–23.

Pentimonti, J., T. Zucker, L. Justice, & J. Kadarvek. 2010. "Informational Text Use in Preschool Classroom Read-Alouds." *The Reading Teacher* 63 (8): 656–65.

Peterson, C.L., B. Jesso, & A. McCabe. 1999. "Encouraging Narratives in Preschoolers: An Intervention Study." *Journal of Child Language* 26 (1): 49–97.

Peterson, C.L., & A. McCabe. 1994. "A Social Interactionist Account of Developing Decontextualized Narrative Skill." *Developmental Psychology* 30 (6) 937–48.

Peterson, C., & A. McCabe. 2004. "Echoing Our Parents: Parental Influences on Children's Narration." In *Family Stories and the Life Course: Across Time and Generations,* eds. M.W. Pratt & B.H. Fiese, 27–54. Mahwah, NJ: Lawrence Erlbaum.

Piasta, S.B. 2023. "The Science of Early Alphabet Instruction: What We Do and Do Not Know." In *Handbook on the Science of Early Literacy,* eds. S.Q. Cabell, S.B. Neuman, & N.P. Terry, 83–94. New York: Guilford.

Piasta, S.B., Y. Petscher, & L.M. Justice. 2012. "How Many Letters Should Preschoolers in Public Programs Know? The Diagnostic Efficiency of Various Preschool Letter-Naming Benchmarks for Predicting First-Grade Literacy Achievement." *Journal of Educational Psychology* 104 (4): 945–58.

Pikulski, J.J. 2006. "Fluency: A Developmental and Language Perspective." In *What Research Has to Say About Fluency Instruction*, eds. S.J. Samuels & A.E. Farstrup, 70–93. Newark, DE: International Reading Association.

Pikulski, J.J., & D. Chard. 2005. "Fluency: The Bridge Between Decoding and Reading Comprehension." *The Reading Teacher* 58 (6): 510–21.

Pila, S., C.K. Blackwell, A.R. Lauricella, & E. Wartella. 2019. *Technology in the Lives of Educators and Early Childhood Programs: 2018 Survey.* Report. Evanston, IL: Center on Media and Human Development, Northwestern University. https://cmhd.northwestern.edu/wp-content/uploads/2019/08/NAEYC-Report-2019.pdf.

Pollard-Durodola, S.D., J.E. Gonzalez, D.C. Simmons, M.J. Davis, L. Simmons, & M. Nava-Walichowski. 2011. "Using Knowledge Networks to Develop Preschoolers' Content Vocabulary." *The Reading Teacher* 65 (4): 265–74.

Poulin-Dubois, D., & J.N. Forbes. 2006. "Word, Intention, and Action: A Two-Tiered Model of Action Word Learning." In *Action Meets Word: How Children Learn Verbs*, eds. K. Hirsh-Pasek & R.M. Golinkoff, 262–85. New York: Oxford University Press.

Poulin-Dubois, D., & T.R. Shultz. 1990. "The Infant's Concept of Category: The Distinction Between Social and Nonsocial Objects." *Journal of Genetic Psychology* 151 (1): 77–90.

Price, J., & A. Kalil. 2019. "The Effect of Mother–Child Reading Time on Children's Reading Skills: Evidence from Natural Within-Family Variation." *Child Development* 90 (6): 688–702.

Price, L.H., A. van Kleeck, & C.J. Huberty. 2009. "Talk During Sharing Between Parents and Preschool Children: A Comparison Between Storybook and Expository Book Conditions." *Reading Research Quarterly* 44 (2): 171–94.

Pulverman, R., K. Hirsh-Pasek, R.M. Golinkoff, S. Pruden, & S.J. Salkind. 2006. "Conceptual Foundations for Verb Learning: Celebrating the Event." In *Action Meets Word: How Children Learn Verbs*, eds. K. Hirsh-Pasek & R.M. Golinkoff, 134–59. New York: Oxford University Press.

Purcell-Gates, V. 1996. "Stories, Coupons, and the TV Guide: Relationships Between Home Literacy Experiences and Emergent Literacy Knowledge." *Reading Research Quarterly* 31 (4): 406–28.

Pyle, N., A.C. Vasquez, B. Kraft-Lignugaris, S.L. Gillam, D.R. Reutzel, A. Olszewski, H. Segura, D. Hartzheim, W. Laing, & D. Pyle. 2017. "Effects of Expository Text Structure Interventions on Comprehension: A Meta-Analysis." *Reading Research Quarterly* 52 (4): 469–501.

Raver, C. 2002. "Emotions Matter: Making the Case for the Role of Young Children's Emotional Development for Early School Readiness." *SRCD Social Policy Report* 16 (3): 3–14.

RCPCH (Royal College of Paediatrics and Child Health). 2019. *The Health Impacts of Screen Time: A Guide for Clinicians and Parents*. London: RCPCH. www.rcpch.ac.uk/sites/default/files/2018-12/rcpch_screen_time_guide_-_final.pdf.

Read, C. 1975. *Children's Categorization of Speech Sounds in English*. Urbana, IL: National Council of Teachers of English.

Real, N., & C. Correro. 2015. "Digital Literature in Early Childhood: Reading Experiences in Family and School Contexts." In *Digital Literature for Children: Texts, Readers, and Educational Practices*, eds. M. Manresa & N. Real, 172–91. New York: Peter Lang.

Repacholi, B.M., & A. Gopnik. 1997. "Early Reasoning About Desires: Evidence from 14- and 18-Month-Olds." *Developmental Psychology* 33 (1): 12–21.

Repaskey, L., J. Schumm, & J. Johnson. 2017. "First and Fourth Grade Boys' and Girls' Preferences for and Perceptions About Narrative and Expository Text." *Reading Psychology* 38 (3): 808–47.

Richman, W.A., & J. Colombo. 2007. "Joint Book Reading in the Second Year and Vocabulary Outcomes." *Journal of Research in Childhood Education* 21 (3): 242–53.

Rideout, V., & M.B. Robb. 2020. *The Common Sense Census: Media Use by Kids Age Zero to Eight, 2020.* Report. San Francisco: Common Sense Media. www.commonsensemedia.org/research/the-common-sense-census-media-use-by-kids-age-zero-to-eight-2020.

Roberts, T.A. 2008. "Home Storybook Reading in Primary or Second Language with Preschool Children: Evidence of Equal Effectiveness for Second-Language Vocabulary Acquisition." *Reading Research Quarterly* 43 (2): 103–30.

Robinson, A. 2020. "Responding to Informational Texts Across the Efferent-Aesthetic Continuum in Preschool." *The Reading Teacher* 73 (4): 265–74.

Rochat, P. 1989. "Object Manipulation and Exploration in 2- to 5-Month-Old Infants." *Developmental Psychology* 25 (6): 871–84.

Rogow, F. 2022. *Media Literacy for Young Children: Teaching Beyond the Screen Time Debates.* Washington, DC: NAEYC.

Roskos, K., & S.B. Neuman. 2011. "The Classroom Environment: First, Last, and Always." *The Reading Teacher* 65 (2): 110–14.

Roth-Hanania, R., M. Davidov, & C. Zahn-Waxler. 2011. "Empathy Development from 8–16 Months: Early Signs of Concern for Others." *Infant Behavior and Development* 34 (3): 447–58.

Rowe, D.W., & M.E. Miller. 2016. "Designing for Diverse Classrooms: Using iPads and Digital Cameras to Compose eBooks with Emergent Bilingual/Biliterate Four-Year-Olds." *Journal of Early Childhood Literacy* 16 (4): 425–72.

Rowe, D.W., L. Piestrzynski, A.R. Hadd, & J.W. Reiter. 2024. "Writing as a Path to the Alphabetic Principal: How Preschoolers Learn That Their Own Writing Represents Speech." *Reading Research Quarterly* 59 (1): 32–56.

Rowe, D.W., A.Y. Shimuzu, & Z.G. Davis. 2022. "Essential Practices for Engaging Young Children as Writers: Lessons from Expert Early Writing Teachers." *Reading Teacher* 75 (4): 485–94.

Rowe, M.L. 2012. "A Longitudinal Investigation of the Role of Quantity and Quality of Child-Directed Speech in Vocabulary Development." *Child Development* 83 (5): 1762–74.

Rowe, M.L., L. Leech, & N. Cabrera. 2017. "Going Beyond Input Quantity: Wh-Questions Matter for Toddlers' Language and Cognitive Development." *Cognitive Science* 41 (Suppl. 1): 162–79.

Rowe, M.L., R. Romero, & K.A. Leech. 2023. "Early Environmental Influences on Language." In *Handbook on the Science of Early Literacy*, eds. S.Q. Cabell, S.B. Neuman, & N.P. Terry, 23–31. New York: Guilford.

Rowe, M.L., & C.E. Snow. 2020. "Analyzing Input Quality Along Three Dimensions: Interactive, Linguistic, and Conceptual." *Journal of Child Language* 47 (1): 5–21.

Ruff, H.A. 1984. "Infants' Manipulative Exploration of Objects: Effects of Age and Object Characteristics." *Developmental Psychology* 20 (1): 9–20.

Rutter, D.R., & K. Durkin. 1987. "Turn-Taking in Mother-Infant Interaction: An Examination of Vocalization and Gaze." *Developmental Psychology* 23 (1): 54–61.

Rvachew, S., K. Rees, E. Carolan, & A. Nadig. 2017. "Improving Emergent Literacy with School-Based Shared Reading: Paper Versus Ebooks." *International Journal of Child-Computer Interaction* 12: 24–29.

Salmon, L.G. 2014. "Factors that Affect Emergent Literacy Development When Engaging with Electronic Books." *Early Childhood Education Journal* 42: 85–92.

Sari, B., H.A. Başal, Z.K. Takacs, & A.G. Bus. 2019. "A Randomized Controlled Trial to Test Efficacy of Digital Enhancements of Storybooks in Support of Narrative Comprehension and Word Learning." *Journal of Experimental Child Psychology* 179: 212–26.

Saxton, M. 2009. "The Inevitability of Child Directed Speech." In *Language Acquisition,* ed. S.H. Foster-Cohen, 62–86. London: Palgrave Macmillan.

Schaeffer, K. 2021. "Among Many US Children, Reading for Fun Has Become Less Common, Federal Data Shows." *Pew Research Center,* November 12. www.pewresearch.org/short-reads/2021/11/12/among-many-u-s-children-reading-for-f un-has-become-less-c ommon-federal-data-shows.

Scherer, E., A. Hagaman, E. Chung, A. Rahman, K. O'Donnell, & J. Maselko. 2019. "The Relationship Between Responsive Caregiving and Child Outcomes: Evidence from Direct Observations of Other-Child Dyads in Pakistan." *BMC Public Health* 19: 252. doi:10.1186/s12889-019-6571-1.

Schickedanz, J.A. 1990. *Adam's Righting Revolutions: One Child's Literacy Development from Infancy Through Grade One.* Portsmouth, NH: Heinemann.

Schickedanz, J.A., & R.M. Casbergue. 2009. *Writing in Preschool: Learning to Orchestrate Meaning and Marks.* 2nd ed. Newark, DE: International Reading Association.

Schickedanz, J.A., & M.F. Collins. 2012. "For Young Children, Pictures in Storybooks Are Rarely Worth a Thousand Words." *The Reading Teacher* 65 (8): 539–49.

Schickedanz, J.A., M.F. Collins, & C. Marchant. 2022. *What Are Preschoolers Thinking? Insights from Early Learners' Misunderstandings.* Cambridge, MA: Harvard Education Press.

Schickedanz, J.A., & L.M. McGee. 2010. "The NELP Report on Shared Story Reading Interventions (Chapter 4): Extending the Story." *Educational Researcher* 39 (4): 323–29.

Sénéchal, M., G. Ouellette, & D. Rodney. 2006. "The Misunderstood Giant: On the Predictive Value of Early Vocabulary to Future Reading." In *Handbook of Early Literacy Research*, Vol. 2, eds. D.K. Dickinson & S.B. Neuman, 173–82. New York: Guilford.

Serafini, F. 2011. "When Bad Things Happen to Good Books." *The Reading Teacher* 65 (4): 238–41.

Share, D.L. 1999. "Phonological Recoding and Orthographic Learning: A Direct Test of the Self-Teaching Hypothesis." *Journal of Experimental Child Psychology* 72 (1): 95–129.

Shanahan, T. 2016. "Thinking with Research: Research Changes Its Mind (Again)." *The Reading Teacher* 70 (2): 245–48.

Sharifinik, M., M. Ahadi, & V. Rahimi. 2021. "Bilingualism and Cognitive and Auditory Processing: A Comprehensive Review." *Iranian Rehabilitation Journal* 19 (3): 231–40.

Shuler, C. 2009. *Pockets of Potential: Using Mobile Technologies to Promote Children's Learning.* Report. New York: The Joan Ganz Cooney Center at Sesame Workshop. www.joanganzcooneycenter.org/wp-content/uploads/2010/03/pockets_of_potential_1_.pdf.

Siegler, R.S., & M.W. Alibali. 2005. *Children's Thinking.* 4th ed. Upper Saddle River, NJ: Prentice Hall.

Simcock, G., & J.S. DeLoache. 2008. "The Effect of Repetition on Infants' Imitation from Picture Books Varying in Iconicity." *Infancy* 13 (6): 687–97.

Simion, F., V. Macchi Cassia, C. Turati, & E. Valenza. 2001. "The Origins of Face Perception: Specific Versus Non-Specific Mechanisms." *Infant and Child Development* 10 (1-2): 59–65.

Smeets, D.J.H., & A.G. Bus. 2014. "The Interactive Animated E-Book as a Word Learning Device for Kindergartners." *Applied Psycholinguistics* 36 (4): 899–920.

Smith, C.R. 2001. "Click and Turn the Page: An Exploration of Multiple Storybook Literacy." *Reading Research Quarterly* 36 (2): 152.

Smith, M.W., J.P. Brady, & L. Anastasopoulos. 2008. *Early Language and Literacy Classroom Observation Pre-K Toolkit.* Baltimore: Brookes.

Smith, R., P. Snow, T. Serry, & L. Hammond. 2021. "The Role of Background Knowledge in Reading Comprehension: A Critical Review." *Reading Psychology* 42 (3): 214–40.

Snow, C.E. 1977. "The Development of Conversation between Mothers and Babies." *Journal of Child Language* 4 (1): 1–22.

Son, S.H.C., & M.F. Tineo. 2016. "Mothers' Attention-Getting Utterances During Shared Book Reading: Links to Low-Income Preschoolers' Verbal Engagement, Visual Attention, and Early Literacy." *Infant and Child Development* 25 (4): 259–82.

Sorce, J., R. Emde, J. Campos, & M. Klinnert. 1985. "Maternal Emotional Signaling: Its Effect on the Visual-Cliff Behavior of 1-Year-Olds." *Developmental Psychology* 21 (1): 195–200.

Spelke, E.S., A. Phillips, & A.L. Woodward. 1995. "Infants' Knowledge of Objects in Motion and Human Action." In *Causal Cognition: A Multidisciplinary Debate,* eds. A.J. Premack, D. Premack, & D. Sperber, 44–77. Oxford: Clarendon Press.

Spinu, L., J. Hwang, & M. Vasilita. 2023. "Differences Between Monolinguals and Bilinguals in Phonetic and Phonological Learning and the Connection with Auditory Sensory Memory." *Brain Science* 13 (3): 488. doi:10.3390/brainsci13030488.

Spira, E.G., S.S. Bracken, & J. Fischel. 2005. "Predicting Improvement After First-Grade Reading Difficulties: The Effects of Oral Language, Emergent Literacy, and Behavior Skills." *Developmental Psychology* 41 (1): 225–34.

Spriet, C., E. Abassi, J. Hochmann, & L. Papeo. 2022. "Visual Object Categorization in Infancy." *Psychological and Cognitive Sciences* 119 (8): e2105866119. doi:10.1073/pnas.2105866119.

Sroufe, L.A., & J.P. Wunsch. 1972. "The Development of Laughter in the First Year of Life." *Child Development* 43 (4): 1326–44.

Stahl, K.A.D. 2012. "Applying New Visions of Reading Development in Today's Classrooms." *The Reading Teacher* 65 (1): 52–56.

Stephens, G., & D. Matthews. 2014. "The Communicative Infant from 0–18 Months: The Social-Cognitive Foundations of Pragmatics Development." In *Pragmatic Development in First Language Acquisition,* ed. D. Matthews, 13–35. Amsterdam, The Netherlands: John Benjamins.

Stern, D., J. Jaffe, B. Beebe, & S.L. Bennett. 1975. "Vocalizing in Unison and in Alternation: Two Modes of Communication Within the Mother-Infant Dyad." *Annals of the New York Academy of Sciences* 263 (1): 89–100.

Stewart, M., & N. Chelsey. 2014. *Perfect Pairs: Using Fiction and Nonfiction Picture Books to Teach Life Science, K–2.* New York: Routledge.

Stewart, M., & M. Correia. 2021. *5 Kinds of Nonfiction: Enriching Reading and Writing Instruction with Children's Books.* New York: Routledge.

Storch, S.A., & G.J. Whitehurst. 2002. "Oral Language and Code-Related Precursors to Reading: Evidence from a Longitudinal Structural Model." *Developmental Psychology* 38 (6): 934–47.

Strouse, G.A., L.A. Newland, & D.J. Mourlam. 2019. "Educational and Fun? Parent Versus Preschooler Perceptions and Co-Use of Digital and Print Media." *AERA Open* 5 (3). doi:10.1177/2332858419861085.

Sweet, A.P., & C. Snow. 2002. "Reconceptualizing Reading Comprehension." In *Improving Comprehension Instruction: Rethinking Research,* eds. C.C. Block, L.B. Gambrell, & M. Pressley, 54–79. Newark, DE: International Reading Association.

Takeuchi, L., & R. Stevens. With B. Barron, E. Branch-Ridley, M. Brooks, H. Cooperman, A. Fenwick-Naditch, S. Fisch, R. Herr-Stephenson, C. Llorente, S. Mehus, S. Pasnik, W. Penuel, & G. Revelle. 2011. *The New Coviewing: Designing Learning Through Joint Media Engagement.* Report. New York: The Joan Ganz Cooney Center Sesame Workshop. www.joanganzcooneycenter.org /wp-content/uploads/2011/12/ jgc_coviewing_desktop.pdf.

Tamis-LeMonda, C.S., Y. Kuchirko, & L. Song. 2014. "Why Is Infant Language Learning Facilitated by Parental Responsiveness?" *Current Directions in Psychological Science* 23 (2): 121–26.

Tamis-LeMonda, C.S., & L. Song. 2012. "Parent–Infant Communicative Interactions in Cultural Context." In *Developmental Psychology,* eds. R.M. Lerner, E. Easterbrooks, & J. Mistry, 143–70. Vol. 6 of *Handbook of Psychology: Developmental Psychology,* 2nd ed., ed. I.B. Weiner. Hoboken, NJ: John Wiley & Sons.

Taumoepeau, M., & T. Ruffman. 2006. "Mother and Infant Talk About Mental States Relates to Desire Language and Emotional Understanding." *Child Development* 77 (3): 465–81.

Taumoepeau, M., & T. Ruffman. 2008. "Stepping Stones to Others' Minds: Maternal Talk Related to Child Mental Language and Emotion Understanding at 15, 24, and 33 Months." *Child Development* 79 (2): 284–302.

Taylor, D., & C. Dorsey-Gaines. 1988. *Growing Up Literate*. Portsmouth, NH: Heinemann.

Teale, W.H. 1986. "Home Background and Children's Literacy Development." In *Emergent Literacy: Writing and Reading*, eds. W.H. Teale & E. Sulzby, 173–206. Norwood, NJ: Ablex.

Teale, W.H., & E. Sulzby, eds. 1986. *Emergent Literacy: Writing and Reading*. Norwood, NJ: Ablex.

Temple, C., M. Martinez, & J. Yokota. 2019. *Children's Books in Children's Hands: A Brief Introduction to Their Literature*. 6th ed. New York: Pearson.

Termine, N.T., & C.E. Izard. 1988. "Infants' Responses to Their Mothers' Expressions of Joy and Sadness." *Developmental Psychology* 24 (2): 223–29.

Tompkins, V., A. Bengochea, S. Nicol, & L. Justice. 2017. "Maternal Inferential Input and Children's Language Skills." *Reading Research Quarterly* 52 (4): 397–416.

Torgesen, J.K. 2004. "Avoiding the Devastating Downward Spiral: The Evidence That Early Intervention Prevents Reading Failure." *American Educator* 28 (3): 6–19, 45–47.

Torr, J. 2023. *Reading Picture Books with Infants and Toddlers: Learning Through Language*. New York: Routledge.

Towell, J.L., L. Bartram, S. Morrow, & S.L. Brown. 2021. "Reading to Babies: Exploring the Beginnings of Literacy." *Journal of Early Childhood Literacy* 21 (3): 321–37.

Treiman, R., J. Cohen, K. Mulqueeny, B. Kessler, & S. Schechtman. 2007. "Young Children's Knowledge About Printed Names." *Child Development* 78 (5): 1458–71.

Turner, K.H., T. Jolls, M.S. Hagerman, W. O'Byrne, T. Hicks, B. Eisenstock, & K.E. Pytash. 2017. "Developing Digital and Media Literacies in Children and Adolescents." *Pediatrics* 140 (Suppl. 2): 122–26.

Ukrainetz, T.A., J.J. Nuspl, K. Wilkerson, & S.R. Beddes. 2011. "The Effects of Syllable Instruction on Phonemic Awareness in Preschoolers." *Early Childhood Research Quarterly* 26 (1): 50–60.

Ünlütabak, B., A. Aktan-Erciyes, D. Yilmaz, S. Kandemir, & T. Göksun. 2022. "Parental Input During Book Reading and Toddlers' Elicited and Spontaneous Communicative Interactions." *Journal of Applied Developmental Psychology* 81 (July-Aug): 101436.

Ungerer, J.A., R. Dolby, W. Brent, B. Barnett, N. Kelk, & V. Lewin. 1990. "The Early Development of Empathy: Self-Regulation and Individual Differences in the First Year." *Motivation and Emotion* 14 (1): 93–106.

Ungerer, J.A., P.R. Zelazo, R.B. Kearsley, & K. O'Leary. 1981. "Developmental Changes in the Representation of Objects in Symbolic Play from 18 to 35 Months of Age." *Child Development* 52 (1): 186–95.

Vaish, A., & T. Sriano. 2004. "Is Visual Reference Necessary? Contributions of Facial Versus Vocal Cues in 12-Month-Olds' Social Referencing Behavior." *Developmental Science* 7 (3): 261–69.

van Kleeck, A., J. Vander Woude, & L. Hammett. 2006. "Fostering Literal and Inferential Language Skills in Head Start Preschoolers with Language Impairment Using Scripted Book-Sharing Discussions." *American Journal of Speech-Language Pathology* 15 (1): 85–95.

Verhallen, M.J.A.J., A.G. Bus, & M.T. De Jong. 2006. "The Promise of Multimedia Stories for Kindergarten Children at Risk." *Journal of Educational Psychology* 98 (2): 410–19.

Vukelich, C., B.J. Enz, K.A. Roskos, & J. Christie. 2020. *Helping Young Children Learn Language and Literacy: Birth Through Kindergarten.* 5th ed. New York: Pearson.

Walle, E.A., P.J. Reschke, & J.M. Knothe. 2017. "Social Referencing: Defining and Delineating a Basic Process of Emotion." *Emotion Review* 9 (3): 245–52.

Walsh, R.L., & K.A. Hodge. 2018. "Are We Asking the Right Questions? An Analysis of Research on the Effect of Teachers' Questioning on Children's Language During Shared Book Reading with Young Children." *Journal of Early Childhood Literacy* 18 (2): 264–94.

Wang, S., L. Kaufman, & R. Baillargeon. 2003. "Should All Stationary Objects Move When Hit? Development of Infants' Causal and Statistical Expectations About Collision Events." *Infant Behavior & Development* 26 (3): 529–67.

Wasik, B.A., A.H. Hindman, & E.K. Snell. 2016. "Book Reading and Vocabulary Development: A Systematic Review." *Early Childhood Research Quarterly* 37 (4): 39–57.

Weinberg, M.K., & E.Z. Tronick. 1996. "Infant Affective Reactions to the Resumption of Maternal Interaction After the Still-Face." *Child Development* 67 (3): 905–14.

Weisleder, A., & A. Fernald. 2013. "Talking to Children Matters: Early Language Experience Strengthens Processing and Builds Vocabulary." *Psychological Science* 24 (11): 2143–52.

Weizman, Z.O., & C.E. Snow. 2001. "Lexical Input as Related to Children's Vocabulary Acquisition: Effects of Sophisticated Exposure and Support for Meaning." *Developmental Psychology* 37 (2): 265–79.

White, L.J., & D.B. Greenfield. 2017. "Executive Functioning in Spanish- and English-Speaking Head Start Preschoolers." *Developmental Science* 20 (1): e12502. doi:10.1111/desc.12502.

WHO (World Health Organization). 2019. *Guidelines on Physical Activity, Sedentary Behaviour, and Sleep for Children Under 5 Years of Age.* Geneva: WHO. https://apps.who.int/iris/handle/10665/311664.

Wigfield, A., J. Gladstone, & L. Turci. 2016. "Beyond Cognition: Reading Motivation and Reading Comprehension." *Child Development Perspectives* 10 (3): 190–95.

Willingham, D.T. 2009. *Why Don't Students Like School? A Cognitive Scientist Answers Questions About How the Mind Works and What It Means for the Classroom.* San Francisco: Jossey-Bass.

Wohlwend, K.E. 2015. "One Screen, Many Fingers: Young Children's Collaborative Literacy Play with Digital Puppetry Apps and Touchscreen Technologies." *Theory Into Practice* 54 (2): 154–62.

Wong Fillmore, L. 1976. "The Second Time Around: Cognitive and Social Strategies in Second Language Acquisition." Unpublished doctoral dissertation, Stanford University.

Wong Fillmore, L. 1991. "Second Language Learning in Children: A Model of Language Learning in Social Context." In *Language Processing in Bilingual Children*, ed. E. Bialystok, 49–69. Cambridge, England: Cambridge University Press.

Yaden, D.B., Jr. 1988. "Understanding Stories Through Repeated Read-Alouds: How Many Does It Take?" *The Reading Teacher* 41 (6): 556–61.

Yesil-Dagli, U. 2011. "Predicting ELL Students' Beginning First Grade English Oral Reading Fluency from Initial Kindergarten Vocabulary, Letter Naming, and Phonological Awareness Skills." *Early Childhood Research Quarterly* 26 (1): 15–29.

Yokota, J., & W.H. Teale. 2014. "Picture Books and the Digital World: Educators Making Informed Choices." *The Reading Teacher* 67 (8): 577–85.

Young, T., P.H. Ricks, & K.L. MacKay. 2023. "Engaging Students with Expository Texts Through Interactive Read-Alouds." *Reading Teacher* 77 (1): 6–15.

Zahn-Waxler, C., M. Radke-Yarrow, E. Wagner, & M. Chapman. 1992. "Development of Concern for Others." *Developmental Psychology* 28 (1): 126–36.

Zambo, D., & C.C. Hansen. 2007. "Love, Language, and Emergent Literacy." *Young Children* 62 (3): 32–37.

INDEX

Page numbers followed by *f* and *t* indicate figures and tables, respectively.

memorized books, 111

mental states of others, 50

message composition, digital, 184–185

misunderstanding of stories, 60–61, 62

mock words

    of 2½- to 3-year-olds, 158–159, 159*f*, 160*f*, 162

    of 3- to 4-year-olds, 164–165, 164*f*

    of 4- to 5-year-olds, 171

    and stages of emergent writing, 130

motivation for learning, 8, 83, 101, 189

motivation of story characters, 35, 50, 58

motor skills. *See* fine motor development; gross motor skills

multilingual learners

    effect of peer interaction on language learning of, 53–55

    and irregularities of letter sounds in English, 115

    phonological awareness in, 108–109, 110

    spelling skills, 190–191

    and whole group story reading, 70–71

multiple story readings, 74–75, 78

N

names

    on labels, in preschool classrooms, 122*t*

    in phonological awareness tasks, 112–114, 115

    writing of, 162–163, 163*f*

narrative intangibles, 35

narratives, 46, 56, 86

National Reading Panel report, 132

Negative Cat (Blackall), 48*f*, 49

newborns, 21, 24, 152

nonbook printed information, 95–97, 96*f*, 97

O

onomatopoeia, 69

onsets, 108, 109, 110, 112, 113

Open Library, 39

oral language skills

    and the decoding process, 10–11

    and early reading-related behaviors, 40, 41*t*

    effect of peers on, 53–55

    group reading and support of, 51–53

    importance of support for, 17

    in infants, 21, 27

    and reading comprehension, 12

overregularization, 176

P

pacing in reading aloud to children, 60–61

painting. *See* drawings and paintings

paralinguistic communications, 24–25

peer interactions and language learning, 53–55

personal affect questions, 66

personal narratives, 34

phonemes

    in blending tasks, 117*t*

    and decoding skills, 10

    and digital games, 113, 119–120

    as speech units, 108–110

    spelling and, 175*t*, 176–177, 190–191

phonological awareness

    beginning sound and rhyme activities, 116*t*–117*t*

    constructive teacher feedback on, 118

    course of acquisition of, 110

    definition of, 106

    initial steps in teaching, 111–113

    letter clue game, 107

    manipulative materials for, 114, 114*f*, 118

    in multilingual learners, 108–109

    name-based tasks for, 113–114, 115, 118

    speech units in words, 108–110

    technology for supporting, 119–120, 120*f*

    See also decoding

picture walks, 58, 71

play materials, 123*f*, 123*t*, 136. *See also* dramatic play

poems, 114, 116*t*

pointing

    finger point reading, 111

    by group reader, 62

    by infants, 27

    and joint attention, 26, 29

    and key word learning, 69

    by toddlers, 31

post office play, 187

pragmatics, 52

predictable books, 34, 47, 111, 116*t*

preschoolers

    drawings of 4- to 5-year-olds, 183, 183*f*

    early literacy practices' contributions to reading foundation, 15, 16*t*

    emergent writing of, 130

    goals for group story reading to, 50–53

    message composition and technology use, 184–185